Literature of Revolution

Norman Geras

Literature of Revolution

Essays on Marxism

VERSO
London • New York

This edition first published by Verso 2017
First published by Verso 1986
© Norman Geras 1986

All rights reserved

The moral rights of the author have been asserted

1 3 5 7 9 10 8 6 4 2

Verso
UK: 6 Meard Street, London W1F 0EG
US: 20 Jay Street, Suite 1010, Brooklyn, NY 11201
versobooks.com

Verso is the imprint of New Left Books

ISBN-13: 978-1-78663-318-7
ISBN-13: 978-1-78663-009-4 (US EBK)
ISBN-13: 978-1-78663-008-7 (UK EBK)

British Library Cataloguing in Publication Data
A catalogue record for this book is available from the British Library

Library of Congress Catalog-in-Publication Data
A catalog record for this book is available from the Library of Congress

Typeset in Plantin by Cover to Cover, Cambridge
Printed in the UK by CPI Mackays Ltd

Contents

To Michael Löwy and Morris Szeftel,
old friends by
whom I have been
encouraged.

Introduction

The essays collected in this volume have appeared during the last fifteen years and deal with topics, concepts and problems in the literature of revolutionary Marxism. They are all concerned more or less directly with exposition and analysis of texts within this tradition as a platform for examining issues that have been, and continue to be, of importance. Written over the course of a decade and a half and for different purposes or occasions, naturally they vary somewhat in style and format as well as by virtue of the content and precise objectives specific to each. But there are also significant connections between them; conceptual or thematic links, continuity and progression of argument, bestowing on them a certain unity, sufficient, I believe, to justify their republication here together.

The essays fall into two groups. Those in Part I are devoted to questions of Marxist philosophy and concern mainly the writings of Marx himself, but also the work of Louis Althusser, the philosopher most influential—for good and ill—in the way Marx was read and understood by a generation of British Marxists from the late 1960s. Part II of the book discusses the thought of Trotsky and, to a lesser extent, that of Rosa Luxemburg and Lenin as well. The focus here is on questions of socialist political theory. With one exception, and that not a complete exception, the preoccupation of the essays in this second group is with the forms of working-class action, organization and democracy.

'The Controversy About Marx and Justice', with which the volume begins, is addressed to the normative foundations of

Marx's thought. Immediately continuous, in that, with at least one of the major concerns of my earlier *Marx and Human Nature: Refutation of a Legend*, it confronts directly and at length what is also a recurring theme in several of the essays that follow it but which they only touch on much more briefly—the presence and importance of the ethical component within Marxism. The issue is approached by way of the recent debate over whether or not Marx considered capitalism to be unjust.

Central to that debate amongst many other matters raised by it is the account given by Marx in *Capital* of the nature of value, the wage contract and exploitation, and the distinction much used by him in giving it, between the outward appearances and the inner reality of capitalist relations of production. This distinction is the subject of the next two essays in the book. 'Fetishism', a very short piece written for a work of reference, is included here as introducing the argument of the longer, following piece in convenient and summary form. 'Essence and Appearance: Aspects of Fetishism in Marx's *Capital*' examines the presuppositions and methodological implications of this pivotal dichotomy, draws attention to ambiguities in and common misunderstandings of it, and emphasizes both its explanatory and critical dimensions. Some of Althusser's theses are criticized in the process and, in particular, his way of construing the relation between Marxist theory and the working class.

The fourth and fifth essays then centre on Althusser's ideas in their own right. 'Louis Althusser' is, again, a shorter piece, included to provide a brief summary and overview of the more extensive explanation and argument it precedes. 'Althusser's Marxism: An Account and Assessment' is, as the title of itself indicates, in large part expository, aiming for as clear a presentation as possible of some unfamiliar, some complex and some obscure ideas. The exposition of them is followed by a critique, partial rather than comprehensive, but in any case enlarging upon the matter broached earlier in the previous essay but one. Althusser's theory of knowledge and science and, within it, his view of the relationship between Marxism itself and the politics and experience of the working class, are judged to be one-sided and idealist.

The grounds for this judgement are further explored in the sixth piece—the last in Part I—which returns to Marx's own thought and a theme argued to be central to it as to classical Marxism more

generally. 'Marxism and Proletarian Self-Emancipation' discusses
the principle that the liberation of the working class must be won
by the working class itself, suggesting that, transparently simple
as it may appear, it carries with it both assumptions and consequences of quite some moment, epistemological as well as political.
The text for a brief talk, this piece only deals with these in the
broadest terms, but it acts as a bridge towards the second group of
essays, sketching out or anticipating issues which they treat of
more thoroughly.

Part II of the book is introduced by the essays, 'Leon Trotsky'
and 'Rosa Luxemburg'. These condense and resume the lives and
principal writings and ideas of their respective subjects, furnish-
ing thereby some general background to the specific topics considered—with reference to his work chiefly but by comparison or
contrast with hers and also Lenin's—in the remainder of the
volume. It may be noted that like the opening essay of the
collection, the material that makes up this second part of it abuts
on that of another of my books, namely, in this instance, *The
Legacy of Rosa Luxemburg*. This is owing not just to the connecting figure of Luxemburg herself but to a substantial number
of continuous preoccupations, cognate and overlapping themes,
arising from the common concern with problems of revolutionary
politics.

'Political Participation in the Revolutionary Thought of Leon
Trotsky', first of the longer items in this section, examines
Trotsky's views on the modes of working-class political activity
and organization, focusing especially on the relationship between
party and class. Across the writings and a span of nearly forty
years, it traces the development of his thinking on these matters,
recording changes of both emphasis and substance, crucial amongst
them the mutation and certain nuances in his assessment of the
conceptions of Lenin. The relation between the pertinent ideas of
the two revolutionaries is then directly the subject of 'Lenin,
Trotsky and the Party'. In more informal accents due to its origin
as a talk, this seeks to isolate the lastingly valid core in Lenin's
theory of party organization from his more peripheral or circumstantial formulations, theoretical infelicities and mistakes; and
likewise to distinguish in the young Trotsky's, and in Luxemburg's,
criticisms of him the valuable insights from a broader error of
political judgement.

These same criticisms form the starting point of the next essay,

'Classical Marxism and Proletarian Representation'. They are the material for reflection on a problem secreted in the two preceding pieces—and in *The Legacy of Rosa Luxemburg*—unsettled and unsettling within their stress upon the democratic norms necessary and proper to the workers' movement; a problem, indeed, recognized here as running the length of the Marxist tradition. It concerns the democratic and pluralist commitment of classical Marxism: the tension between that and its habitual way of talking about class and party. Through close analysis of the texts in which Trotsky and Luxemburg set forth their strictures of Lenin and some reference back to the writings of Marx and Engels, the essay brings this problem into the open, proffers some tentative hypotheses about its theoretical and historical roots, and identifies the boundary that must be crossed as a precondition of resolving it.

The volume closes with the article, 'Literature of Revolution'. Though concerned once again with the work of Trotsky and therefore taking in his ideas on organization, revolution and the like along the way, it is rather different in scope and aim from the foregoing items. It considers Trotsky's strength and abilities as a writer; in psychological observation and individual portraiture, in representation of the socialist movement and its organizations, in the description of revolutionary ferment; in general. The book, *1905*, and other of his earlier writings are assessed from this point of view. His work gives us, it is argued, not only theory and history of revolution but also in a certain sense a literature of it. The essay refers Trotsky's achievement in this to the moral dimension of the socialist project and concludes with a discussion of the relation between form and content in socialist political writing.

These essays are reprinted here almost exactly as they have previously appeared. It stands to reason that in reviewing the writings of fifteen years, one is made more clearly aware of changes in one's thinking, comes across things one would no longer put in quite the same way, and so on. I felt it best, however, to leave these pieces as they were, entrusting change and qualification to other work, and have made only a very few and very minor emendations which do not affect anything of substance. The one exception to this is the talk, 'Lenin, Trotsky and the Party'. The version in which it originally appeared was unsatisfactory, because inadequately edited from an actual transcript and referred to me too late for anything to be done about this. Consulting the written notes from which the talk was given, I have taken the opportunity provided by this volume to make some small corrections and to eliminate repetition, redundancy and clumsiness. Even so, it is substantially the same text and argument that remain here also, albeit in a somewhat more polished form.

In the light of the generally abstentionist editorial policy just described, there are three features of the contents of this collection that I think it advisable briefly to remark on. First, the article, 'Essence and Appearance', was written with a greater confidence in Marx's theory of value than I now find it possible to have in view of recent work and controversy in this area. This need not deprive it of whatever merits it possesses by way of expounding and clarifying Marx's ideas but is nevertheless a change of view that it is proper to register. Secondly, in two or three places in the earliest of these essays, expression is given to what one might call a transformationist conception of the nature of humankind: the view that the character of human beings varies both through history and across different societies and cultures. In itself, there is nothing wrong with that. Indeed, it asserts an important truth. But it has become a cliché of a lot of Marxist writing, and unqualified, as here at the sites in question, it tends to be accompanied by another, for its part false, namely that there is no room within Marxist theory, and nor is there any such thing as, a universal human nature. This falsehood is the target of my *Marx and Human Nature* and the shift towards the saner position there argued for is reflected in a couple of the more recent of the essays herein.

Thirdly, where and to the extent that they are addressed to the issue, these essays collectively underwrite what it would be most accurate to describe as a qualified Leninism. Some readers of this volume may feel that the particular qualification which is the upshot of the penultimate of them, 'Classical Marxism and Proletarian Representation', is of a kind and weight sufficient to undo what it is supposedly qualifying, so setting that essay at odds with the others around it. This qualification, embodied in the essay's pluralist conclusion, is unquestionably important and it does sit uneasily with the idea of Leninism conceived by the generality of both its enemies and its adherents. But it should be noted and noted carefully that if it qualifies the authentic tradition of

Leninism, it does so only because and by virtue of qualifying the broader Marxist tradition to which Leninism belongs and, if the truth be told, the socialist tradition virtually as a whole. For, the pluralist thesis of that essay is developed not through a critique of Lenin's ideas but precisely—and by premeditation—through pointing out a certain limitation also in those of Lenin's critics and of his and their intellectual forbears, one therefore that they, all of them, shared with him and with others, from then to now, too many to be counted. So, an important qualification of Leninism (to speak only for the moment of that) it certainly is, but it is in exactly the same spirit as the others that are made in these pages, a spirit styled elsewhere in them as being one of 'critical continuity and respect', and in which the respect and the continuity are at least as significant as the criticism, as the necessary theoretical development. It has absolutely nothing to do with the shameless flight from and denigration of Lenin's political legacy that are the norm and fashion today with so many on the left and so many who used to know better.

An introduction of this kind is obviously not the place for attempting a balanced, up-to-date reassessment of that legacy. But so much, at least, can be said. The concept and the project of a socialist party, as an indispensable precondition of actual socialism, is as valid now as ever. A *party* (or plurality of such parties, should it through the dynamic and interplay of socialist politics so turn out): democratic and organized, of effective size and weight within the given national context, capable of unifying and representing at the political level the issues, the campaigns and the movements that will make up its (or their) programme and active constituency. And *socialist*: not in any sectarian or exclusivist sense, but in the minimal sense, only, of meaning business and being willing to go through to the end. As things stand in Britain today, more or less everything in this respect is still to be done. For such a formation to come into being, it will need to be in tune with its own time and with the needs and capacities and all that is positive in the culture of its potential members and supporters. Insistence upon the purity or even soundness of its Leninist— and Trotskyist or indeed other uniquely identifying—principles, practices or general lineage will here be out of place. This must be, within the broadest limits of what it is meaningful to call by the name, a socialism open and plural, critical and undevout, receptive to every healthy impulse, current or idea. By the very same token, however, a socialism today that is not completely, and to the very roots of its being, honest has not got a hope. And a socialist politics that thinks just to turn its back on the Leninist tradition as entirely foreign, spent or null, or that distorts and denounces it, is not an honest politics. It is a collusion with the lies of socialism's worst enemies: at best ignorance and delusion; at worst the language of those in the way of making their peace with the rule of capital.

Open to the variety and the wealth of contemporary socialism, the socialist party of today—in effect, of tomorrow or the day after—will not want to insist on its Leninist credentials and will not as such be Leninist. But if it *is* socialist, nor will it be anti-Leninist. For it will have to make a faithful and fair accounting of the great traditions of socialism, be able and willing to draw and to build on everything that is good in them. This is not a matter of mere sentiment or even justice, though these things have their importance amongst the ingredients of socialist integrity. It is a political necessity. We socialists have to make use of every decent resource available to us, intellectual as well as material. The struggle for socialism has not been and is not so easy that we can afford to waste them. We must extract the positive from the negative, the strengths from the limitations, in the several lineages and currents within socialism's past. The notion that so central and powerful, international and internationalist, and fertile a tradition of Marxist political thought as Leninism can now just be left behind, this is not one that can be taken seriously or treated with any great respect.

So much, then, by way of signalling some changes of viewpoint. Given the degree of inconstancy of intellectual and moral commitment in recent times, it may be apt to conclude this introduction with a few observations consequential upon the fact that these are all changes situated firmly within the boundaries of a Marxist outlook, within the theory of history and social revolution developed by the likes of Marx, Luxemburg, Lenin and Trotsky, those figuring most centrally in these essays. For, the flight from Leninism aforementioned has been part of a more general process of decampment which has carried many erstwhile Marxists altogether away, while inflecting the conceptions of many others so considerably to the right as to have left them with a Marxism of only the most residual and precarious sort. This collection is subtitled, unimaginatively perhaps but accurately,

'Essays on Marxism'. They would not have been written nor would I be reprinting them here if not for the conviction that Marxist thought remains the best point of departure for the socialist project, contains the indispensable basis for an adequate understanding of the social world. As such, it is due both precise and critical study. And if this leads to the need for qualification and development, then so be it; that is perfectly normal and natural and necessary. But qualification and development is what it is, not a pretext for just hauling down the flag.

There is a whole chorus of voices today—how many of them, yesterday, advocates of the blindest dogmas and enthusiasms?[1]— ready to tell you, and in tones from the hand-wringing to the most brazen, that Marxism is full of problems and unresolved questions, gaps, weaknesses and areas inadequately researched; as if there were some other body of ideas or social-scientific methodology of which this were not true, some superior alternative theory. Marxism *is* full of problems and unresolved questions, gaps, weaknesses and areas inadequately researched. But somebody who gives this as the basis for abandoning or disembowelling it does not give a reason. They give an excuse. The choice they make thereby is an intellectual one, to be sure, but it is also, in the largest sense, a moral choice. It reposes on a double form of amnesia: of content and of context.

Amnesia of content consists in taking what was formerly dismissed and rejected under one sort of designation, for example, reformism or social democracy, Fabianism, Kautsky or Bernstein, and attempting to resurrect it thinly disguised under another, realism or post-Marxism—or even hegemony, simultaneously honoured and abused. It is the politics that dare not speak its own genuine name and pedigree, wanting the political benefit of something less discredited. Amnesia of context arises from forgetting, seemingly in the very instant of beginning to wash one's hands of the classical Marxist heritage, even its most elementary truths, in particular that the evolution of ideas has a material basis and environment. Ideas, of course, do also have a logic and a certain autonomy of their own and there is intellectual change that is thoroughly necessary and progressive, a part of the

1. See, in this connection, the very pertinent comment of Tamara Deutscher on Isaac Deutscher's essay, 'The Ex-Communist's Conscience', in her introduction to Isaac Deutscher, *Marxism, Wars and Revolutions*, Verso, London 1984, p. xxv.

development of knowledge. But it is impossible for anyone whose Marxism was not merely skin-deep in the first place to pretend that this is all that life is about. They should not simply presume, without hesitation or scruple, that they are in the process of moving forward just because they are moving on. If only out of a minimal respect for their own past, they ought to consider what might be the extraneous pressures upon their thought, whether of age or status, or of the general political context in which they are obliged to move. There have, in truth, been two 'Great Moving Right Shows' taking place since the late 1970s. One concerns Thatcher and Reagan and the somewhat bleak time. The other is closer to home. Many have already departed with the cold wind that has been blowing to the right. Others have been carried sufficiently far that at any decisive turning point they are likely to go the wrong way. Still others may yet return. The tradition of Marxist socialism will progress with or without them.

I have taken the title for this volume from the last of the pieces collected here, altering the sense of it, however, in doing so. On the essay, it referred to the literary power and quality of Trotsky's writing. On the volume as a whole, it is meant only to convey that the component essays are concerned with a number of the texts of revolutionary Marxism, with a literature of revolution in this sense. The title, of course, echoes that of one of Trotsky's famous books. No arrogance or inflated claim is intended in the echo. It is a small tribute to a great and much reviled revolutionary.

Over the period and the different abodes and circumstances in which these essays were composed, one constant has been the indispensable moral support and encouragement of Adèle Geras, my wife. I record my deep gratitude here. Not yet born when I wrote the earliest of them, our children, Sophie and Jenny, have done whatever they could to help ever since they were. I thank them both, too.

Manchester, January 1986.

Acknowledgements

The essays in this volume have appeared previously as follows:
1. 'The Controversy About Marx and Justice' in *New Left Review* 150, March/April 1985; 2. 'Fetishism' in Tom Bottomore (ed.), *A Dictionary of Marxist Thought*, Basil Blackwell, Oxford 1983; 3. 'Essence and Appearance: Aspects of Fetishism in Marx's *Capital*' in *New Left Review* 65, January/February 1971; 4. 'Louis Althusser' as 2 above; 5. 'Althusser's Marxism: An Account and Assessment' in *New Left Review* 71, January/February 1972; 6. 'Marxism and Proletarian Self-Emancipation' in *Radical Philosophy* 6, Winter 1973; 7. 'Leon Trotsky' in Justin Wintle (ed.), *Makers of Modern Culture*, Routledge & Kegan Paul, London 1981; 8. 'Rosa Luxemburg' as 2 above; 9. 'Political Participation in the Revolutionary Thought of Leon Trotsky' in Geraint Parry (ed.), *Participation in Politics*, Manchester University Press, Manchester 1972; 10. 'Lenin, Trotsky and the Party' in *International* 4, No. 2, Winter 1977; 11. 'Classical Marxism and Proletarian Representation' in *New Left Review* 125, January/February 1981; 12. 'Literature of Revolution' in *New Left Review* 113-114, January/April 1979.

For kind permission to reprint them here I am most grateful to these journals and the editors and publishers of these works.

I

Mainly Marx

1.

The Controversy About Marx and Justice

1984

In this essay I review a fast growing sector of the current literature on Marx and the controversy that has fuelled its growth. During the last decade or so, the keen interest within moral and political philosophy in the concept of justice has left its mark on the philosophical discussion of his work. It has left it in the shape of the question: did Marx himself condemn capitalism as unjust? There are those who have argued energetically that he did not; and as many who are equally insistent that he did—a straightforward enough division, despite some differences of approach on either side of it. To prevent misunderstanding, it is worth underlining at the outset that the question being addressed is not that of whether Marx did indeed *condemn* capitalism, as opposed just to analysing, describing, explaining its nature and tendencies. All parties to this dispute agree that he did, agree in other words that there is some such normative dimension to his thought, and frankly, I do not think the denial of it worth taking seriously any longer. The question is the more specific one: does Marx condemn capitalism in the light of any principle of *justice*?

I shall survey the case for thinking he does not and the case for thinking that he does; the textual evidence adduced and supporting argument put forth on behalf of each. Given the extent of the literature being surveyed—some three dozen items (all but one of which have appeared since 1970; and incidentally, of largely, indeed overwhelmingly, North American provenance, twenty-one of the twenty-four authors cited here either writing or hailing from that continent)—each case as I present it is a kind of composite. No one of its proponents necessarily makes use of all the texts and arguments I shall enumerate and they sometimes emphasize or formulate differently those that they do use in common. Still, I give what I hope is an accurate overall map of this dispute, before going on to venture my own judgement on it. The main body of the essay falls, therefore, into three parts. First, I review the texts and arguments put forward by those who deny that Marx condemned capitalism as unjust. Second, I review the texts and arguments put forward by those who claim he did so condemn it. I try in these two sections to present each case broadly as made, with a minimum of critical comment. Third, I then offer some conclusions, and argument in support of them.[1]

1. For convenience of reference, bibliographical details of the literature under review are assembled here. In subsequent citation I then give just the author's name (followed, where there is more than one publication by the same author, by an identifying numeral in parenthesis as designated below in this note) and page number(s). Several of the articles are cited from the following collections: M. Cohen, T. Nagel and T. Scanlon (eds.), *Marx, Justice, and History*, Princeton 1980; K. Nielsen and S. C. Patten (eds.), *Marx and Morality* (*Canadian Journal of Philosophy*, Supplementary Volume VII, 1981); J. R. Pennock and J. W. Chapman (eds.), *Marxism* (*Nomos* XXVI), New York and London 1983. Contributors to the debate may be grouped as follows:

[1] Those according to whom Marx did not criticize capitalism as unjust: D. P. H. Allen, (1) 'Is Marxism a Philosophy?', *Journal of Philosophy*, 71, 1974, pp. 601–612, (2) 'Marx and Engels on the Distributive Justice of Capitalism', in Nielsen and Patten, pp. 221–250; G. G. Brenkert, (1) 'Freedom and Private Property in Marx', in M. Cohen et al., pp. 80–105 (reprinted from *Philosophy and Public Affairs*, 8, No. 2, Winter 1979, pp. 122–147), (2) *Marx's Ethics of Freedom*, London 1983, ch. 5; A. Buchanan, (1) 'Exploitation, Alienation and Injustice', *Canadian Journal of Philosophy*, IX, No. 1, March 1979, pp. 121–139, (2) *Marx and Justice*, London 1982, ch. 4 (a revised version of 'The Marxian Critique of Justice and Rights', in Nielsen and Patten, pp. 269–306); L. Crocker, 'Marx's Concept of Exploitation', *Social Theory and Practice*, Fall 1972, pp. 201–215; S. Lukes, (1) 'Marxism, Morality and Justice', in G. H. R. Parkinson (ed.), *Marx and Marxisms*, Cambridge 1982, pp. 177–205, (2) 'Morals', in T. Bottomore (ed.), *A Dictionary of Marxist Thought*, Oxford 1983, pp. 341–342, (3) *Marxism and Morality*, Oxford 1985, chs. 3–5; R. W. Miller, (1) 'Marx and Aristotle: A Kind of Consequentialism', in Nielsen and Patten, pp. 323–352, (2) *Analyzing Marx*, Princeton 1984, chs. 1 and 2; R. C. Tucker, *The Marxian Revolutionary Idea*, London 1970, ch. 2 (which is reprinted from C. J. Friedrich and J. W. Chapman (eds.), *Justice* (*Nomos* VI), New York 1963, pp. 306–325); A. W. Wood, (1) 'The Marxian Critique of Justice', in M. Cohen et al., pp. 3–41 (reprinted from *Philosophy and Public Affairs*, 1, No. 3, Spring 1972, pp. 244–282), (2) 'Marx on Right and Justice: A Reply to Husami', in M. Cohen et al., pp. 106–134 (reprinted from *Philosophy and Public Affairs*, 8, No. 3, Spring 1979,

Before getting under way, however, there is one indispensable preliminary and that is to sketch briefly a part of the theoretical background to this debate, the general lines of Marx's account of capitalist exploitation. One may speak for this purpose of the 'two faces' of it distinguishable in the wage relation. The first and more benign of them is seen in the sphere of circulation, where there is according to Marx an exchange of equivalent values, wages on the one side for labour-power on the other. The workers sell their commodity—the capacity to work—and from the capitalist they receive in exchange, in the form of wages, the value of the commodity they sell, which is to say the value of what goes into producing it, of the things workers consume by way of their

pp. 267–295), (3) *Karl Marx*, London 1981, Part 3, (4) 'Marx and Equality', in J. Mepham and D. H. Ruben (eds.), *Issues in Marxist Philosophy*, Volume 4, Brighton 1981, pp. 195–221, (5) 'Justice and Class Interests', *Philosophica* (Ghent), 33, 1984 (1), pp. 9–32.

[II] Those according to whom Marx did criticize capitalism as unjust: R. J. Arneson, 'What's Wrong With Exploitation?', *Ethics*, 91, January 1981, pp. 202–227; G. A. Cohen, (1) 'Freedom, Justice and Capitalism', *New Left Review*, 126, March/April 1981, pp. 3–16, (2) Review of *Karl Marx* by Allen W. Wood, *Mind*, XCII, No. 367, July 1983, pp. 440–445; J. Elster, (1) 'Exploitation, Freedom, and Justice', in Pennock and Chapman, pp. 277–304, (2) *Making Sense of Marx*, Cambridge 1985, ch. 4; M. Green, 'Marx, Utility, and Right', *Political Theory*, 11, No. 3, August 1983, pp. 433–446; R. Hancock, 'Marx's Theory of Justice', *Social Theory and Practice*, 1, 1971, pp. 65–71; Z. I. Husami, 'Marx on Distributive Justice', in M. Cohen et al., pp. 42–79 (reprinted from *Philosophy and Public Affairs*, 8, No. 1, Fall 1978, pp. 27–64); P. Riley, 'Marx and Morality: A Reply to Richard Miller', in Pennock and Chapman, pp. 33–53; C. C. Ryan, 'Socialist Justice and the Right to the Labour Product', *Political Theory*, 8, No. 4, November 1980, pp. 503–524; H. van der Linden, 'Marx and Morality: An Impossible Synthesis?', *Theory and Society*, 13, No. 1, January 1984, pp. 119–135; D. van de Veer, 'Marx's View of Justice', *Philosophy and Phenomenological Research*, 33, 1973, pp. 366–386; G. Young, (1) 'Justice and Capitalist Production: Marx and Bourgeois Ideology', *Canadian Journal of Philosophy*, VIII, No. 3, September 1978, pp. 421–455, (2) 'Doing Marx Justice', in Nielsen and Patten, pp. 251–268.

[II*] A group not altogether distinct from [II] but rather more tentative, expressing reservations of one sort or another about the interpretation of [I] without directly challenging it: N. Holmstrom, 'Exploitation', *Canadian Journal of Philosophy*, VII, No. 2, June 1977, pp. 353–369; W. L. McBride, 'The Concept of Justice in Marx, Engels, and Others', *Ethics*, 85, 1975, pp. 204–218; J. H. Reiman, 'The Possibility of a Marxian Theory of Justice', in Nielsen and Patten, pp. 307–322; W. H. Shaw, 'Marxism and Moral Objectivity', in Nielsen and Patten, pp. 19–44; R. J. van der Veen, 'Property, Exploitation, Justice', *Acta Politica* (Amsterdam), 13, 1978, pp. 433–465.

historically defined subsistence. What they receive from the capitalist, Marx goes out of his way to insist, is the full equivalent in value of what they sell and so involves no cheating. The second and uglier face of the relationship now shows itself, however, in the sphere of production. Here the workers, whose labour is itself the source of the value that commodities contain, will have to work longer than the time which is necessary to reproduce the value of their own labour-power, longer than is necessary to replace the value of the wage they have received. They will perform, that is to say, surplus labour, and the surplus-value they create thereby will be appropriated by the capitalist as profit. Labour-power in operation creates a value greater than the value labour-power itself embodies and is sold for. The two faces by turns reveal their contrasting features across the pages of *Capital*, complementary aspects of the wage relation: in the sphere of circulation, an equal exchange freely contracted; in the sphere of production, the compulsion to labour some hours without reward.

This, then, is the character of capitalist exploitation. Does Marx think it unjust?

I. Marx Against Justice

(i) A first and, on the face of it, compelling piece of evidence against supposing so is that he actually says it is not. Once the purchase of labour-power has been effected, according to Marx, this commodity belongs to the capitalist as of right, and so therefore does its use and so do the products of its use.[2] Or, expressed from the worker's point of view, 'As soon as his labour actually begins, it has already ceased to belong to him.'[3] The capitalist, Marx says in the passage most often referred to in this connection, has paid for the value of labour-power, and the fact that the use of the latter now creates a greater value, this 'is a piece of good luck for the buyer, but by no means an injustice

2. Karl Marx, *Capital*, Volume 1 (Penguin edition), Harmondsworth 1976, pp. 292, 303, and *Theories of Surplus Value*, Moscow 1968–72, Volume 1, p. 315.
3. *Capital* 1, p. 677.

towards the seller.'[4] Similarly: 'The fact that this particular commodity, labour-power, possesses the peculiar use-value of supplying labour, and therefore of creating value, cannot affect the general law of commodity production. If, therefore, the amount of value advanced in wages is not merely found again in the product, but augmented by a surplus-value, this is not because the seller has been defrauded, for he has really received the value of his commodity; it is due solely to the fact that this commodity has been used up by the buyer.'[5]

(ii) Consistently with this denial that the wage relation is unjust, Marx also rails against socialists who want for their part to appeal to considerations of justice. The best known occasion is his polemic, in *Critique of the Gotha Programme*, against the notion of a fair distribution of the proceeds of labour. 'What is a "fair distribution"?' he asks pointedly. 'Do not the bourgeois assert that the present-day distribution is "fair"? And is it not, in fact, the only "fair" distribution on the basis of the present-day mode of production? Are economic relations regulated by legal conceptions or do not, on the contrary, legal relations arise from economic ones? Have not also the socialist sectarians the most varied notions about "fair" distribution?' Shortly afterwards, he refers to such notions as 'obsolete verbal rubbish' and 'ideological nonsense about right and other trash so common among the democrats and French Socialists'—the gist of all of which seems clear enough.[6] Again, in a letter of 1877, he writes contemptuously of 'a whole gang of half-mature students and super-wise diplomaed doctors who want to give socialism a "higher, idealistic" orientation, that is to say, to replace its materialistic basis (which demands serious objective study from anyone who tries to use it) by modern mythology with its goddesses of Justice, Liberty, Equality, and Fraternity.'[7] On the one occasion when Marx himself makes use of some phrases about rights and justice —in his Inaugural Address to, and Preamble to the Rules of, the

4. *Capital* I, p. 301.
5. *Capital* I, p. 731. See also the 'Notes on Adolph Wagner' in Karl Marx, *Texts on Method* (T. Carver ed.), Oxford 1975, p. 216.
6. Karl Marx and Frederick Engels, *Selected Works*, Moscow 1969–70, Volume 3, pp. 16, 19.
7. Karl Marx and Frederick Engels, *Selected Correspondence*, Moscow n.d., pp. 375–6; see also *Capital* I, pp. 178–9 n. 2.

First International—he explains carefully in a letter to Engels: 'I was obliged to insert two phrases about "duty" and "right" into the Preamble to the Rules, ditto about "truth, morality and justice", but these are placed in such a way that they can do no harm.'[8]

(iii) What motivates the above polemics, as well as Marx's denial of any injustice in the wage relation, is perhaps already evident. It is what is suggested to many, including those whose interpretation we are presently rehearsing, by another formulation from *Critique of the Gotha Programme*; namely, that 'Right can never be higher than the economic structure of society and its cultural development conditioned thereby.'[9] Standards of justice, this may be taken to mean, are relative or internal to specific historical modes of production. It is not merely that they are generated by these— that juridical relations and the 'forms of social consciousness' corresponding to them 'originate in the material conditions of life'[10]—but that, in addition, they are only applicable to and valid for them. The only principles of justice which are appropriate to judging a particular mode of production are those that in fact 'correspond' to it, that are functional to sustaining and legitimating it. In the words of another much quoted passage: 'It is nonsense for Gilbart to speak of natural justice in this connection [interest payment on loans—NG]. The justice of transactions between agents of production consists in the fact that these transactions arise from the relations of production as their natural consequence. The legal forms in which these economic transactions appear as voluntary actions of the participants, as the expressions of their common will and as contracts that can be enforced on the parties concerned by the power of the state, are mere forms that cannot themselves determine this content. They simply express it. The content is just so long as it corresponds to the mode of production and is adequate to it. It is unjust as soon as it contradicts it. Slavery, on the basis of the capitalist mode of production, is unjust; so is cheating on the quality of commodi-

8. *Selected Correspondence*, p. 182; and see *Selected Works* 2, pp. 18–20, for the phrases in question.

9. *Selected Works* 3, p. 19.

10. Karl Marx, *A Contribution to the Critique of Political Economy*, London 1971, p. 20.

ties.'[11] Now, if by relativism in this regard we understand a conception in which what is just is simply a matter of subjective viewpoint, then Marx's conception may be said not to be a relativist one. It has, on the contrary, a firmly objective basis, since it construes the standards of justice appropriate to any society as being so by virtue of the real social function they perform.[12] It remains relativist, however, in the different sense of tying every principle of justice to a specific mode of production in the way described, and thus rendering each such principle unfit to provide a basis for trans-historical judgement. On this account of things, there cannot be an independent standard of justice, external to capitalism, yet appropriate to assessing it. There can be no principle transcending historical epochs and in the light of which Marx would have been able to condemn capitalism as unjust.

(iv) We can put the same point in another way. Moral norms and notions come within the compass of Marx's theory of ideology. Not only, therefore, do ideas about justice, but so does morality more generally, belong to the superstructure of any social formation. As *The German Ideology* has it, 'Morality, religion, metaphysics, and all the rest of ideology as well as the forms of consciousness corresponding to these, thus no longer retain the semblance of independence.'[13] It is not consistent with his views on ideology that Marx should have found capitalist society to be unjust by reference to historically quite general norms of justice.[14]

Reformism

(v) Justice being an essentially distributive value, it is argued furthermore, to attribute to Marx a concern with it is to inflect his critique of capitalism in a direction he explicitly repudiated and leads to a reformist conclusion he did not accept. For it focuses

11. *Capital*, Volume III (Penguin edition), Harmondsworth 1981, pp. 460–1; see also *Capital* I, p. 178.

12. Wood (1), pp. 18–19, (3), pp. 131–2.

13. Karl Marx and Frederick Engels, *Collected Works*, London 1975ff., Volume 5, pp. 36–7.

14. Brenkert (1), p. 90, (2), pp. 150, 154–5.

attention too narrowly on the distribution of income and the differentials within it: on the share of the social product received by the workers, the inadequate level of their remuneration. And it suggests that their exploitation might be eliminated by alteration and regulation of this sphere, in other words, merely by reforms in the distribution of income. As we know, however, for Marx exploitation is in the very nature of capitalism, integral to its relations of production on which the distribution of income largely depends. His preoccupation is with this more fundamental issue of the production relations and the need for a thoroughgoing revolution in them. As important as they are, reforms in the matter of wage levels simply cannot lead to the abolition of exploitation.[15] So, Marx chides the authors of the Gotha Programme with having made a fuss about 'so-called *distribution*'. The distribution of 'the means of consumption' cannot be treated independently of the mode of production.[16] So too, in *Wages, Price and Profit*, he speaks of 'that false and superficial radicalism that accepts premises and tries to evade conclusions', and he goes on: 'To clamour for *equal or even equitable retribution* on the basis of the wages system is the same as to clamour for *freedom* on the basis of the slavery system. What you think just or equitable is out of the question. The question is: What is necessary and unavoidable with a given system of production?' Later in the same work Marx proclaims, 'Instead of the *conservative* motto, "*A fair day's wage for a fair day's work!*" they [the workers—NG] ought to inscribe on their banner the *revolutionary* watchword, "*Abolition of the wages system!*"'[17]

(vi) The focus on distributive justice, some say, is also reformist in another way. It leads back from Marx's materialist enterprise of seeking the real revolutionary tendencies which will overturn the capitalist order to projects of moral enlightenment and legal reform. As one commentator puts this, it 'directs attention toward confused abstract ideals of justice and away from concrete revolutionary goals.'[18] The line of thought here is that for Marx it is a form of idealism to believe historical progress occurs through

15. See Tucker, pp. 50–1; Wood (1), p. 27; Buchanan (1), p. 134, (2), pp. 56–7.
16. *Selected Works* 3, pp. 19–20.
17. *Selected Works* 2, pp. 56–7, 75.
18. Buchanan (1), p. 134.

a change for the better in people's moral or juridical ideas. Such a change is secondary, derivative of the transformations in society's production relations. What counts, therefore, is to identify the actual historical tendencies that make for this sort of transformation and the social forces and movements at work that are capable of consummating it. Relative to this materialist task, a critique of capitalism in the name of justice represents a retreat— just equipping the would-be revolutionary, determined and passionate as may be, 'to deliver the keynote address at the next Democratic Convention'.[19]

(vii) Principles of justice are, in any case, precisely *juridical* principles. As such, they have their place within that whole institutional apparatus of state, law, sanctions and so on, by which obligatory modes of conduct are imposed upon the members of a social order. According to Marx, however, a communist society will not have this sort of apparatus. The state here withers away. Communism as envisaged by him cannot then be seen as realizing a juridical principle like one of distributive justice, as conforming to and institutionalizing this where capitalism is to be criticized for violating it.[20]

Beyond Scarcity

(viii) A communist society as Marx envisages it, indeed, is a society beyond justice. That is the claim of the commentators whose case we are presenting and the main textual authority for it is the same section from *Critique of the Gotha Programme* we have already cited, in which Marx speaks his mind about 'fair distribution' and about 'right'. For, in that context, he also anticipates two sorts of distributional criterion for the different phases of a post-capitalist society and discusses them in a way these commentators take to prove their point. For convenience, I refer hereafter to the two principles involved as, respectively, the *contribution principle* and the *needs principle*. The former will apply, Marx thinks, during an earlier period of emergent communism, 'still stamped with the birth marks of the old society'. After some

---

19. Wood (1), p. 30 – and see also (2), p. 133, (3), p. 143.
20. Wood (1), pp. 26–7, 30; Lukes (1), p. 198.

necessary deductions from the total social product have been made—for infrastructural and similar social purposes and the provision of public goods—each individual will receive from it, by way of means of personal consumption, an amount in proportion to his or her labour contribution. Each will be rewarded, therefore, according to an equal standard, constitutive of a situation of 'equal right'. But this is an equal right, Marx says, 'still constantly stigmatized by a bourgeois limitation'. Though it no longer permits class differences or privileges, nevertheless by measuring people solely according to their labour contribution, it allows those relatively well endowed, whether with physical or with intellectual ability, to benefit from the greater contribution they can thereby make, and it entails, conversely, for those with relatively large needs or responsibilities, greater burdens and disadvantages than others will have to bear: '*It is, therefore, a right of inequality, in its content, like every right.* Right by its very nature can consist only in the application of an equal standard; but unequal individuals (and they would not be different individuals if they were not unequal) are measurable only by an equal standard in so far as they are brought under an equal point of view, are taken from one *definite* side only, for instance, in the present case, are regarded *only as workers* and nothing more is seen in them, everything else being ignored.' Such a one-sided approach, so to speak levelling the complex individuality of persons, is unavoidable, Marx holds, in the initial stage of communism. Only in a later period will it be possible to implement the needs principle, better able, this, to match each person's individuality: 'In a higher phase of communist society, after the enslaving subordination of the individual to the division of labour, and therewith also the antithesis between mental and physical labour, has vanished; after labour has become not only a means of life but life's prime want; after the productive forces have also increased with the all-round development of the individual, and all the springs of co-operative wealth flow more abundantly—only then can the narrow horizon of bourgeois right be crossed in its entirety and society inscribe on its banners: From each according to his ability, to each according to his needs!'[21]

Now, it is argued in the light of these passages that the needs

21. *Selected Works* 3, pp. 16–19.

principle—which I shall render henceforth: 'From each according to their ability, to each according to their needs!'—is not a principle of distributive justice; and that in the higher phase of communism Marx speaks of, the very circumstances, of scarcity and conflict, that make such principles necessary will no longer exist. The formula is not intended by him as a principle of justice, so the argument goes, since it is clear here that he regards principles of justice, and concepts of rights associated with them, as inadequate by their nature, unable in their generality and formalism, indeed unable owing to their egalitarianism, to take account of the specific individuality of each person. The needs principle is not such a general or formal rule, because it does not subsume people under any equal standard or point of view but takes them in their specificity and variety. It is not, some even suggest, a prescriptive principle at all but simply a description of how things will eventually be. When Marx talks, therefore, of 'the narrow horizon of bourgeois right' being crossed, we must take him to mean that it is considerations of rights and justice as such that are transcended and left behind; 'to mean, not merely that there will be no more *bourgeois* right, but that there will be no more *Recht*, no more legal and moral rules.'[22] This possibility is based upon the hypothesis of a progressive disappearance of those conditions which create the need for codes of rights and norms of distributive justice. It is predicated, that is, on the elimination of scarcity and of other sources of human conflict, or at least on their diminution to a point of insignificance. With increasing material productivity yielding an abundance of resources; with less selfish, more sympathetic and generous interpersonal attitudes and qualities; with more harmonious and co-operative relationships all round—what from Hume to Rawls have been perceived as 'the circumstances of justice' will be present no more. If Marx sees this communist society as being 'higher' than all preceding social forms, then obviously, given what has gone before, this cannot mean he regards it as *more just*. No, it is higher according to some other standard of value.[23]

22. Lukes (1), p. 200.
23. For this paragraph, see Tucker, p. 48; Brenkert (1), p. 91, (2), pp. 153, 162; Buchanan (1), p. 139, (2), pp. 57–9; Lukes (1), pp. 198–203, (3), chs. 3 and 4; Wood (2), p. 131, (3), pp. 138–9, (4), pp. 203–11; Miller (1), pp. 338–9; Allen (1), p. 609.

(ix) For—finally, in our review of this side of the argument—Marx *is* committed to certain other values. As was made clear at the very beginning, no one here is denying that he condemned capitalism, and he did so in the light precisely of values other than justice: the most commonly mentioned in this connection being freedom; but also self-realization, well-being and community.[24] Unlike norms of justice, it is held, such values are not wholly relative or internal to historically specific modes of production and so are able to serve as universal criteria of judgement. There is a subordinate dispute, 'on this side of the line' as it were, as to whether they are themselves also *moral* values or are, rather, values of a different, non-moral sort, but I shall ignore that issue as of secondary significance, in view of the position I take in the last section of this essay on the principal issue of disagreement.

II. Marx for Justice

(i) If Marx sees no injustice or fraud in the wage paid by the capitalist to the labourer, then that is because these two, as he insists, exchange fully equivalent values. However, it is only in the narrow and preliminary perspective of the circulation process (so says our second group of interpreters in reply) that he does treat the wage relation as an exchange of equivalents. Only within the sphere of exchange itself, where commodities are bought and sold, and only in accordance with the criteria internal to it, with the law of value which governs the purchase and sale of commodities, does Marx depict the relation in that way. Once he moves forward, the wage contract behind him, to deal with the surplus labour that must be rendered by the worker to the capitalist within the production process, and once he sets this individual relationship in its broader class context, with the capitalist class facing the workers and exploiting them repeatedly and continuously, he goes on to represent the wage relation as *not* in fact an exchange of equivalents, not a genuine exchange at all. That the capitalist advances anything in exchange for labour-power, let

24. See Tucker, p. 50; Wood (1), pp. 34–41, (2), pp. 119–28, (3), pp. 125–30, 138; Brenkert (1), pp. 81–6, 93–105, (2), ch. 4 and pp. 155–7; Allen (1), pp. 609–11; Lukes (1), p. 201, (2), p. 342, (3), chs. 3 and 5; Miller (2), chs. 1 and 2.

alone something of an equivalent value, this, Marx now says, is 'only illusory' and a 'mere semblance' or 'form'.[25] It is an 'appearance', a 'mere pretence'.[26] There is no true equivalence in the exchange, for the worker must perform more labour than that which is necessary to replace the value of the wage; and thus Marx speaks of the surplus labour involved as done 'gratis' for the capitalist and as 'uncompensated', or often calls it simply 'unpaid labour'.[27] And the exchange is only an apparent one anyway since the capitalist just contributes to it what has been appropriated —gratis!—from the product of the labour of other workers. As Marx puts it in *Capital*: 'The exchange of equivalents, the original operation with which we started, is now turned round in such a way that there is only an apparent exchange, since, firstly, the capital which is exchanged for labour-power is itself merely a portion of the product of the labour of others which has been appropriated without an equivalent; and, secondly, this capital must not only be replaced by its producer, the worker, but replaced together with an added surplus. The relation of exchange between capitalist and worker becomes a mere semblance belonging only to the process of circulation, it becomes a mere form, which is alien to the content of the transaction itself, and merely mystifies it. The constant sale and purchase of labour-power is the form; the content is the constant appropriation by the capitalist, without equivalent, of a portion of the labour of others which has already been objectified, and his repeated exchange of this labour for a greater quantity of the living labour of others.'[28]

There is a parallel to be noted here between Marx's treatment of the apparent equivalence in the wage contract and his treatment of the freedom the worker enjoys in choosing to enter that contract. For the worker may appear to do this quite voluntarily and the sphere of circulation to be, therefore, 'a very Eden of the innate rights of man . . . the exclusive realm of Freedom, Equality, Property and Bentham'.[29] But the reality is different and, again, not so benign: 'the "free" worker', Marx writes,

25. Karl Marx, *Grundrisse*, Harmondsworth 1973, pp. 458, 509, 551, 674.

26. *Theories of Surplus Value* III, pp. 92–3, and I, p. 316.

27. *Capital* I, pp. 346, 680; and pp. 672, 689, 691, 693, 714, 715, 728, 729, 732, 733, 757, 769, 771; *Capital* III, p. 509; *Theories of Surplus Value* II, p. 29; *Grundrisse*, pp. 570–1.

28. *Capital* I, pp. 729–30.

29. *Capital* I, p. 280.

'makes a voluntary agreement, that is, he is compelled by social conditions to sell the whole of his active life, his very capacity for labour'; and 'the period of time for which he is free to sell his labour-power is the period of time for which he is forced to sell it.'[30] As, in the one case, unilateral appropriation of the labour of others is the reality behind an appearance of equal exchange, so in the other, compulsion is the real content of the appearance of voluntary contract: 'capital . . . pumps out a certain specific quantum of surplus labour from the direct producers or workers, surplus labour that it receives without an equivalent and which by its very nature always remains forced labour, however much it might appear as the result of free contractual agreement.'[31] The supposed justice *of* the wage relation is comparable, then, to the worker's freedom *in* it. It is an appearance whose real content or essence is a radically different one. It is asserted by Marx provisionally and in the context only of the circulation process where capitalist and worker treat with one another exclusively as individuals, but is then revealed in due course as mere appearance, within the overall perspective of the relations of, and in, production, a perspective this, by contrast, of the relationship of class to class.[32]

Exploitation as Theft

(ii) But if Marx, so to speak, takes back his assertion of an equivalence in this matter, does he also clearly take back his denial that there is any injustice involved? Does he say in fact, and in defiance of his own strictures of other socialists, that the real and exploitative content of the wage relation is *unjust* or is in violation of anyone's *rights*? In so many words he does not, but in effect—this case continues—he does. For he often talks of the capitalist's appropriation of surplus-value in terms of 'robbery', 'theft' and the like, which is tantamount to saying that the capitalist has no right to appropriate it and that his doing so is,

30. *Capital* I, pp. 382, 415.
31. *Capital* III, pp. 957–8; see also *Grundrisse*, pp. 247–9, 464.
32. This is the argument of Holmstrom, pp. 366–8; Husami, pp. 66–7; Young (1), pp. 441–50; Ryan, pp. 512–13; Arneson, pp. 218–19—and of my own 'Essence and Appearance: Aspects of Fetishism in Marx's *Capital*', see below at pp. 77–8, 82.

therefore, indeed wrongful or unjust. Thus, referring in one place to the surplus product as 'the tribute annually exacted from the working class by the capitalist class', Marx goes on: 'Even if the latter uses a portion of that tribute to purchase the additional labour-power at its full price, so that equivalent is exchanged for equivalent, the whole thing still remains the age-old activity of the conqueror, who buys commodities from the conquered with the money he has stolen from them.'[33] That is not a maverick usage on Marx's part. On the contrary. He also speaks of the annual surplus product 'embezzled from the English workers without any equivalent being given in return', and he says that 'all progress in capitalist agriculture is a progress in the art, not only of robbing the worker, but of robbing the soil.'[34] He refers to 'the booty pumped out of the workers' and 'the total surplus-value extorted . . . the common booty' and 'the loot of other people's labour'.[35] The prospective abolition of capitalist property he describes as 'the expropriation of a few usurpers.'[36] And the wealth produced under capitalism, he says, is based on the 'theft of alien labour time'.[37] Now it is perfectly possible, of course, to use the language of robbery without intending, for one's own part, any charge of injustice and wrong. One may mean by it simply to invoke, and not to endorse, some prevailing or conventional standard of rightful ownership. Thus, Robin Hood stole from the rich to help the poor, and so forth. But the whole point here is that according to Marx, as should be clear enough by now, exploitation is not robbery by prevailing and conventional standards, wrong by the norms of capitalist society. This point has been well put by Jerry Cohen: 'since . . . Marx did not think that by capitalist criteria the capitalist steals, and since he did think he steals, he must have meant that he steals in some appropriately non-relativist sense. And since to steal is, in general, wrongly to take what rightly belongs to another, to steal is to commit an injustice, and a system which is "based on theft" is based on injustice.'[38]

33. *Capital* I, p. 728.

34. *Capital* I, pp. 761, 638.

35. *Capital* I, p. 743; *Capital* III, pp. 312–13; *Theories of Surplus Value* II, p. 29.

36. *Capital* I, p. 930.

37. *Grundrisse*, p. 705. For a more ambiguous, and disputed, passage, see *Texts on Method*, p. 186 — and Wood (2), pp. 115–6; Young (2), pp. 259–60.

38. Cohen (2), p. 443; and see Husami, pp. 45, 63; Young (1), pp. 431–3; Ryan, p. 513; Elster (1), pp. 291–3, (2), ch. 4; van der Linden, pp. 128–9.

Some see it as significant, moreover, that in his discussion of primitive capitalist accumulation in the concluding part of the first volume of *Capital*, Marx should have emphasized, amongst other violent and bloody methods, the robbery that marked this process too—robbery of 'all their own means of production' from the direct producers, theft of the common lands from the people.[39] Not right and labour, as in the idyll of political economy, but 'In actual history . . . conquest, enslavement, robbery, murder, in short force, play the greatest part.'[40] This actual history may not be decisive from a purely theoretical point of view, since one could envisage a capitalism with clean origins or at least with cleaner origins than these, and it is capitalism in general, and by its very nature, that falls foul of Marx's charge of wrong, irrespective of how salubrious or otherwise its origins. Nevertheless, if he highlighted the robbery that actually occurred, he did so in order to draw attention to capitalism's unjust historical foundation. And since the context of this condemnation is precisely a transition period between modes of production, it shows surely, against what is argued on the other side, that not every standard of justice was, for him, internal to a particular mode of production.[41]

(iii) From what Marx says about capitalist robbery, therefore, we can infer a commitment to independent and transcendent standards of justice, and further evidence of the same thing is provided by his way of characterizing the two principles of distribution that he anticipates for post-capitalist society. I shall come presently—at II (viii)—to the interpretation of the second of them, the needs principle, that responds to what we have seen the other group of commentators aver about it. Of import here is that, and how, Marx ranks these principles relative both to what precedes them historically and to one another. The contribution principle, by which distribution of consumption goods is based exclusively on the labour one has done, he explicitly calls an 'advance'. This principle—where 'no one can give anything except his labour, and . . . nothing can pass to the ownership

39. *Capital* I, pp. 875, 885, 889, 895.
40. *Capital* I, p. 874.
41. See Arneson, p. 204; Cohen (1), p. 15; and–especially on this last point–Young (2), pp. 262–3.

of individuals except individual means of consumption'—is a superior one, then, to the norms of capitalist distribution. But on the other hand, because, as was earlier explained, it takes no account either of differential individual endowment or of differential needs, Marx says also that it possesses 'defects' relative to the needs principle which will eventually replace it, so that we must take the needs principle as being a yet superior one. He proposes, in other words, a hierarchy of distributive principles; and as they are not ranked by him according to any extrinsic standard of value, it is a reasonable supposition that he simply sees some principles as fairer or more just than others intrinsically, on a trans-historical standard of justice.[42]

Moral Realism

(iv) Marx's seemingly relativist statements in this area are not, in fact, what many have taken them to be. They are statements not of moral relativism but rather, as we may call this, of moral realism. That standards of right are, for him, sociologically grounded or determined means that the norms people believe in and live by will be powerfully influenced by the nature of their society, their class position in it, and so on. It means, more particularly, that what standards of right can actually be implemented effectively and secured—this is constrained by the economic structure and resources of the given society. It does not mean that the standards to be used in evaluating or assessing a society must necessarily also be constrained by the same economic configuration; that the only valid criteria of assessment are those actually prevalent, those harmonious with the mode of production.[43] Marx's assertion that right cannot be 'higher than the economic structure' is a case in point. Its context makes clear that it is a realist, not a relativist, one. He first speaks of the contribution principle as an advance over capitalism, then explains why it is defective nonetheless, and says that the defects are inevitable, however, during the first phase of communism. Then he makes

42. See *Selected Works* 3, pp. 18–19; and Hancock, p. 66; van de Veer, p. 373; Husami, p. 58; Arneson, pp. 214–15; Riley, pp. 39–42; Elster (1), pp. 290–1, 296, (2), ch. 4.

43. van de Veer, pp. 371–3; Holmstrom, p. 368; Husami, pp. 49–51; Arneson, p. 216; Shaw, p. 28; Hancock, pp. 66–7.

the statement in question and says, immediately afterwards, that the different conditions of a higher phase of communism will permit the implementation of the needs principle. Implanted in this context, Marx's statement is plausibly one concerning the real prerequisites of achieving progressively higher or more advanced standards of right. It is obviously not a statement that there can be no higher or lower in this matter on account of each such standard being relative to its appropriate economic structure.[44]

(v) There is nothing at all either reformist or contrary to the cast of Marx's thought, it is argued in addition, about a preoccupation with distribution as such. He does object to any over-restricted focus upon the social *division of income*, but that is because he sees the latter as more or less a consequence of the relations of production, and it is both politically misguided and theoretically senseless to condemn the necessary effects of a cause which is itself left uncriticized. On any broader view of distribution, however, Marx is clearly concerned with it: with the distribution of free time, of opportunities for fulfilling activity, of unpleasant or rebarbative work; with the distribution of welfare more generally, of social and economic benefits and burdens. And he is concerned, in particular and above all, with the distribution of productive resources, on which according to him this wider distribution depends. That is clear even in the passage of *Critique of the Gotha Programme* from which his putative anti-distributive orientation is usually derived. For, insisting that the distribution of means of consumption cannot be viewed as independent of the mode of production, Marx speaks of the mode of production as itself a kind of—more basic—distribution: 'the distribution of the conditions of production'.[45] His belittling of the 'fuss' about distribution, therefore, is aimed at distribution too narrowly construed and not in general. His own attention to the production relations is precisely a preoccupation with distribution, with for him the most fundamental one of all, namely that of the means of production; and as such this preoccupation is revolutionary *par excellence*.[46]

44. *Selected Works* 3, pp. 18–19.
45. Ibid.
46. van de Veer, p. 376; Husami, p. 75; Cohen (1), pp. 13–14; Arneson, pp. 222–5; van der Veen, p. 455.

(vi) Equally, there is nothing inherently reformist or idealist, from Marx's point of view, in criticism of capitalism by appeal to ethical norms or ideals, like justice. True, if such is the sole and self-sufficient, or even the principal, burden of a critical discussion of capitalism, then he does find it so wanting, but while clearly inadequate for him as an impulse to, or instrumentality of, revolutionary change, moral criticism and argument are in no way incompatible with the sort of materialist analysis—of the real historical tendencies towards revolution—that he sees as indispensable. In conjunction with that analysis, and with the actual movement and the struggles of the workers against capitalism, and with the social and economic transformations which these struggles and other developments bring about, a normative critique is perfectly in place and the denial of this just a form of what is called economism. Moral censure and justification are certainly the accompaniment of, and arguably they are a relatively independent contribution to, processes constituting the human agency of revolutionary change, the formation of a desire and a consciousness for socialism.[47]

(vii) So, whatever else may be the force of categorizing principles of justice and right as juridical ones, the categorization is unacceptably narrow if it is meant to bind them indissolubly to the existence of law, in a strict and positivist sense. They are, of course, as Marx knew well, standardly embodied in legal codes, backed up by the apparatus of enforcement that is a part of the state. However, such principles can be too, in the first instance, simply ethical ones concerning what is and what is not a morally defensible distribution of goods and bads; and it is possible to conceive their realization without the paraphernalia of state coercion. If these points do not make a juridical conception, then Marx had, or he *also* had, a non-juridical conception of justice.[48]

The Needs Principle

(viii) That is what the principle, 'From each according to their ability, to each according to their needs!', amounts to. It is in

47. Holmstrom, p. 368; Husami, pp. 53–4; Ryan, p. 516; Elster (2), ch. 4.
48. Husami, pp. 78–9; Shaw, pp. 41–2; Riley, pp. 49–50 n. 40.

substance a principle of distributive justice even if its attainment is envisaged together with the death of the state. There are some differences worth noting in the way this is argued, amongst the writers whose interpretation is being outlined, but the common ground is that, whether knowingly or not, Marx retains a notion of rights even for the higher phase of communism. Severe as his *Critique of the Gotha Programme* may be about a certain sort of formalism exemplified by the contribution principle, the strictures there do not finish by disposing of all types of right, or of general rules as such. They simply reveal, in effect, what rights and rules Marx finds morally inadequate. As one commentator has written, 'it is only the horizon of bourgeois right, not that of rights *überhaupt*, that is superseded in the transition to the higher stage.'[49] The general rule, indeed, marked down for this higher stage is the fulfilment of individual needs, and the right that it generalizes a right, amongst other things, to the means of personal development or self-realization. Its complement (expressed in the first half of the famous slogan) is that each person makes an effort commensurate with her or his abilities, in taking on a share of the common tasks. If they succeed, these standards, in making good the defects of the principle they supplant—which, sensitive only to the magnitude of labour contribution, gives out larger rewards to greater capabilities and talents—this is not because they are free of either the generality or the prescriptive force characteristic of rights. It is only because Marx obviously regards need and effort as morally more appropriate, in a word *fairer*, criteria of distribution than individual endowment. Why else should he say of the contribution principle that 'it tacitly recognizes unequal individual endowment and thus productive capacity as natural privileges',[50] whilst looking forward to the implementation of the needs principle, quite happy therefore to countenance its recognition of unequal need, forgoing with respect to this any such talk of privilege? The element of plain good fortune in the possession of great or exceptional abilities he clearly does not see as meriting any larger reward than is inherent in the very exercise and enjoyment of them. That Marx himself thinks of the needs principle as less formalistic, or more concrete, than the one it

49. Arneson, p. 216; see also van de Veer, p. 372, and compare the text to n. 22 above.

50. *Selected Works* 3, p. 18.

supplants, more exactly attuned, morally speaking, to the specific individuality of each person, does not for all that undo its generality as a normative principle.

Now, it is just because of the idea of its greater responsiveness to the specificity of every individual that some of the writers who view the needs principle, along the above lines, as a standard of right and justice, agree nevertheless, with those who reject that view, that it is not a principle of equality: under it, different individuals are accepted as being, by definition, unequal individuals.[51] Others—a majority—of these writers, however, do not agree. Marx must be understood, they think, as proposing, in place of a false equality, a truer or a better one. For, the sole charge laid by him, by way of its aforesaid 'defects', against the contribution principle, is in essence that it yields unjustifiable inequalities, unequal rewards based on differences in individual ability that are for him of no moral relevance. What Marx foresees in its stead is equality not in the sense of a right to equivalent rewards for equivalent amounts of labour, nor yet in the sense of the right of each person to exactly the same things or to an identical share of social wealth; it is, rather, an equality of self-realization—everyone's right, equally, to the means of his or her own.[52] As for the prospect of an eventual abundance of resources, this is either not discussed at all here or else, acknowledged as the precondition of giving effect to the needs principle, obviously not thought incompatible with construing the latter as a principle of distributive justice. Only one writer explicitly—though another perhaps implicitly—treats the assumption of unconditional abundance as a problematic one.[53]

(ix) The claim, finally, that Marx's condemnation of capitalism rests on values such as freedom and self-actualization, though not on any conception of justice, involves an inconsistent usage of his texts. Whether these other values are said themselves to constitute an ethic ('of freedom') or morality ('of emancipation'), or are regarded, on the contrary, as being non-moral goods,[54] it makes

51. Riley, pp. 39–43; Husami, p. 61.

52. Hancock, pp. 69–70; Arneson, pp. 214–16; Reiman, pp. 316–17, 321–2; Elster (1), p. 296, (2), ch. 4; Green, pp. 438–42.

53. Respectively Elster and – with the appearance of some inconsistency – Reiman.

54. Respectively, here, Brenkert, Lukes and Wood.

no difference in this matter; the claim sets up a distinction in his thought between two sorts of values: on the one hand, those—to do with rights and justice—necessarily dependent on and relative to historically particular social formations and hence unsuitable for the revolutionary criticism of them; on the other hand, those—like freedom and self-realization—not so dependent or relative and apt consequently for critical use. The distinction is unfounded. To the extent that Marx does postulate an ideological limitation or relativity of values, his theory of ideology is perfectly general in its reach, encompassing every sort of normative concept and not only ideas about justice. Sociology of normative belief in attempting to explain the historical bases of different values, it is consistent, however, with his also making evaluative judgements of univeral range on his own behalf. Marx does, of course, condemn capitalism for its unfreedom, oppression, coercion, but so does he in substance condemn it for its injustice. And just as, conversely, he does indeed identify principles of justice that are internal to and functional for the capitalist mode of production, so also does he identify conceptions of freedom and of self-development historically relative in exactly the same way.[55] To take account only of texts in which he does the first is in the circumstances exegetically arbitrary.[56]

III. Marx Against Marx

In the face of two so opposed construals of a single author's meaning, each apparently supported by a plethora of both direct citation of, and inferential reasoning from, his works, it is probably as well to begin by posing, point-blank, the question of whether a definitive resolution of this issue is possible by reference only to the letter of Marx's texts. I think there are reasons for doubting that it is. I shall mention two such, at any rate, one a consideration of a general kind, the other a more specific doctrinal point.

The first is that Marx was not a moral philosopher and there is more than likely to be some incoherence in what he gives out on these matters. To say he was no moral philosopher actually

---

55. See *Collected Works* 6, pp. 464, 499–500, and *Grundrisse*, pp. 487–8, 651–2.

56. Young (2), pp. 266–8; Arneson, pp. 219–20; Husami, pp. 52–3.

understates the relevant point. For, it is not just that he was primarily something else, scientific historian, critic of political economy, theoretician of proletarian revolution, or what have you; but in any case mere non-practitioner of moral philosophy and neutrally disposed towards it. It is that Marx, as is well known, was quite impatient and dismissive of overt theoretical reflection about normative questions, condescending only rarely to engage in it himself. He was hostile, not neutral, towards the explicit elaboration of socialist ethical theory, disdained in this area the kind of rigorous examination of problems and concepts he so insisted upon elsewhere. At the same time, and despite this, like just about everyone else he was given to the use of moral judgement. Normative viewpoints lie upon, or just beneath the surface of, his writings, and they lie there abundantly, albeit in an unsystematic form. This being so, some, perhaps even major, inconsistency here on his part is not to be excluded. The details of our two antithetical interpretations do at least suggest the possibility of it.

The second reason needs more extended exposition. It concerns what I should like to call the 'dialectical play' indulged in by Marx as to whether or not the wage relation constitutes an exchange of equivalents. Does it? The answer is: yes and no. Viewed as an exchange of commodities in the market, it does. The capitalist pays for the value of labour-power; the worker gives this commodity and receives, in exchange, a wage of equal value. But, viewed as a relation in production, the wage relation is not an exchange of equivalents. For, here the worker has still to give something: not in the sense of selling it, since the sale has already been concluded, but in the sense of personal effort; and this personal effort is the substance of a value that is larger than the value of the wage. The same thing can be expressed in other terms. Does the accumulation of value and capital which takes place result from labour that is the capitalist's? Yes and no. The labour which is its source belongs to the capitalist, for it has been bought and paid for; but it is not the labour of his (more rarely, her) own body, not the sweat of his (or her) brow. It is, if you like, labour that the capitalist owns but not the capitalist's own labour. Now, there is nothing mysterious about all this (leave alone whether the theory of value that it depends on is defensible) — it is spelled out plainly by Marx himself and careful readers of *Capital* have no trouble grasping it. Considered from one point of view, the wage relation is an exchange of equivalents and the accumulation of capital due only to the use of what is the capitalist's. Considered from another point of view, the wage relation is not an exchange of equivalents and the accumulation of capital is due to the labour of the worker. The two points of view are simply that, two different angles of vision on a single phenomenon. They depend on two different senses of what counts as an exchange of equivalents. They are in no way contradictory, but mutually consistent parts of the doctrine that labour is the source and substance of all value: that labour-power, sold for what it is worth as a commodity, in operation creates something that is worth more.

An Equivocal Dialectic

Which of them, however, is the appropriate point of view in the present context, the controversy about Marx and justice? Those according to whom he sees no injustice in the wage relation privilege the first, that there is an exchange of equivalents.Many (not all) of those according to whom he does regard the wage relation as unjust privilege the second, that there is not. Each side says, in effect, '*This* point of view is the only one relevant to the question of whether or not capitalism is for him unjust.'[57] But what of Marx himself? Well, Marx has it both ways, and that is at least one root of the difficulty. Note, here, that the problem is *not* that he affirms both points of view. As has just been said, they are mutually consistent parts of one doctrine. The problem is that he equivocates as to which of them is the one relevant to the moral question, so that it is legitimate in a way for each side to claim, about the two different perspectives: Marx *really* means us to adopt this one. For, he does say that, so far as justice is at issue, all that matters is that equal values are exchanged, in accordance with the laws of commodity production, and he thereby legitimates the view of one side in this dispute. But then, by a piece of dialectical wizardry in Chapter 24 of the first volume of *Capital*, he has these same laws turning into their very opposite. In his own words, 'the laws of appropriation or of private property, laws based on the production and circulation of commodities, become

57. See, for example, Allen (2), pp. 234–7, and Young (2), pp. 263–6.

changed into their direct opposite through their own internal and inexorable dialectic.' He speaks here, similarly, of the occurrence of a 'dialectical inversion'. The exchange of equivalents has now become, accordingly, only apparent, not an exchange of equivalents—in fact theft. A passage from the *Grundrisse* tells us, in the same vein, that 'the right of property undergoes a dialectical inversion, so that on the side of capital it becomes the right to an alien product.'[58] If the laws of commodity production and exchange have actually turned into their opposite, then that legitimates the view of the other side in this dispute as well, that, when all is said and done, there is no genuine equivalence or reciprocity here.

But this turning into opposites is just a logical trick, or more generously perhaps—though that point stands—the enjoyment of intellectual paradox and surprise. It is a game with the two different senses of equivalence. Nothing, in fact, changes into its opposite in this matter. Everything persists. In so far as the laws of commodity production require that equal values be exchanged in the market, they are, and this remains so when labour-power is sold as a commodity. And in so far as these laws allow that labour-power may indeed be sold as a commodity, being itself alienable, they allow *ab initio* a relation other than, but consistent with, equal exchange in the market, a relation in which the capitalist uses the worker to reap a profit over the wage, while the worker for her or his part simply works, just giving the portion of value that the other just takes. The right of property involved is always a right of persons to use what they own, thus what they have paid the value of in exchange; and it is, consistently with that, always a right to profit from the labour of others. Both the equivalence or reciprocity and the lack of it are there from beginning to end. Marx knows all this—it is, after all, his own theory—and he says as much even in expounding the 'dialectical inversion'. But, as is so often the way with it, the dialectic here only muddies the water. A thing cannot be its opposite. If the wage relation is an exchange of equivalents and just, then that, finally, is what it is, and this can be maintained, even to the point of extreme stubbornness,[59] in the face of Marx clearly speaking otherwise. But if it

58. *Capital* I, pp. 725–34 (the quoted material appears at pp. 729, 730 n. 6, 734); *Grundrisse*, p. 458.

59. See, for instance, Wood (3), p. 256 n. 21, and the apt comment on it by Cohen, (2), p. 443.

does indeed turn into its direct opposite, then it is not, finally, an exchange of equivalents or just, and therefore Marx cannot really mean what he says when he says that it is. The confusion amongst his commentators is a fruit, then, of his own: of his prevarication over which perspective, equivalence or non-equivalence, really counts for this purpose; of the consequent willingness and ability to assert, to all appearances in his own voice, both that the wage relation is not unjust and that it is theft. There are other and perhaps more important causes of Marx's confusion, causes I shall come to shortly. But the path is certainly smoothed for it by his use in this context of the language of the dialectic.

In view of these considerations, any attempt to resolve the central issue in dispute must bring with it some measure of reconstruction beyond mere exegesis, and I will contend for my own part that the most cogent such reconstruction broadly vindicates those who say Marx did think capitalism unjust. It gives them the better of this argument. The enterprise requires that one be as faithful as possible to the spirit of all the pertinent texts, both those already adduced on each side and others to be cited in what follows. One should not deny the elements of confusion and inconsistency in them, a common though not a universal temptation in this debate. Rather, acknowledging their presence there, one should seek to make the best sense that can be made of them. A reconstruction along these lines, however, broadly vindicates the view that Marx thought capitalism unjust, because it is better able to explain the apparent evidence to the contrary than are those who gainsay that he did able to explain what speaks against them. The issue turns, in my opinion, on two questions. Each of them is sorely embarrassing to the case I shall henceforth here oppose, and neither has elicited a satisfactory response from its proponents. On the principle that a good test of any intellectual position is the answers it has to the strongest questions that can be put against it, the view that Marx did not condemn capitalism as unjust must be judged to be uncompelling, for all the passages from his work seemingly in its favour. I shall, in any case, now take the two crucial questions in turn, interposing between them, though, what I think needs to be conceded on account of those passages. First, I endorse the claim, against inadequate attempts to explain such talk of his away, that in characterizing exploitation as robbery, Marx was impugning the justice of it. Second, I qualify this claim in the light of his own disavowal of a critique of capitalism in the name of justice. Third, I argue that the counter-claim, that his real critique was, instead, one on behalf of freedom and self-actualization, bears within it a fatal logical flaw: probed, this reveals, at the heart of his very critique on behalf of these other values, a concern for distributive justice.

'Explanations'

Why then, firstly, does Marx use 'robbery' and cognate terms in describing the realities of capitalism, unless it is because he thinks them unjust? The force of this question is not lost on those who deny that he thinks so and, in general, they do not flinch from responding to it.[60] Nor are they short of suggested answers. On the contrary, they offer, between them, a surprisingly large number. I shall set down their suggestions here. (1) In some of the usages in question, Marx has in mind the theft, not of surplus-value, but of the worker's health or time. (2) As regards the robbery involved in particular in the primitive accumulation of capital, this has the 'straightforward' sense that some people took what did not belong to them: wrong, therefore, according to prevailing standards of rightful ownership, it does not necessarily entail a charge of injustice on Marx's own part. (3) Similarly, but with regard now to capitalist exploitation in general, this is robbery only on bourgeois society's own conceptions of justice, and not by any standard that he himself entertains. At any rate, 'it appears that' the passages under discussion can be accounted for in this way. (4) Marx's model here might be a relationship of more or less regular plunder, as of a conquering from a conquered people, and in that case 'it is not so clear that' the robbery is unjust, since, being regular, such plunder must be based on existing material possibilities, hence correspond to the given mode of production, and if it corresponds to the mode of produc-tion, then it is, we know, just, on Marx's conception of justice. (5) His talk of theft and the like is aimed in fact at the disguised coercion, or merely at the coercion, whether disguised or open, rather than at the injustice of capitalist exploitation. (6) Or it is

---

60. But see Tucker, p. 46; having perhaps overlooked the relevant material, he says that Marx and Engels 'do not admit that profit derived from wage labour under the capitalist system is "theft"'.

'rhetoric pure and simple', 'Marx . . . speaking figuratively', or 'speaking falsely', misrepresenting his own view of things. (7) In any event, it simply cannot be taken as levelling a charge of injustice on the basis of a principle that transcends capitalism, for Marx's views on ideology prohibit him from doing that.[61]

The secret of these attempted explanations is discovered in the last of them. It might be thought that the plurality of their number testifies to the soundness and security of the interpretation of Marx they are deployed to defend, able to throw so much against a potentially damaging criticism. But it only testifies, in fact, to the feebleness of each one. If the texts themselves pointed to some strong and obvious explanation, then the authors of the above suggestions might have been expected to converge on it. In the absence of this, they do the best they can, each in his own particular way. The first three suggestions merit some detailed individual comment. Briefer and more generalized treatment then disposes of the rest of them.

As to (1), Marx does sometimes say that capital robs the workers of their time and health, or that it 'usurps' these things.[62] But, with respect to the passages in dispute in this debate, that accounts only partially for one or two of them, as open-minded readers may satisfy themselves. The main point of these passages is the theft of surplus labour and surplus-value. More importantly, even where it is time and health that is the point, does not this, as one commentator has observed, 'show *a: least* that in Marx's view capitalist production essentially involves the theft of the worker's time and health, and is for *that* reason unjust?'[63] As for (2), the argument has some logical force but is for all that wanting. That is, it is possible that, in speaking of the robbery that marked the dawn of capitalist society, Marx meant only to register the violation of pre-existing property rights and not himself to condemn it; to record a wrong by the then prevailing standards rather than injustice by his own. Abstractly considered, therefore, the circumstance that he was dealing with a transition between modes of production does not in itself conclusively prove that he sub-

61. See, for (*1*): Allen (2), p. 248; for (*2*): Brenkert (2), p. 148; for (*3*): Buchanan (2), pp. 187–8 n. 31; for (*4*): Wood (2), pp. 117–18, (3), pp. 137–8; for (*5*): Wood (2), p. 119, (3), p. 138, and Brenkert (2), pp. 147–8; for (*6*): Allen (2), pp. 246–9; for (*7*): Brenkert (2), pp. 149–50.

62. *Capital* 1, pp. 375–6, 553, 591, 599.

63. See the references at notes 33–37 above, and Young (2), pp. 256–8.

scribed to some trans-historical principle of justice. He might simply have been speaking relative to positive property rights.[64] But what tells us that this abstract possibility is a fact—that Marx in reality did mean what he possibly might have meant? Nothing does, absolutely nothing in the relevant texts. On the contrary, the passion of his treatment of primitive accumulation indicates the opposite, that his description of this process is also a denunciation of the brutal methods it involved. We are offered no reason here for thinking that his talk of robbery was not intended in his own name—unless inconsistency with the view that he did not consider capitalism to be unjust can itself be counted as such a reason. The argument, in other words, is merely an explanation of convenience. It responds to a need that must be met if that view is to be sustained, and has no independent textual foundation.

The same goes for the argument—(3)—that, in calling capitalist exploitation 'robbery', Marx implicitly invokes standards of justice internal to capitalism and records an injustice relative only to these. Since he never says explicitly that exploitation is unjust, whether by standards internal to capitalism or by standards external to it, how do we know that such is the burden of the robbery passages? We do not. It just 'appears that' they can be accounted for in that way. What appears, however, to others is Marx himself simply saying that the capitalist robs the worker, and as the passages themselves give not so much as a hint of any appeal to someone else's norms of justice, saying it in his own right. It is again, not the texts, but the needs of the interpretation that are the real foundation of the argument. I shall digress briefly to point out that the latter is part of a subordinate difference amongst those who concur that Marx does not himself view capitalism as unjust. Some of them claim that he does, at least, see it as unjust by its own criteria.[65] It is true that he seeks to expose an ideology of bourgeois society according to which the worker receives full recompense for all the value his or her labour-power creates. The worker, Marx holds, receives the equivalent only of some of that value, of a part of it equal to the value of labour-power itself. However, this is all that the capitalist is required to pay according to the laws of commodity production and exchange,

64. See text to n. 41 above.

65. See Allen (1), pp. 603–7, (2), pp. 240–1; Buchanan (1), p. 138, (2), pp. 54–5.

and it is these which Marx plainly takes as the real standard of bourgeois right in this matter. If, therefore, the ideology is a deception or hypocrisy, the relation between capitalist and worker still satisfies what are for him the sole effective juridical norms of capitalist exchange.[66] So the claim is unconvincing. But, convincing or not, it makes no difference: it cannot establish that when he terms exploitation, repeatedly—without qualification— 'robbery', 'theft', 'embezzlement', and surplus-value 'loot' or 'booty', and capitalists 'usurpers', this does not imply that, right or wrong by bourgeois society's standards, exploitation is an injustice by Marx's own lights. It cannot establish it save via the pure presumption that exploitation cannot be that, on account of other things he says, which is the presumption generating speculation as to what else these usages might mean.

Double-Counting

And this is the crux of it all. What we have here are precisely ad hoc and speculative attempts to explain away material that embarrasses the interpretation of Marx these writers favour. They are speculative attempts because there is nothing in the robbery passages themselves, or in their context, to confirm that they in fact have the character attributed to them in the explanations suggested. Detailed consideration of the remainder of these would involve unwarranted repetition. (7) just *asserts* that the talk of robbery cannot carry a charge of injustice, on the basis of this presumption of consistency. Doubtless on the same basis, (6) equally, and very conveniently, just discounts such talk as rhetoric and self-misrepresentation. (5) is a quite arbitrary displacement; 'robbery' has a meaning distinct from 'coercion' and we are given no reason to believe either that Marx was ignorant of the distinction or that he chose to overlook it. And the tautological inadequacy of (4) is manifest. It tells us in essence, albeit with a tentativeness surely due to its own inadequacy, that 'it is not so clear that' Marx regards this particular form of robbery as unjust, because we know that it is for him *not* unjust if it corresponds, as regular plunder necessarily would, to the prevailing mode of production. But the question remains, why then does he charac-

66. Ryan, p. 510; Brenkert (2), pp. 139–40.

terize it as robbery? This attempt at a response, like all the others, is just based on a kind of exegetical double-counting: there must be some such explanation as these, for we already *know* that Marx says capitalist exploitation is not unjust and so he cannot *really* mean robbery. One can just as well reason, as others in effect do: we *know* he thinks exploitation is robbery, so he cannot *really* mean it is not unjust. Either way the reasoning begets a forced and conjectural reading of some passages from Marx's work, a reading strained against the evidence internal to them.

The assumption of some consistency is, of course, a rational principle of textual interpretation. Where an author's work reveals the clear commitment to a certain intellectual position and we nevertheless find there also some few formulations which seem to contradict that, interpretative charity demands that we should inquire whether the inconsistency is not merely an apparent one or seek some other way of explaining the formulations in question. Elsewhere, for example, I have myself argued that Marx obviously did have a concept of 'human nature' and that the one lonely—and ambiguous—passage which has encouraged many to believe otherwise is susceptible to such treatment and must be given it. The same applies to a single phrase, concerning 'uninterrupted revolution', in Lenin's writings before 1917, a phrase often used to denature the sense of his conception of the Russian revolution up to that year.[67] However, the assumption of consistency has its limits. It cannot be absolute. Otherwise, one will simply presume complete theoretical coherence where it may be lacking. When not just one or a few formulations, but a whole body of formulations, arguments, concepts, stands in the way of one of a thinker's putative intellectual commitments, then an assumption of full consistency is no longer either rational or justified. The whole of section II of this essay, and the literature there summarized, is testimony to the fact that this is the case with respect to Marx's disavowal of any critique of capitalist injustice. In such circumstances, the argument that he cannot have held one viewpoint because to have done so would have been inconsistent with another he affirmed, is not a good one.

In the absence, therefore, of any convincing answer to the

67. See *Marx and Human Nature: Refutation of a Legend*, Verso, London 1983, and in particular the remarks at pp. 57–8; and *The Legacy of Rosa Luxemburg*, Verso/NLB, London 1976, pp. 70–100.

question, why Marx should have called exploitation 'robbery' if not because he considered it unjust, one must accept the most natural reading of the passages where he so characterizes it, which is that he did consider it unjust. To treat exploitation as theft is to treat the appropriation of surplus-value and, with it, capitalist property rights as wrongs. That such was Marx's view of things, however, is a claim that has to be qualified—and this brings me to the second part of my argument. For one can no more wish away the material that is troubling to this claim than one can Marx's talk of robbery. He does explicitly deny that there is injustice in the relationship between capitalist and worker, eschews and derides any appeal on behalf of socialism to the language of rights or justice, and appears more generally to underwrite a conception wherein standards of justice are merely relative to each mode of production. Some commentators have been tempted to propose that it is in fact this sort of material which is not to be taken at face value: that his denial of any injustice in the wage relation is made 'tongue-in-cheek' or with satirical, 'ironic' intent; that he means by it to say simply—this is what is called or what is taken to be just, or this is what is just by capitalist criteria, or this is a mere appearance of justice inasmuch as the exchange to which it relates is itself a mere appearance; and that, correspondingly, the object of his impatience with socialist appeals to notions of what is just or fair is only the rhetoric of justice and not its substance.[68] In other words Marx, on these proposals, is either not speaking literally and seriously here or not speaking in his own voice. As I have already intimated, I think the temptation to have recourse to this kind of explanation is mistaken. It gives us a mirror-image of the procedure of those who would explain away Marx's assertions of robbery, just switching from one side of the intellectual profile to the other the values of what he means literally and what he does not; conveniently discounting, exactly as do writers of the opposite viewpoint, what cannot readily be accommodated within the interpretation proffered: in the present case, not the charge of theft but rather the relativizing discourse about justice.

68. Holmstrom, p. 368; Husami, pp. 45, 67; Arneson, pp. 217–18; Young (1), pp. 441, 446, (2), p. 252; van de Veer, pp. 369–70.

An Unacknowledged Thought

But the procedure is equally unconvincing with respect to this. On internal textual evidence Marx speaks in these matters both seriously and for himself. It is true, to be sure, that it is on criteria internal to capitalism that his judgement of the equity of the wage relation is based. But then, according to the *only* direct and explicit statements Marx makes concerning justice, it is precisely and solely such internal and, thus, relative criteria that are relevant to deciding what is just and what is not. If the relation is just by capitalist standards, it is also just on the only explicit conception of justice that Marx himself puts forward. There is at any rate no conscious irony involved—if one does not, in the manner I have criticized, simply presume that there *must* be, given other things we know. So far as his own intentions are concerned, Marx has to be taken as meaning both that the wage contract is not unjust according to the appropriate, internal, bourgeois standards and—therefore!—that it is not unjust according to him, that is, according to the relativist definition of justice to which he expressly commits himself. From this it should be clear that I do not believe it possible plausibly to dispose of all of what I have termed his relativizing discourse by representing it as only apparently that and really something else. It may be true of some of his statements standardly read as relativist ones that they are not. The argument, in particular, that the proposition, 'Right can never be higher than the economic structure of society', signifies rather a sober moral realism, seems to me from the details of the proposition's context to be a cogent one, in any case no less plausible than the common relativist interpretation of these words. More generally, such a sense of or care for moral realism is unquestionably an important dimension of Marx's thought, thereby also of the problem under discussion, and it is one to which I shall later advert. All the same, I think it idle to hope to liquidate, by appeal either to this or to other considerations, what is at the very least a strong tendency on his part, one that pervades his mature writings, whatever else he may *also* do or say inconsistently with it; a tendency to relativize the status of norms and values, and whose most incontrovertible manifestation is the treatment of these as ideological, hence superstructural and merely derivative, without independent validity or trans-historical reach.

Is there, then, no way of resolving the conflict between Marx's explicit statements that are the product and reflection of this tendency and his implicit charge that capitalism is unjust, borne by, amongst other things, his usage of the terminology of robbery? I believe there is, although what I propose has itself an air of paradox about it. Not only is it perfectly coherent, however; it is the virtually mandatory conclusion in the light of all the relevant textual evidence. The proposal is: Marx did think capitalism was unjust but he did not think he thought so.[69] This is because in so far as he indeed thought directly about and formulated any opinion concerning justice, which he did only intermittently, he expressed himself as subscribing to an extremely narrow conception of it. The conception was narrow in two respects: associating justice, firstly, in more or less legal positivist fashion, with prevailing or conventional juridical norms, the standards internal to each social order; and associating it, secondly, with the distribution of consumption goods or, as this relates to capitalism, the distribution of income, and hence with a too partial focus upon the process of exchange in the market. This double association is manifest in the material cited at I (i) through I (v) above and it is obvious why on the basis of it Marx should have treated the wage contract as not unjust and justice as not a revolutionary notion. But it is these two conceptual associations that are, along with the 'dialectical inversion' discussed earlier, the source of his confusion.[70]

For neither of them is obligatory in estimating the justice of a society, which is to say that there are alternative and broader conceptions of distributive justice than they define. One may consider what is proper in virtue of a supposed set of *moral*, rather than legal or conventional, rights or entitlements—the rational content of notions of natural right—and one may also take

69. Two other writers make this point: see Cohen (2), pp. 443–4–also (1), p. 12–and Elster (1), pp. 289–90, 303 n. 44, (2), ch. 4. Oddly, so does a third, Steven Lukes, from the other side of the debate: his essay on the subject, however, minimizes the force of the point, consigning to a footnote Marx's belief that capitalism was unjust and simply declaring it an 'unofficial' view; and while his book appears to concede a larger place in Marx's thinking to this unofficial view, the appearance is basically deceptive since Lukes does not in fact concede what really matters here, that the belief in question shows Marx's attachment to some *non-relativist* standards of justice. See Lukes (1), p. 197 n.83, (3), ch. 4.

70. See also, in connection with this paragraph and the next, Hancock, p. 66; Shaw, pp. 41–2; Ryan, pp. 516–17; van der Veen, pp. 434, 448, 455.

account, in doing so, of the distribution of advantages and disadvantages quite generally, including here consequently the distribution of control over productive resources. And that is exactly what Marx does and does frequently, even if the concept, 'justice', is not expressly present to his mind and under his pen when he does it. Not compelled by the aforementioned conceptual associations, we can legitimately say, therefore, that inasmuch as he obviously finds the distribution of benefits and burdens under capitalism morally objectionable, impugning the capitalist's right to the best of it, he does think capitalism is unjust. Implicit in his work is a broader conception of justice than the one he actually formulates, notwithstanding the fact that he never himself identifies it as being such. This is not a question of simply imputing to Marx something alien to his own ways of thought. On the contrary, it is *he* who clearly, albeit *malgré lui*, challenges the moral propriety of the distributive patterns typical of capitalism — distribution in this context, mark you, taken in its widest sense — and that he does not realize what he is doing in challenging it, precisely criticizing capitalism as unjust, is merely a confusion on his part about the potential scope of the concept of justice and thus neither here nor there so far as the substance of the issue is concerned. The challenge, by its nature, cannot be anything else than a critique of injustice. We have seen this with respect to the matter of robbery: to say that that is what capitalists are engaged in just *is*, so long as one has no well-founded alternative explanation of its meaning, to question their right to what they appropriate and so the justice of that appropriation. We may now go on to adduce further confirmation of the resolution of this controversy I have here proposed, by examining how things stand with the third matter for discussion previously signalled: Marx's commitment to the values of freedom and self-development.

The Distribution of Freedom

It is this commitment, remember, that is urged upon us, by those who deny his attachment to considerations of justice, as being the real basis of his condemnation of capitalism. But such a delineation of putative alternatives is a false one, as immediately becomes clear if we proceed to put the second of the two questions I have said are embarrassing to the case these writers make.

Whose freedom and self-development or self-realization are at issue? The answer to this question, Marx's answer, is—tendentially everybody's. Tendentially, because of course for Marx universal freedom can only come through class struggle, the dictatorship of the proletariat, a transitional economic formation and so on, in the course of which there should be, certainly, a progressive enlargement of freedom and of opportunities for individual self-realization, but only over time and in the face of social and also material obstacles. Everybody's, however, because it is after all a universal freedom and self-development that he both envisages and looks forward to at the end of the line. And this is to say that it is the distribution and not just the extent of these, not just the aggregate quantity so to speak, that matters to him. Communist society is a better society in Marx's eyes and capitalism condemned by him at least partly because of the way in which the former makes such 'goods' available to all where the latter allots them unevenly and grossly so. His concern with distribution in the broad sense, in other words, takes in the very values said to distance him from any preoccupation with justice, so that these do not in truth supply the foundation of a separate and alternative critique of capitalism. His critique in the light of freedom and self-actualization, on the contrary, is *itself* in part a critique in the light of a conception of distributive justice, and though it is so in part only, since there is also an aggregative aspect involved, Marx clearly believing that communism will provide greater freedoms overall than has any preceding social form,[71] the identity is none the less real or important for all that.

Considering, indeed, this point's logical centrality to the whole controversy, it is surprising how little discussion there has been of it in the literature here being reviewed. For it vitiates a claim quite fundamental to the 'anti-justice' interpretation. That Marx does care about distribution broadly construed has, as I have made clear, been effectively argued by opponents of this. But the theoretical hole, the incoherence, in the interpretation that is revealed once the goods themselves of freedom and self-development are seen to fall within the scope of this distributive concern of his is something noted by few commentators and then only fleetingly, in passing.[72] In any event, the distributive dimension

71. Here I disagree with Arneson, pp. 220-1.
72. See Arneson, pp. 220-1; Riley, p. 50 n. 40-and cf. Hancock pp. 68-9.

of Marx's treatment of these values may now be documented. I cite material relevant both to the distribution of advantages and disadvantages in general and to the distribution of freedom and self-development in particular.

In *The German Ideology*, Marx refers to the proletariat as 'a class . . . which has to bear all the burdens of society without enjoying its advantages'. One sort of advantage he has in mind is evident from the following, in the same work:'All emancipation carried through hitherto has been based . . . on restricted productive forces. The production which these productive forces could provide was insufficient for the whole of society and made development possible only if some persons satisfied their needs at the expense of others, and therefore some—the minority—obtained the monopoly of development, while others—the majority—owing to the constant struggle to satisfy their most essential needs, were for the time being (that is, until the creation of new revolutionary productive forces) excluded from any development.'[73] This disparity is also registered in the later, economic writings. Marx speaks on one occasion, for example, of 'the contradiction between those who have to work too much and those who are idlers' and of its projected disappearance with the end of capitalism.[74] Amplifying the point in *Capital* itself, he writes: 'The intensity and productivity of labour being given, the part of the social working day necessarily taken up with material production is shorter and, as a consequence, the time at society's disposal for the free intellectual and social activity of the individual is greater, in proportion as work is more and more evenly divided among all the able-bodied members of society, and a particular social stratum is more and more deprived of the ability to shift the burden of labour (which is a necessity imposed by nature) from its own shoulders to those of another social stratum. The absolute minimum limit to the shortening of the working day is, from this point of view, the universality of labour. In capitalist society, free time is produced for one class by the conversion of the whole lifetime of the masses into labour-time.'[75]

Some readers will think they detect, in Marx's way of putting things here, the signs of a definite evaluative attitude to the

73. *Collected Works* 5, pp. 52, 431–2.
74. *Theories of Surplus Value* III, p. 256.
75. *Capital* I, p. 667.

distributive imbalance he describes, and they will be right to think so. Lest it be said, however, that this thought is just prompted by their, and my, own intellectual predilections, not by anything Marx himself says, we can point to other passages of the same general type, in which a charge of moral wrong is not merely signalled obliquely but there black on white. Thus, speaking, in a famous summary paragraph, of the cumulative processes of capitalist development, Marx says *inter alia*: 'Along with the constant decrease in the number of capitalist magnates, who usurp and monopolize all the advantages of this process of transformation, the mass of misery, oppression, slavery, degradation and exploitation grows.'[76] Note: the capitalists not only monopolize all advantages, they also *usurp* them, which is just to say that they have no right to what they monopolize. And included under this rubric of the usurpation of advantages is, once again, self-development; in the *Grundrisse* Marx writes: 'Since all *free time* is time for free development, the capitalist usurps the *free time* created by the workers for society.'[77] So, the distribution of advantages, amongst them free time and free development, and also, conversely, of burdens, is morally illegitimate, and this entails a commitment to some more acceptable, some fairer, distribution of both the first and the second.

That such indeed is what Marx is committed to, another and a better standard of distributive justice than prevails under capitalism, is also brought out clearly in a passage from the third volume of *Capital*, concerning capitalism's 'civilizing' mission. He states first: 'It is one of the civilizing aspects of capital that it extorts this surplus labour in a manner and in conditions that are more advantageous to social relations and to the creation of elements for a new and higher formation than was the case under the earlier forms of slavery, serfdom, and so on.' Then, proceeding to elaborate on this statement, Marx says immediately after it: 'Thus on the one hand it leads towards a stage at which compulsion and the monopolization of social development (with its material and intellectual advantages) by one section of society at the expense of another disappears.'[78] It could not be more direct. The social formation in prospect is 'higher', and it is higher in part because

76. *Capital* I, p. 929.
77. *Grundrisse*, p. 634.
78. *Capital* III, p. 958.

compulsion disappears, but *also* because so does the monopolization of social development by some at the expense of others. The
positive distributive principle that is implicit in this judgement is
spelled out by Marx elsewhere. He refers, in the first volume of
Capital, to: 'those material conditions of production which alone
can form the real basis of a higher form of society, a society in
which the full and free development of every individual forms the
ruling principle.'[79] Or, in the celebrated formula of the *Communist
Manifesto*: 'In place of the old bourgeois society, with its classes
and class antagonisms, we shall have an association, in which the
free development of each is the condition for the free development of all.'[80]

Justice and Class Interests

So soon, therefore, as the ambit of 'distribution' is extended to
cover the generality of social advantages, especially the relative
availability of free time, time, that is, for autonomous individual
development, itself a crucial component in Marx's conception of
human freedom, it becomes evident that his critique of capitalism
is motivated by distributive considerations, at least amongst
others. Do those who claim that he did not think capitalism
unjust have any persuasive answer to this apparent evidence
against their claim? None that I have been able to discover. In
fact, for the most part they do not even attempt one, either
ignoring or being unaware of the problem for them here. Taking
those who do have something to say about this, however, we may
quickly pass over, as not worthy of serious attention in view of the
texts just cited, the bare assertion of one author that 'Marxist
freedom' should not be thought of as a social good to be distributed. Those texts, I submit, suffice to show the opposite. We
can be nearly as quick with the argument of the same author that,
since the capitalist like the worker is in a significant sense unfree
so long as capitalism persists, it is not the point of Marx's critique
that the former enjoys freedoms which the latter lacks.[81] It is
unquestionably true, on the doctrine of alienation, that everybody

---

79. *Capital* 1, p. 739.
80. *Collected Works* 6, p. 506.
81. See Brenkert (2), p. 158, for both arguments.

is to some degree unfree under capitalism. But the passages I have quoted demonstrate, equally, that it is also part of Marx's criticism of this society that it privileges some with advantages, opportunities for free development included, which others are denied, by contrast with what he envisages as the principle of a communist society.

More space needs to be given to the only substantial attempt at a counter-argument in this matter. It is to be found in a recent paper by Allen Wood, whose earlier articles played so prominent a part in stimulating the whole debate. Wood concedes that Marx 'clearly objects to the prevailing distribution of such entities as effective control over the means of production, leisure time, and the opportunity to acquire education and skills'; but such objection, he claims, cannot be counted a criticism of capitalism as unjust, since to be that it would have to be urged on the basis of 'disinterested or impartial considerations' and it is not consistent with what Wood calls the 'class interests thesis' that Marx should have urged it on this kind of basis. The class interests thesis, part and parcel of historical materialism, is stated thus: 'Marx believes that our actions are historically effective only in so far as they involve the pursuit of class interests, and that the historical meaning of our actions consists in their functional role in the struggle between such interests.' For a rational or self-conscious historical agent, Wood argues, practical recognition of this thesis is incompatible with taking justice, in the sense of impartially grounded distributive principles, as a primary concern.[82]

Two things may be said in response to Wood's argument. The first is that the incompatibility it alleges is open to question. It is Marx's belief, certainly, that where there are classes and class struggle, disinterested or impartial consideration of the interests of everyone is merely an ideological illusion, and he aligns himself unambiguously with one set of interests, the proletariat's, against those of its exploiters. The goal of communism, furthermore, he treats as being in the interests of the proletariat and absolutely not in the interests of the capitalist, as a capitalist, and it is a goal for him that cannot be effectively secured except on the basis of proletarian interests and of the social and political movement that pursues them. However, to limit the 'historical meaning' of action along this path to its functional role within a struggle so character-

82. Wood (5), pp. 12–13, 15, 19 and *passim*.

ized, just one sectional interest against another, is radically to diminish, to impoverish, the sense which Marx himself —everywhere—gives it. For, as partial and as 'interested' as he unashamedly proclaims it to be, such action also has a universal aspect, in virtue of the character of its historical objective, of what the proletariat's struggle is a struggle *for*. This universality, I have already said, is tendential; it cannot be immediate. Some genuine social interests, of really existing people, first of all the interest of the beneficiaries of exploitation in its continuance, are not allowed by Marx morally to count for anything. That is the truth in Wood's argument. But if the proletariat's struggle for its own interests can still be viewed as being of ultimately universal significance, it is just and indeed because, considered from an impartial and disinterested standpoint, the goal of this struggle, 'the free development of all', is for Marx a moral advance on the sectional monopoly of social advantages that capitalism entails. Is it, after all, a feature special to his intellectual outlook that in the pursuit of just arrangements, the interests some will have in the preservation of injustices from which they benefit must be set aside? Scarcely. In returning to someone what rightfully belongs to her, you may legitimately disregard, so far as it is only justice that is at issue, any interest that, say, I may have in holding on to it. Nor, for the rest, is there anything in itself remarkable about the fact that the historical objective or ideal which Marx adumbrates he also sees as not being immediately or straightforwardly realizable, but rather as mediated by obstacles, opposed by vested interests, as something therefore that must be fought for through a long and difficult process on which 'causes' other than the ideal in view will inevitably leave their mark. This is in the nature of many political ends and it is a problem for everyone, although some give themselves the luxury of pretending that it is not.[83]

The second thing to say is that even if one does not—as I do— contest the incompatibility Wood argues there to be between the so-called class interests thesis and any too central preoccupation with disinterested principles of justice, but grants him it for the sake of exhausting exegetical possibilities, it will not suffice for his defensive purpose. For it only shows that if Marx expressed a commitment to disinterested distributive principles, he did so

83. See my 'Bourgeois Power and Socialist Democracy: On the Relation of Ends and Means', *The Legacy of Rosa Luxemburg*, ch. IV.

inconsistently with other beliefs he held. It cannot show that he did not *in fact* express such a commitment, because he in fact did, as is manifest from the textual evidence assembled above. Wood himself in some sort acknowledges the existence of this evidence. In his own words, 'Marx often describes the results of the communist revolution in terms which suggest that if one accepts the description, then one has reasons for considering these results as impartially or disinterestedly good. For example, Marx claims that the revolution will put an end to alienation, that it will enable *every member of society* to develop his or her capacities, that it will promote community and solidarity between people, and that it will facilitate the expansion of human productive powers and the *universal* satisfaction of human needs.'[84] But then the passages in which these claims are made are promptly discounted as 'the liturgy which self-styled "Marxist humanism" never tires of chanting'. Sharp stuff, but what is its justification? What, in other words, saves Wood from giving their due weight to the passages which he himself so aptly characterizes? Well, just the class interests thesis and other passages said to be its consequence, and which he takes—wrongly, but we have decided here to let this pass—as evincing a contempt on Marx's part for humanitarianism. Exegetically, however, it is no more legitimate to set aside the first sort of passage for not squaring with the second than it would be to set aside the second sort, therefore the class interests thesis itself, for not squaring with the first. If the object is to understand Marx's own thought, as for Wood it emphatically is, then the only proper procedure would be to register a large inconsistency there. Simply to decide that the apparent evidence of a disinterested concern with the distribution of human goods— and, *Wood says it*, such is what the texts in question suggest— cannot really be what it gives every appearance of being, is to indulge in that double-counting we have already, in the matter of robbery, uncovered and dismissed.

On this issue as on that, proponents of the 'anti-justice' interpretation default. They are unable satisfactorily to answer the questions they must, unable to explain the data they must, if they are to render plausible the interpretation they propose. Their account of Marx, one must conclude, is mistaken. The negative part of my critique of it is here completed, and it remains only to

84. Wood (5), p. 21; my emphasis.

spell out positively what the substance of the conception of justice is that is implicit in his writings. The strands of it already run through the foregoing discussion and it is just a matter now of trying to draw them out more clearly.

The Conditions of Production

Fundamental to that conception is that there is no moral right to the private ownership and control of productive resources.[85] Treating exploitation as theft, Marx challenges the legitimacy of some people being in a position to appropriate the surplus product of social labour, and he thereby challenges the legitimacy of the system of property rights whose consequence such appropriation is. The positive titles to property embodied in capitalist law, therefore, are condemned as unjust by reference to a generalized moral entitlement—to control over the means of production—which for him has precedence over them. Some will doubtless find it mildly shocking that I attribute to Marx what is in effect a notion of natural right, and this is understandable in view of his overt hostility to the natural rights tradition. Consider, however, how he regards the private ownership of land: 'From the standpoint of a higher socio-economic formation, the private property of particular individuals in the earth will appear just as absurd as the private property of one man in other men. Even an entire society, a nation, or all simultaneously existing societies taken together, are not the owners of the earth. They are simply its possessors, its beneficiaries, and have to bequeath it in an improved state to succeeding generations, as *boni patres familias*.'[86] What *can* he be saying? That no one owns or that no one can own land? But Marx knows all too well that individuals both can and do privately own it. Their positive legal titles to such ownership are no mystery to him. That no one, then, legal titles notwithstanding, *truly* owns it—truly *owns* it—in the sense of having a right to it which *legitimately* excludes others? Exactly. He is saying no more nor less than that people are not morally entitled to exclusive use of the productive resources of the earth; saying that private ownership of these constitutes a wrong. What else

85. See Cohen (1), p. 13; Ryan, p. 521.
86. *Capital* III, p. 911.

could his meaning be? There is even, according to the above passage ('They . . . have to bequeath it in an improved state . . .'), a moral obligation in this matter to later generations. The same judgements are betrayed by the tenor of other, similar texts. Thus, in connection with rent, Marx writes that 'the tremendous power [of] landed property when it is combined together with industrial capital in the same hands enables capital practically to exclude workers engaged in a struggle over wages from the very earth itself as their habitat. One section of society here demands a tribute from the other for the very right to live on the earth.' And of capitalist agriculture he says: 'instead of a conscious and rational treatment of the land as permanent communal property, as the *inalienable* condition for the existence and reproduction of the chain of human generations, we have the exploitation and the squandering of the powers of the earth.'[87]

Taken together with the language of usurpation and robbery, passages like these put beyond doubt Marx's conviction that the 'distribution of the conditions of production' in capitalist society is unjust.[88] Now, I have said that this conviction is fundamental to his conception of justice, but it does not exhaust it. The normative principle it entails, that of collective democratic control over productive resources, is complemented by another, the needs principle, covering the distribution, broadly speaking, of individual welfare, with this second principle seen by Marx as the eventual consequence of realizing the first. And I do not agree with a suggestion which has been made on both sides of the

87. *Capital* III, pp. 908, 948–9–my emphasis.
88. The bland assertion according to which (once again) 'it appears that' Marx's criticisms of capitalism are not based on any conception of 'productive-distributive' justice – and by this the assertion's author has in mind just what I have argued for in the text – is itself based, it appears, on his forbearing to give us some account of these passages. See Buchanan (2), pp. 59–60. And it is, candidly, no more than a desperate intellectual ruse to say – see Brenkert (2), p. 162 – that, collective property being 'a qualitatively different institution' from private property, it has to be regarded simply as something radically new, not as a different, more just arrangement, a *redistribution*, of the means of production. This is the discourse of the pure, unconstrained 'leap' and quite foreign to Marx's own sense of the continuities of history which, despite all novelty and change, and the growth in human productive powers, make the comparative analysis of social institutions a rational enterprise. The 'distribution of the conditions of production' (see text to n. 45 above) is, unproblematically, a trans-historical category for him.

debate that it is not the particular content of the needs principle, or of any other distributive principle which might govern access to individual welfare in a classless society, that is of moment, but just the fact that any such principle will be the result of collective democratic decision.[89] I do not agree with this because one can easily imagine distributive norms or practices which, endorsed by the most democratic procedures of a social collective, will be morally objectionable nonetheless. Not to put too fine a point on it: a stable majority, whatever the basis of its self-definition, arbitrarily, regularly and over an extended period votes advantages and benefits for its members and relative disadvantages for the members of some minority, whatever, in turn, the basis of its identification.[90] Of course, Marx himself plainly did *not* envisage the possibility that a classless society might so combine collective control over the conditions of production with sheer moral arbitrariness in the distribution of welfare. Whether that was simply a sign of utopian optimism on his part, as non-socialists and perhaps even some socialists may be likely to think, or rather evidence of a bold, far-sighted realism, is an issue that may be left aside, for the point here is a different one. It is that if Marx himself upholds the principle of collective control over resources with the clear expectation that its implementation will have a certain kind of further distributive consequence and will not have a certain other kind of distributive consequence for the enjoyment of basic human goods, then it is a strange caprice to make abstraction from this expectation concerning distributive consequences and impute to him an ethical conception in which it is just collective control that matters, more or less irrespective of the nature of its ulterior distributive results. Such results must surely participate in defining the value he attaches to a future communist society. It is, in any case, a fact that he expressly formulates a principle to cover them.

So I take the principle he formulates, 'From each according to their ability, to each according to their needs!', as also integral to his notion of a just society and I want now to say something additional to the arguments reported at II (viii), in defence of construing it thus as a standard of distributive justice. There are essentially two reasons advanced against regarding it as such, and

89. See Crocker, p. 207, and Ryan, pp. 521–2.
90. A less 'extreme' example is given by Arneson, p. 226.

I shall consider these in turn. They are: (A) that the needs principle is not a standard of equality but meant on the contrary to respond to the unique individuality of each person, to the variety of personal character and need, and is therefore a formula for treating people differentially; and (B) that by anticipating a time when 'all the springs of co-operative wealth flow more abundantly', Marx envisages an end to scarcity and so to the very circumstances requiring principles of justice.[91]

Needs and Equality

As to (A), attention should be drawn to another text that is of interest in this connection, yet neglected in the argument over Marx's meaning in *Critique of the Gotha Programme*. For there is also a passage in *The German Ideology* which, from the standpoint of a sort of needs principle, takes issue with a version of the contribution principle, criticizing the view 'that the "possession" and "enjoyment" of each should correspond to his "labour"'. 'But one of the most vital principles of communism, a principle which distinguishes it from all reactionary socialism, is . . . that differences of *brain* and of intellectual ability do not imply any differences whatsoever in the nature of the *stomach* and of physical *needs*; therefore the false tenet, based upon existing circumstances, "to each according to his abilities", must be changed, in so far as it relates to enjoyment in its narrower sense, into the tenet, *"to each according to his need"*; in other words, a *different form* of activity, of labour, does not justify *inequality*, confers no *privileges* in respect of possession and enjoyment.'[92] What this passage rejects, it rejects precisely as justifying inequality, and therefore the needs principle which it commends by contrast cannot reasonably be regarded as anything but a standard of equality. The passage, however, was probably written by Moses Hess and not by Marx and Engels, who are thought only to have edited the chapter of *The German Ideology* from which it comes.[93] Needs are here construed, moreover, in an explicitly narrow sense, as basic physical needs, and as I shall argue shortly, one

91. See I (viii) above.
92. *Collected Works* 5, pp. 537–8.
93. See Ibid., pp. 586 n. 7, 606 n. 143.

cannot take that as having been Marx's intention in *Critique of the Gotha Programme*. We must be circumspect, then, as to what may legitimately be made of this passage in the present context. It would plainly be wrong to jump, without more ado, to the conclusion that, because of the manifestly egalitarian import of lines penned some thirty years earlier by another hand, the kindred formulations of Marx in the later text just have to be of identical import. But if such quick certainty would be unwarranted on our part, we may fairly ask how, in the light of these lines, the diametrically opposite certainty can be warranted on the part of those insisting that the principle he puts forward is not one of equality. The need for circumspection here cuts both ways. And these commentators, it should be noted, simply ignore this passage from *The German Ideology*.

Exercising all due care and caution, we are entitled nonetheless to make the following observations about it. First, there is no other passage in the Marx-Engels Works that has so obvious a bearing on the famous slogan from *Critique of the Gotha Programme* as this one does, notwithstanding the assumption concerning its probable authorship. Second, it provides a salutary reminder that the tenet, 'to each according to their needs', was already part of the tradition of socialist discourse before Marx himself employed it. Third, the passage shows that this tenet was understood by others as a principle of equality and that one of these others, an erstwhile collaborator, openly proposed it as such within a work that was intended to bear Marx's name. These three points must surely suffice to open anyone's mind to there being at least a reasonable possibility—let us say no more yet than that—that Marx in turn espoused the principle in question out of a similar, egalitarian concern. In any case, fourthly and decisively, between the earlier passage from *The German Ideology* and the text of *Critique of the Gotha Programme* there is an undeniable internal likeness which confirms that this possibility is a fact. For just as the burden of the former is that 'differences of . . . intellectual ability' and thus of 'labour' cannot justify *'inequality'* or *'privileges'*, so part of the burden of the latter is to find fault with the contribution principle because 'it tacitly recognizes unequal individual endowment and thus productive capacity as natural privileges' and so amounts to *'a right of inequality'*.[94]

94. *Selected Works* 3, p. 18.

Consideration of the earlier passage, therefore, just serves to highlight the fact that when Marx speaks of the 'defects' of the contribution principle, he clearly refers to inequalities entailed by it which are morally unacceptable in his eyes. That he does this, and in accordance, we can now see, with a pre-existing tradition of argument, supports the claim that the needs principle as he presents it is a principle of equality. It is obviously true, on the other hand, that in envisaging equal treatment from one point of view, that principle necessarily countenances unequal treatment from other points of view. All people, equally, will be able to satisfy their needs. But the means of consumption will not be divided into exactly equivalent individual shares; even equal labour contributions will not, or will not invariably, be matched by such shares being of the same size; some but not all, only those who need them, will have access to expensive drugs or medical treatment; and so forth. There is nothing unusual in this, however. The same applies to absolutely every substantive conception of social justice or principle of equality. If distribution is to be according to some standard of need, then people who make the same labour contribution, or people for that matter of the same height or born under the same astrological sign, may well not receive equivalent resources. But, likewise, if distribution is according to some standard of achievement or merit, then those with identical needs or who have made similar efforts may just as well find that their needs are not equally provided for or their efforts not equally rewarded, as the case may be. It is indeed a truism of the philosophical analysis of both justice and equality that the *formal* principle involved here—'Treat like cases alike and different cases commensurately with their differences'—is practically useless until one has specified *substantive* criteria regarding what sort of likenesses and what sort of differences are morally relevant; what kind of equality it is, in other words, that matters. Marx for his part comes down in favour of need, and against 'individual endowment', as the decisive criterion. There is no question that, in doing so, he himself emphasizes how adoption of this criterion—responding to the specific needs of each individual—must, *in some senses*, mean unequal individual treatment. It is a mistake, however, to get carried away by this emphasis of his, as are so many of the contributors to this debate. For they cannot, simply by verbal fiat, stipulate that there is not then *any* sense in which equal consideration and treatment are involved. There is, and Marx shows himself aware of it in the way he criticizes the contribution principle. The needs of all, irrespective of individual endowment, irrespective also of such other and many differentiating characteristics as will be judged to be morally irrelevant—the needs of all equally, therefore, are to be met.

Communist Abundance

We may turn now to (B), the argument that since the prospective abundance of communist society will 'permit everyone's needs to be fully satisfied',[95] principles of distributive justice will have become redundant there. There will no longer be any necessity for authoritative norms or rules that lay down what sort of distribution is fair, and thus the needs principle as proposed by Marx cannot be taken for one. The argument does not withstand close scrutiny. Some critical reflection on the concept of 'abundance', which means also on the concept of human 'needs', will show what is wrong with it. To this end, the following passage supplies a useful background to Marx's thinking on the subject. 'Man is distinguished from all other animals by the limitless and flexible nature of his needs. But it is equally true that no animal is able to restrict his needs to the same unbelievable degree and to reduce the conditions of his life to the absolute minimum.'[96] Now, when Marx anticipates the springs of wealth flowing 'more abundantly', what is his idea of abundance? He does not say directly. Indeed, there is no evidence that he gave the question any very rigorous consideration. We are obliged, in trying to answer it, to see what can be extrapolated from any texts that may be relevant—as accords with my earlier remarks about the need to find the best reconstruction we can. But there are, in any event, only three pertinently different 'possibilities' here, the terms of the above passage providing us with a convenient framework for distinguishing what they are. (a) There is abundance relative to an 'absolute minimum', a bare physical subsistence, definition of needs. (b) There is, at the other end of the scale, abundance relative to a 'limitless and flexible' notion of needs; in the sense, that is, of everyone being able to have or do whatever

95. Wood (4), p. 211; and see also Lukes (1), p. 201.
96. 'Results of the Immediate Process of Production', Appendix to *Capital* I, p. 1068.

they might conceivably feel themselves as needing to. (c) And there is abundance relative to some standard of 'reasonableness' —there could, of course, be more than one such standard— intermediate between (a) and (b).

We can discount (a) on the grounds that there is a lot of textual evidence that it is not Marx's notion for a communist society. He thinks in terms not of a minimum standard but of the expansion of individual needs.[97] And he has in mind particularly needs of individual self-realization. This is clear from, amongst much else that could be cited, his reference in *Critique of the Gotha Programme* itself to 'the all-round development of the individual' and from the contrast he draws in *Capital* when he refers to 'a mode of production in which the worker exists to satisfy the need of the existing values for valorization, as opposed to the inverse situation, in which objective wealth is there to satisfy the worker's own need for development'.[98] The needs principle as Marx construes it is not distinct from the other principle we have seen that he enunciates —namely, the 'free development' of each and of all[99]—but rather encompasses it and is not therefore to be understood in any minimalist sense. We can discount (b), on the other hand, on the grounds that it is absurd; it is not really a possibility at all. For 'flexible' needs are one thing, but 'limitless' needs quite another. If by way of means of self-development you need a violin and I need a racing bicycle, this, one may assume, will be all right. But if I need an enormously large area, say Australia, to wander around in or generally use as I see fit undisturbed by the presence of other people, then this obviously will not be all right. No conceivable abundance could satisfy needs of self-development of this magnitude, given only a modest incidence of them across some population, and it is not difficult to think of needs that are much less excessive of which the same will be true. While it will not do simply to take it as a matter of course that Marx cannot have entertained an absurdity, it is also not legitimate to impute this sort of thing to him without some textual basis for doing so, and there is no such basis. His reflections in the third volume of *Capital* on the persistence of 'the realm of necessity' betoken an altogether more sober vision of communist abundance.[100]

97. *Capital* III, pp. 959, 986–7, 1015–16; *Capital* I, p. 667.
98. See text to n. 21 above, and *Capital* I, p. 772.
99. See text to notes 79 and 80 above.
100. *Capital* III, p. 959.

We are bound, consequently, to conclude in favour of (c), that this is abundance relative to some standard of 'reasonable' needs which, large and generous as it may be possible for it to be, still falls short of any fantasy of abundance without limits. It might be said against the reasoning by which I have reached this conclusion that the very fact that the principle under discussion is a needs principle rules out the kind of fantastic and extravagant individual requirements hypothesized in the last paragraph. Marx means precisely needs, not any old wants or fancies. But this point changes nothing at all. It is only another route to the same conclusion. So long as the relevant notion of needs covers more than 'the absolute minimum', as we have seen for Marx it does, the distinction between what may properly be counted the needs of communist women and men and what are merely wants, whims or fancies will require a standard of differentiation. It makes no difference whether this is said to distinguish reasonable from unreasonable needs, or needs *tout court* from wants and the rest. The substance is the same. There is still a determinate standard this side of unqualified abundance.

If we now ask how a standard of 'reasonableness' vis-à-vis the satisfaction of needs might be maintained without overt conflict, there are again two suggestions that we can safely reject. (i) It could be coercively imposed by a state-type body or other institution of social control. We know that this is not what Marx envisaged. (ii) The standard, if such it can be called in these circumstances, might simply be a spontaneous, unreflected one. That is to say, it might just 'so happen' that the needs of different individuals are, everywhere and always, of such a kind and such a level as to be all satisfiable in a harmonious way. I think there are good reasons for doubting that this was Marx's view of the matter. For one thing, it does not sit well with the idea of an economy subject to conscious regulation, of a *planned* use and distribution of resources. For another, the very idea of spontaneity here is open to question. These individuals will after all be 'social individuals', so that their overall needs cannot just, 'primitively', *be* thus and so. The prospect, in any case, of there never being any potentially conflicting needs of individual self-development is scarcely imaginable. So much the worse for a conception of communism that does depend on it. There is, finally, (iii) the supposition that though there can be no primitively-given co-ordination or harmony of individual needs and though these might well sometimes potentially conflict, there will be authoritative social norms, including distributive ones, which people more or less voluntarily accept. Still plenty utopian enough for many tastes, this is a more realistic supposition and it renders Marx's principle from *Critique of the Gotha Programme* in effect one of distributive justice. It is supported by at least these aspects of his thought: that although the state, in the Marxist sense of that term, withers away, public institutions in which the community collectively deliberates and decides on its common affairs will still exist; and that though labour will have become 'life's prime want',[101] there will continue to be a 'realm of necessity', in other words some work also that is not free creation or self-realization but 'determined by necessity and external expediency', a burden Marx explicitly envisages being shared by everyone, with the obvious exception of the very young, the very old, the infirm and so on[102] —even if shared only according to relative ability.

The claim, for the rest, that 'From each according to their ability, to each according to their needs!' is not meant as any kind of norm but is merely a *description* of the future,[103] is not very plausible in the light of the fact that Marx speaks of a communist society inscribing it on its banners, no less, and with an exclamation point at that.

Conclusion

The viewpoint I have criticized in this essay may be regarded as a bogus solution to a genuine problem in Marx's thought. The problem is an inconsistency—or paradox[104]—in his attitude to normative questions. Disowning, when he is not actively ridiculing, any attachment to ideals or values, he is nevertheless quite free in making critical normative judgements, author of a discourse that is replete with the signs of an intense moral commitment. The 'anti-justice' interpretation attempts to smooth away this contradiction by representing its two sides as just applicable

101. See text to n. 21 above.
102. *Capital* III, pp. 959, 986–7, 1015–16; *Theories of Surplus Value* III, p. 256; and see also the text to n. 75 above.
103. See I (viii).
104. See Lukes (3), for a clear statement of the paradox as well as this solution to it.

to different things: what Marx disowns and derides is justice, rights; the ideals of freedom, self-realization, community—these he invokes and affirms. It is a spurious resolution. The obstacle cannot be so easily levelled. Early and late, Marx's denials in this matter (efforts of repression, so to speak, of the normative dimension of his own ideas) are quite general in scope. Thus, in *The German Ideology*: 'Communism is for us not a *state of affairs* which is to be established, an *ideal* to which reality [will] have to adjust itself. We call communism the *real* movement which abolishes the present state of things.'[105] Similarly, twenty-five years on in *The Civil War in France*, the workers 'have no ideals to realize, but to set free the elements of the new society with which old collapsing bourgeois society itself is pregnant.'[106] Not, then, be it noted, the ideal of freedom or of self-actualization *as opposed to* the ideal of justice: *no* ideals to realize, just the immanent movement and that is that. The generality of this negation leaves its mark, in fact, at the most strategic conceptual point, mocking the very disjunction of which some commentators here make so much. In the *Communist Manifesto*, a hypothetical opponent is imagined as charging that communism 'abolishes eternal truths, it abolishes all religion and all morality.' The response to the charge is not a rebuttal of it, but the acknowledgement that the communist revolution 'is the most radical rupture with traditional property relations; no wonder that its development involves the most radical rupture with traditional ideas.' But what are the eternal truths actually mentioned as being, with 'all morality', candidates for abolition? I quote: 'Freedom, Justice, etc.'[107]

Marx's impatience with the language of norms and values is global in range. And yet he himself, despite it, does plainly condemn capitalism—for its oppressions and unfreedoms and also, as the argument of this essay has been, for its injustices. Denied publicly, repressed, his own ethical commitments keep returning: the values of freedom, self-development, human well-being and happiness; the ideal of a just society in which these things are decently distributed. One can perhaps go some way

105. *Collected Works* 5, p. 49; and cf. p. 247.
106. *Selected Works* 2, p. 224.
107. *Collected Works* 6, p. 504. Allen Wood overlooks this conjunction in his use – consequently misuse – of this passage. See Wood (2), p. 128, (3), p. 129, and the comment of Arneson, p. 221.

towards explaining this pervasive contradiction. But that does not mean either explaining it away or justifying it. It should be recognized, on the contrary, as a real and deep-seated inconsistency on Marx's part and one with not very happy effects. Some of these may have been innocent enough: the many socialists who have simply followed him in the same obfuscation, confusing both themselves and others, in one breath denying the normative standpoint clear as noonday in what they say in the next. Not so innocent, within the complex of historical causes of the crimes and tragedies which have disgraced socialism, is the moral cynicism that has sometimes dressed itself in the authority of traditional 'anti-ethical' pronouncements. Marxists should not any longer continue to propagate the aboriginal self-contradiction and confusion in this area, but must openly take responsibility for their own ethical positions, spell them out, defend and refine them. A properly elaborated Marxist conception of justice—to take only the example that is most relevant to this debate—would not be at all premature.

A certain salutary impulse, even so, can be detected in, and partially accounts for, Marx's disavowal of all commitment to ethical principle. It is what I have referred to earlier as a sense of moral realism. Expressed negatively in a distaste for easy moral rhetoric, *mere* moralizing, unconstrained by objective knowledge of historical realities, its positive core is the conviction that ideals alone are an insufficient tool of human liberation and the consequent dedication to trying to grasp the material preconditions of this (historically unavoidable alienations, unfreedoms and injustices included)[108] and the social agencies capable of bringing it about. Such a historical sense, all that is entailed by it in the work of Marx, is no small thing: it is Marx's strength, his greatness. The strength, I had better repeat, does not make good or excuse the deficiency. Normative analysis and judgement can be put in their proper place, a necessary if circumscribed one, without exaggerated denial or dismissive scorn. But it is relevant to remark upon the strength together with the deficiency, all the same. For there has been, and there is, no shortage of moral philosophy which, innocent of course of Marx's particular failure in this matter and generally delighted to be able to point it out, is guilty of a greater irresponsibility of its own: minute analysis of

108. See Hancock, pp. 66–7; Cohen (1), p. 16.

the right, the good, the just and what have you, conceptually *nice and far* from the messy throng, the scarred history of toil and comfort, power and protest, fear, hope, struggle. The contemporary discussion of precisely justice provides ample illustrative material, in the several conceptions of just social arrangements proffered in conjunction with more or less nothing, sometimes actually nothing, on how these might conceivably be achieved. The last and the largest paradox here is that Marx, despite everything, displayed a greater commitment to the creation of a just society than many more overtly interested in analysis of what justice is.[109]

109. I should like to thank Michael Evans for comments of his on Marx's slogan from *Critique of the Gotha Programme*; and Jon Elster, Steven Lukes and Richard Miller for permitting me to see work before it was published.

2.

Fetishism
1982

In capitalist society, Marx argues, material objects have certain characteristics conferred on them in virtue of the prevailing social relations, and take on the appearance that such characteristics belong to them by nature. This syndrome, pervasive of capitalist production, he calls fetishism, its elementary form being the fetishism of the commodity, as repository, or bearer, of value. His analogy is religion, in which people bestow upon some entity an imaginary power. However, the analogy is inexact, for the properties bestowed on material objects in the capitalist economy are, Marx holds, real and not the product of imagination. But they are not natural properties. They are social. They constitute real powers, uncontrolled by, indeed holding sway over, human beings; objective 'forms of appearance' of the economic relationships definitive of capitalism. If these forms are taken for natural, it is because their social content or essence is not immediately visible but only disclosed by theoretical analysis.

Although it is not always appreciated, Marx's doctrine of fetishism and his theory of value are indissolubly linked. They highlight the peculiar form that is assumed by expended labour in bourgeois society. Labour itself is universal to human societies. But it is only with the production and exchange of commodities, generalized under capitalism, that it gains expression as an objective property of its own products: as their value. In other types of economy, both communal and exploitative, labour can be recognized directly for what it is, a social process. It is overtly regulated and co-ordinated as such, whether by authority or by agreement.

Under capitalism, by contrast, individual producers of commodities work independently of one another and what co-ordination there is comes about impersonally—behind their backs so to speak—via the market. They all function within an elaborate division of labour. Yet this social relation between them is only effected in the form of a relation between their products, the commodities they buy and sell; the social character of labour appears only indirectly, in the values of those commodities, whereby, being all equally embodiments of labour, they are commensurable. Things become the bearers of a historically specific social characteristic.

The illusion of fetishism stems from conflation of the social characteristic and its material shapes: value seems inherent in commodities, natural to them as things. By extension of this elementary fetishism, in the role of money one particular thing, for example gold, becomes the very incarnation of value, pure concentrate apparently of a power that, in fact, is social. Similarly, in capital fetishism, the specific economic relations that endow means of production with the status of capital are obscured. The powers this commands, all the productive potentialities of social labour, appear to belong to it naturally, a mystifying appearance whose supreme expression is capital's capacity, even without assistance from productive labour, to generate interest.

In the properties conferred upon the objects of the economic process, therefore, veritable powers which render people subject to the latter's dominance, the peculiar relationships of capitalism wear a kind of mask. This gives rise to illusions concerning the natural provenance of these powers. Yet the mask itself is no illusion. The appearances that mystify and distort spontaneous perception of the capitalist order are real; they are objective social forms, simultaneously determined by and obscuring the underlying relations. This is how capitalism *presents itself*: in disguise. Thus the reality of social labour is concealed behind the values of commodities; thus, too, wages conceal exploitation since, equivalent only to the value of labour-power, they appear to be an equivalent for the greater value that labour-power in operation creates. What is actually social appears natural; an exploitative relationship seems to be a just one. It is the work of theory to discover the essential hidden content in each manifest form. However, such forms or appearances are not thereby dissolved. They last as long as bourgeois society itself. With communism, according to Marx, the economic process will be transparent to, and under the control of, the producers.

3.

Essence and Appearance: Aspects of Fetishism in Marx's *Capital*

1969

'Vulgar economy . . . everywhere sticks to appearances in opposition to the law which regulates and explains them. In opposition to Spinoza, it believes that "ignorance is a sufficient reason"' (I, 307).[1] '. . . Vulgar economy feels particularly at home in the estranged outward appearances of economic relations . . . these relations seem the more self-evident the more their internal relationships are concealed from it' (III, 797). '. . . The philistine's and vulgar economist's *way of looking at things* stems . . . from the fact that it is only the direct *form of manifestation* of relations that is reflected in their brains and not their *inner connection*' (Marx to Engels, 27 June 1867). 'Once for all I may here state, that by classical Political Economy, I understand that economy which, since the time of W. Petty, has investigated the real relations of production in bourgeois society, in contradistinction to vulgar economy, which deals with appearances only' (I, 81). 'It is the great merit of classical economy to have destroyed this false appearance and illusion . . . this personification of things and conversion of production relations into entities, this religion of everyday life . . . nevertheless even the best spokesmen of classical economy remain more or less in the grip of the world of illusion which their criticism had dissolved, as cannot be

1. References to *Capital* give the volume number (Roman) and the page number (Arabic) of the edition published by Lawrence and Wishart, London, 1961–2. The letters of Marx and Engels can be found in the *Selected Correspondence* (Moscow n.d.).

otherwise from a bourgeois standpoint, and thus they all fall more or less into inconsistencies, half-truths and unsolved contradictions' (III, 809).

In this manner does Marx, on many occasions, specify the distance separating vulgar economy from classical political economy, and *a fortiori* from his own critique of the latter, providing us at the same time with a conception of the minimum *necessary* condition to be satisfied by any work aspiring to scientific status: namely, that it uncover the reality behind the appearance which conceals it. The intention of this article is to deal with a group of problems (in particular, the problem of fetishism) related to Marx's formulations of this requirement and to the systematic recurrence of its appropriate terminology— appearance/essence, form/content, illusion/reality, phenomena/ hidden substratum, form of manifestation/inner connection, and so forth. It should, however, be made clear at the outset that scarcely anything is said about the development of Marx's views on these questions, hence about the relation between the *Economic and Philosophical Manuscripts* of 1844 and *Capital*; and, about the relationship between Hegel and Marx, nothing at all. Thus the process of Marx's intellectual formation and development is set to one side, and these problems are considered only as they emerge in *Capital* itself, at the interior of what is a more or less finished, more or less coherent structure of thought.

The Theoretical Foundation of *Capital*

If we begin, then, with what I have called the minimum necessary condition of Marx's science, this methodological requirement to which he assigns an exceptional importance, the first question which arises is as follows: what is its theoretical foundation? What establishes its necessity? At all events, it is hardly an arbitrary construction on Marx's part. The text of *Capital* provides us with two kinds of answer. In one, it is revealed as the common requirement of *any* science.

'. . . a scientific analysis of competition is not possible before we have a conception of the inner nature of capital, just as the apparent motions of the heavenly bodies are not intelligible to any but him, who is acquainted with their real motions, motions which are not directly perceptible by the senses' (I, 316).

'That in their appearance things often represent themselves in inverted form is pretty well known in every science except Political Economy' (I, 537).

'. . . all science would be superfluous if the outward appearance and the essence of things directly coincided' (III, 797).

In such passages Marx presents the conceptual distinction between appearance and reality as a form of *scientificity as such*, by notifying us that the method he is applying in political economy is simply a general requirement for arriving at valid knowledge, one which he has taken over from the other sciences where it has long been established. Taken on its own, this answer is not entirely satisfactory. It makes of Marx's primary methodological injunction—to shatter the obviousness of immediate appearances—an abstract procedural rule which must form part of the equipment of every science, regardless of the content of that science, of the nature of its object of study. Taken on its own, this answer does not yet specify why it is appropriate to extend the methods of astronomy to the subject matter of political economy. For this reason we put it in parenthesis for the moment, though it should be borne in mind since it will be reconsidered at a later stage of the argument.

We proceed to Marx's second answer which is of a different order altogether from the first. This answer is, of course, contained in the doctrine of fetishism. For the latter specifies those properties of Marx's object of study itself which imperiously *demand* that appearances be demolished if reality is to be correctly grasped. It analyses the mechanisms by which capitalist society necessarily appears to its agents as something other than it really is. The notion of fetishism raises quite complex problems, which will be developed presently, but even now it should be clear that we have in this second answer a theoretical foundation for the distinction, essence/appearance, and its variations, which was lacking in the first. The relation between methodological injunction and object of study is no longer one of externality, as is the case with an abstract rule applicable to any content whatsoever. It is, rather, what may be termed a *relation of adequacy* between object and method, the character of the latter being determined by the structure of the former. It is because there exists, at the interior of capitalist society, a kind of internal rupture between the social relations which obtain and the manner in which they are experienced, that the scientist of that society is confronted with the necessity of constructing reality against appearances. Thus, this necessity can no longer be regarded as an arbitrary importation into Marx's own theoretical equipment of something he merely extracted from other pre-existing sciences. And the passages quoted at the beginning of this essay are seen to lead, by a short route, to the heart of the notion of fetishism.

It is enough to consult any standard commentary on Marx to see that this notion is not free from ambiguity or confusion, and to some extent this is also true of Marx's own exposition in the first chapter of *Capital*. It seems necessary, therefore, to adopt an analytic procedure, in an attempt to isolate different aspects of the concept and to examine them separately, even if such a procedure runs the risk of fragmenting what Marx conceived to be a unified phenomenon. For, if it enables us to clarify the aspects, taken separately, the chances of understanding their relations to one another, that is to say, of reconstituting them as a whole, are thereby enhanced. An initial distinction, one which is clear enough, between two aspects of fetishism is provided by the text of *Capital* itself: '. . . a definite social relation between men . . . assumes, in their eyes, the fantastic form of a relation between things' (1, 72); '. . . their own social action takes the form of the action of objects, which rule the producers instead of being ruled by them' (1, 75).

In capitalist society the phenomenon of fetishism imposes itself on men (*a*) as mystification and (*b*) as domination. Clearly the two aspects are intimately related, inasmuch as men are in no position to control, rather than submit to, social relations which they do not correctly understand. And that they are so related is reflected in subsequent literature on the subject where they are normally run together. Thus Garaudy writes: 'The relations between men take on the appearance of relations between objects . . . Things rule the men who have created them.' And Sweezy: '. . . the real character of the relations among the producers themselves is both distorted and obscured from view . . . the world of commodities has, so to speak, achieved its independence and subjected the producers to its sway.'[2] However, for the reasons stated, I

2. Roger Garaudy, *Karl Marx: The Evolution of his Thought*, London 1967, p. 125; Paul Sweezy, *The Theory of Capitalist Development*, London, 1946, p. 36. Cf. also George Lukács, *Histoire et Conscience de Classe*, Paris, 1960, pp. 110–13 and Sidney Hook, *Towards the Understanding of Karl Marx*, London, 1933, p. 162.

intend as far as possible to maintain the distinction, and to treat mystification and domination separately, taking the latter first although the former is more directly pertinent to the problem of appearance and reality and also more problematic. No discussion of fetishism can ignore this feature of domination altogether, and it may perhaps be appropriate to clear it out of the way.

The Role of Alienation in *Capital*

What we have to deal with here is not domination in general but a historically specific form of domination. It differs, for example, from the relations of 'personal dependence' which Marx identifies as characteristic of the European middle ages (I, 77), and this for two reasons: whereas there the domination is undisguised, under capitalism it is concealed; secondly, and more to the point here, it is precisely an *impersonal* kind of domination exercised by the totality of economic relations over *all* the agents of capitalist society, embracing also the capitalist whose overriding interest is the extraction of as much surplus labour as possible from the worker. He too cannot be held 'responsible for relations whose creature he socially remains' (I, 10; Preface to the First German Edition). It is unnecessary to rehearse all the aspects of this impersonal domination—the independence of the production process vis-à-vis the producers, the past labour of the worker confronting him as a hostile power in the shape of capital, the instruments of labour employing the worker rather than vice versa, the drudgery and stupefaction of work, and so on. All these are comprised by the concept of alienation. However, in *Capital* this is a historical concept of alienation. Its social and historical premises are precisely economic relations based on the production and exchange of commodities.

This is brought out clearly in the following passages: 'The owners of commodities . . . find out, that the same division of labour that turns them into independent private producers, also frees the social process of production and the relations of the individual producers to each other within that process, from all dependence on the will of those producers, and that the seeming mutual independence of the individuals is supplemented by a system of general and mutual dependence through or by means of the products' (I, 107–8).

Political Economy 'has never once asked the question why labour is represented by the value of its product and labour-time by the magnitude of that value. These formulae, which bear it stamped upon them in unmistakable letters that they belong to a state of society, in which the process of production has the mastery over man, instead of being controlled by him, such formulae appear to the bourgeois intellect to be as much a self-evident necessity imposed by Nature as productive labour itself' (1, 80–1).

Here, the roots of the phenomena grouped under the term alienation are located in specific social relations, and not in the fact that there is an ideal essence of man, his 'species-being', which has been negated or denied. And this is the difference that separates *Capital* from certain passages in the *Economic and Philosophical Manuscripts*,[3] even though there, too, Marx deals with such features of capitalist society as the domination of the worker by his product and the stultifying character of his work.[4] In place of a concept of alienation founded on an essentialist anthropology, we have one tied to the historical specificity of forms of domination.

To this extent, those discussions of fetishism which simply take for granted the complete unity between the *Manuscripts* and *Capital*,[5] are of dubious value, conflating as they do two concepts of different theoretical status. And when Lukács, in his discussion of fetishism, speaks of one-sided specialization 'violating the human essence of man' (op. cit., p. 128), he is guilty of the same conflation. On the other hand, Althusser has proposed a reading of fetishism in which, of the two aspects that have been distinguished, namely, mystification and domination, only the former is treated. The notion of men being dominated by their own products has vanished (almost) without trace. Such an interpretation demands, of course, that the concept of fetishism be regarded as entirely unrelated to, and independent of, that of alienation,[6] and the latter is accordingly dismissed as 'ideological'

3. T. B. Bottomore ed., *Karl Marx: Early Writings*, London, 1963, pp. 126–8.

4. Ibid., pp. 122–5.

5. E.g. Garaudy, pp. 52–63 and 124–7.

6. J-C. Forquin, 'Lecture d'Althusser' in *Dialectique Marxiste et Pensée Structurale*, special number of *Les Cahiers du Centre d'Etudes Socialistes*, 76–81, February–May, 1968, p. 27.

and 'pre-Marxist'.[7]

In this reading Althusser is guilty, in the first place, of violating the text of *Capital*, as the following passages make clear: '. . . the character (*Gestalt*) of independence and estrangement (*entfremdet*) which the capitalist mode of production as a whole gives to the instruments of labour and to the product, as against the workman, is developed by means of machinery into a thorough antagonism' (I, 432).

'Since, before entering on the process, his own labour has already been alienated (*entfremdet*) from himself by the sale of his labour-power, has been appropriated by the capitalist and incorporated with capital, it must, during the process, be realized in a product that does not belong to him (*in fremdem Produkt*)' (I, 570–1).

'Capital comes more and more to the fore as a social power, whose agent is the capitalist. This social power no longer stands in any possible relation to that which the labour of a single individual can create. It becomes an alienated (*entfremdete*), independent, social power, which stands opposed to society as an object, and as an object that is the capitalist's source of power' (III, 259).

And even were the term 'alienation' altogether absent, there are enough passages where the *concept*, and all the phenomena it embraces, are presented, to invalidate Althusser's reading of *Capital* on this point.[8]

However, it is not only a question of the validity of the interpretation of Marx. There are serious theoretical consequences as well. For in Althusser the concept of alienation, as that form of domination engendered by capitalist relations of production, is replaced—and here is its surviving trace—by the notion of men as the mere functionaries, or bearers (Träger), of the relations of production which determine their places and their functions.[9] What Marx regards as a feature specific to *capitalist* relations of production, Althusser articulates as a *general* proposition of historical materialism. Thus de-historicizing the concept of alienation in a manner quite strange for a Marxist author (for how is this different from the fault of the classical political economists

7. Louis Althusser, *For Marx*, London, 1969, p. 239.

8. For example I: 112, 310, 360–1, 422–3, 645. There is an excellent discussion of the relation between the *Manuscripts* and *Capital* in Ernest Mandel, *La Formation de la Pensée Economique de Karl Marx*, Paris, 1967, pp. 151–79.

9. 'The Object of Capital', in *Reading Capital*, London, 1970, p. 180.

who regard commodity production as eternal?) he makes it impossible to comprehend, from his perspective, those passages in which Marx anticipates a future social formation where, precisely, men will control their relations of production, rather than be controlled by them, where they will, therefore, cease to be mere functionaries and bearers. We shall see later on that Althusser commits an exactly parallel error in relation to the other aspect of fetishism, mystification. For the moment it is sufficient to observe that, in his legitimate anxiety to be done with the anthropological concept of alienation, he throws out the historical concept as well, de-historicizing it in a 'new' way.

The Reality of Value Relations

Returning now to the problem of essence/appearance and the mystificatory aspect of fetishism, it will be well to make a secondary distinction: between (a) those appearances, or forms of manifestation, in which social relations present themselves and which are not mystificatory or false *as such*, inasmuch as they do correspond to an objective reality; they become mystified only when regarded as products of nature or of the subjective intentions of men; and (b) those appearances, or forms of manifestation, which are quite simply false, illusions in the full sense, corresponding to no objective reality. This distinction governs what follows. (Unless, therefore, it is made explicit, the term 'appearance' should not be taken to mean 'mere, that is, false, appearance'. The same goes for the word 'form'.) And it is a helpful one to the extent that it enables one to avoid the kind of confusion into which many accounts of fetishism fall, and of which the following passage by Karl Korsch is an example: 'The value relations appearing in the exchange of the products of labour as "commodities" are essentially not relations between things, but merely an imaginary expression of an underlying social relation between the human beings who co-operate in their production. Bourgeois society is just that particular form of the social life of man in which the most basic relations established between human beings in the social production of their lives become known to them only after the event, and even then only in the reversed form of relations between things. By depending in their conscious actions upon such imaginary concepts, the members of modern "civilized" society are really, like the savage by his fetish, controlled by the work of their hands.'[10]

While there is much here that is unobjectionable (e.g. value relations as the product of social relations, men dominated by their own creations), it is incorrect to describe value relations as imaginary. As I shall try to show, Marx does not do so. Such a description is dangerously close, though Korsch manages to keep his distance, to a purely subjectivist explanation of fetishism, of the kind given by Berger and Pullberg when, in an article on the sociology of knowledge, they formulate the following stupefying definition: '. . . alienation is the process by which man forgets that the world he lives in has been produced by himself.'[11] What they themselves 'forget' is that, if forgetfulness were all that was involved, a reminder should be sufficient to deal with the constituent problems of alienation.

How is it then with Marx? What is in question at the moment are the following forms of manifestation: that labour is represented by the value of its product, labour-time by the magnitude of that value, and social relations by the value relations between commodities. For Marx, neither values nor value relations are imaginary. They are not illusory appearances, but *realities*. This point cannot be emphasized too strongly. It represents a first step towards understanding what is involved in fetishism. Thus he writes: '. . . the labour of the individual asserts itself as a part of the labour of society, only by means of the relations which the act of exchange establishes directly between the products, and indirectly, through them, between the producers. To the latter, therefore, the relations connecting the labour of one individual with that of the next appear, not as direct social relations between individuals at work, but as *what they really are*, material relations between persons and social relations between things' (1, 73. My emphasis).

It is in the light of this statement that the ambiguous footnote which occurs shortly afterwards should be interpreted: 'When, therefore, Galiani says: Value is a relation between persons . . . he ought to have added: a relation between persons expressed as a relation between things' (1, 74).

10. Karl Korsch, *Karl Marx*, New York, 1963, p. 131.
11. P. Berger and S. Pullberg, 'Reification and the Sociological Critique of Consciousness', *New Left Review*, No. 35, January–February, 1966, p. 61.

This means, not that a relation between persons takes on the illusory appearance of a relation between things, but that where commodity production prevails, relations between persons really do take the form of relations between things. This is the specific form of capitalist social relations; other societies, both pre- and post-capitalist, are characterized by social relations of a different form. A moment's consideration of the defining relations of capitalist society—capitalist/worker, producer-of-/consumer-of-commodities—is enough to verify this. For the capitalist, the worker exists only as labour-power, for the worker, the capitalist only as capital. For the consumer, the producer is commodities, and for the producer the consumer is money. Althusser is therefore correct to insist that the social relations of production are not, and are not reducible to, simple relations between men.[12] And the reply of one of his critics—that they are, but mediated by things[13]—is not so much a counter-statement as a restatement of the same thing. It should, however, be borne in mind that the objects, namely commodities, the value relations between which are the form taken by capitalist social relations, are social and not natural objects.

It is just because these value relations are neither imaginary nor illusory but real, that Marx is able to make the following judgement: 'The categories of bourgeois economy . . . are forms of thought expressing *with social validity* the conditions and relations of a definite, historically determined mode of production, namely, the production of commodities' (1, 76. My emphasis).

At the same time Marx describes these forms of thought as absurd. But what kind of absurdity is it? 'When I state that coats or boots stand in a relation to linen, because it is the universal incarnation of abstract human labour, the absurdity of the statement is self-evident. Nevertheless, when the producers of coats and boots compare those articles with linen, or, what is the same thing, with gold or silver, as the universal equivalent, they express the relation between their own private labour and the collective labour of society in the same absurd form' (1, 76). It is the absurdity not of an illusion, but of reality itself, and to this extent it is an absurdity which is true.

12. 'The Object of Capital', p. 174.
13. S. Pullberg, 'Note pour une lecture anthropologique de Marx' in *Dialectique Marxiste et Pensée Structurale*, p. 145.

The Social Reality Behind Fetishized Relationships

Having insisted on the *reality* of value, and of the objective form taken on by capitalist social relations, the form, that is to say, of a relation between objects, we further specify them by emphasizing that they are *social* realities. This determination Marx himself makes quite clear: 'If . . . we bear in mind that the value of commodities has a purely social reality, and that they acquire this reality only in so far as they are expressions or embodiments of one identical social substance, namely, human labour, it follows as a matter of course, that value can only manifest itself in the social relation of commodity to commodity' (I, 47). '. . . the coat, in the expression of value of the linen, represents a non-natural property of both, something purely social, namely, their value' (I, 57). Further, by a third specification, it is necessary to recognize value and the objective form of social relations as *historically specific* social realities, and not just social realities in general. From this, three important conclusions are to be derived.

1. The distinctions, form/content, appearance/essence, retain their significance for the analysis and explanation of these realities, but on condition that the first term of each opposition is not taken to be synonymous with illusion. Because the forms taken by capitalist social relations, their modes of appearance, are historically specific ones, they are puzzling forms, they contain a secret. The reasons why social relations should take such forms, rather than others, are not self-evident. It requires a work of analysis to discover them, to disclose the secret, and, in doing this, it reveals the contents of these forms and the essence of these appearances. At the same time, the content explains the form, and the essence the appearances, which cease thereafter to be puzzling. But this must not be regarded as a journey from illusion to reality. It is rather a process of elucidating one reality by disclosing its foundation in and determination by another. Thus the form of value (namely, exchange-value) and the object character of social relations is not dissolved or dissipated by Marx as an illusion, but its content is laid bare: the individuals working independently and producing use-values not for direct consumption but for exchange. It is the commodity form itself which is responsible for the enigma (I, 71), and its solution therefore requires an analysis of that form. Similarly, Marx uncovers the content of surplus-value by indicating its source in the surplus labour-time of the worker. He

thus discovers *its* secret. Bourgeois political economy, itself unable to hit upon this secret, except in the New World (I, 774) and, even there, without drawing the necessary conclusions, takes the only other road open to it. It de-historicizes value and surplus-value, makes of them products of nature, and, in parallel fashion, regards the impersonal and objective form of capitalist social relations as an entirely natural state of affairs. It thus transforms the properties possessed by commodities, capital, etc., qua *social* objects, into qualities belonging *naturally* to them as things. *This* is the root and beginning of the mystification of fetishism.

2. It is not that something imaginary has been endowed with the quality of reality. The mechanism of mystification consists in the collapsing of social facts into natural ones. In this way, the value form is fetishized. This is expressed most clearly by Marx in a passage in the second volume, where he refers to: '. . . the fetishism peculiar to bourgeois Political Economy, the fetishism which metamorphoses the social, economic character impressed on things in the process of social production into a natural character stemming from the material nature of those things' (II, 225).

There is, however, no shortage of examples of Marx observing this metamorphosis in relation to particular features of capitalist society. Thus he writes of the productive power of social labour: '. . . co-operation begins only with the labour-process, but they [the workers] have then ceased to belong to themselves . . . Hence, the productive power developed by the labourer when working in co-operation, is the productive power of capital . . . Because this power costs capital nothing, and because, on the other hand, the labourer himself does not develop it before his labour belongs to capital, it appears as a power with which capital is endowed by Nature' (I, 333).

And of money: 'What appears to happen is, not that gold becomes money, in consequence of all other commodities expressing their values in it, but, on the contrary, that all other commodities universally express their values in gold, because it is money . . . These objects, gold and silver, just as they come out of the bowels of the earth, are forthwith the direct incarnation of all human labour. Hence the magic of money' (I, 92).[14]

And of interest-bearing capital: 'It becomes a property of

14. Cf. I, 57–8.

money to generate value and yield interest, much as it is an attribute of pear-trees to bear pears' (III, 384).

Now, it is in order to undo the mystifying effects of this meta-morphosis that Marx insists: '. . . capital is not a thing, but rather a definite social production relation, belonging to a definite historical formation of society, which is manifested in a thing and lends this thing a specific social character' (III, 794).[15]

The demystification is achieved by means of a denaturation. But this is not the same thing as a de-objectification. Pending the destruction of bourgeois society, capital remains an objective form, a social object, whose content and essence are accumulated labour, which dominates the agents of that society, and it must be comprehended as such.

It should further be noted that the *false* appearances to which the fetishization of forms gives rise are yet 'something more and else than mere illusions'.[16] By this I mean that they are not attributable simply to a failure of perspicacity on the part of the social agents, to some act of 'forgetfulness', with its source in purely subjective deficiencies. In every case where Marx presents us with an example of fetishization, he goes to great pains to indicate the roots and raison d'être of the resulting illusions in the reality itself. Briefly, most, though not all, of his indications can be subsumed under the following general kind of explanation: in capitalist society, the social relations between the producers take the form of objective qualities belonging to their products, namely, commodities; there is nothing, however, in the com-modity which indicates that these qualities which it actually possesses as a commodity (say, money) do not belong to it as a thing (gold); the collapse into nature is therefore itself perfectly 'natural', that is, comprehensible. If then the social agents experi-ence capitalist society as something other than it really is, this is fundamentally because capitalist society *presents itself* as some-thing other than it really is. As Maurice Godelier has put it: 'It is not the subject who deceives himself, but *reality* which deceives *him*.'[17]

3. We have seen that one type of mystification consists of

---

15. Cf. I, 766.

16. Henri Lefebvre, *The Sociology of Marx*, London, 1968, p. 62.

17. M. Godelier, 'System, Structure and Contradiction in *Capital*', *Socialist Register*, 1967, p. 93.

reducing the social objectivity of the forms of capitalist relations to a natural objectivity. This mystification is fetishism. However, Marx also exposes a second type of mystification, one which involves a reduction of these forms, in the opposite direction, from social objectivity to social *subjectivity*. This occurs when they are declared to be imaginary, fictional forms. While this is not fetishism, indeed, may be regarded as an over-reaction against it, it is nevertheless a mystification: 'The act of exchange gives to the commodity converted into money, not its value, but its specific value-form. By confounding these two distinct things some writers have been led to hold that the value of gold and silver is imaginary . . . But if it be declared that the social characters assumed by objects, or the material forms assumed by the social qualities of labour under the regime of a definite mode of production, are mere symbols, it is in the same breath also declared that these characteristics are arbitrary fictions sanctioned by the so-called universal consent of mankind. This suited the mode of explanation in favour during the eighteenth century. Unable to account for the origin of the puzzling forms assumed by social relations between man and man, people sought to denude them of their strange appearance by ascribing to them a conventional origin' (I, 90–1).

Thus, the fact that the material forms of capitalist social relations are not natural ones, does not deprive them of their objectivity, that is to say, of their character of being objects, which become independent vis-à-vis the social agents, dominate them according to their own laws, and cannot be ascribed to human subjectivity, either as their source or as their explanation. Such an ascription, whether it be seen as an agreement—convention, consent, social contract—or as a failure of consciousness—act of forgetting, lack of insight, trick of the imagination—has this theoretical consequence: it spirits away the uncontrolled, and fundamentally uncontrollable, character of these objects, these forms of capitalist social relations. For, in the first case, it is sufficient to undo the agreement, make new agreements, work out new conventions, in order to handle the contradictions of capitalism. Marx is plunged into liberal political theory or its poorly disguised variant, social-democratic reformism. In the second case, a new act of consciousness, a reappropriation of the world in thought, serves the same purpose. Marx is plunged into Hegel.

Pure Appearance: The Wage Form

I have dealt, so far, with those forms of capitalist social relations, those modes of appearance in which they present themselves, which are not illusory as such, but are subject to two kinds of transformation which render them mystificatory: they are fetishized, that is, grounded in nature, or given an idealistic explanation. I come now to the forms which are illusory in the full sense, appearances which are *mere* appearances. First and foremost here, because it is an illusory form which is itself the source of a number of other illusions, is the wage form. In this, the value of labour-power is transformed in such a way that it takes on the (false) appearance of the value of labour. It 'thus extinguishes every trace of the division of the working day into necessary labour and surplus-labour, into paid and unpaid labour' (1, 539). Which is to say, it conceals the *essential* feature of capitalist relations, namely, exploitation. The latter is based on the difference between the value of labour-power, for which the capitalist pays in order to use it for a given time, and the greater value which the same labour-power in operation creates during that time. But since, in the wage form, what appears to happen is that the capitalist pays, not for the labour-power, but for the labour, the inequality of the exchange is falsely disguised as an equal exchange.

Those passages where Marx refers to the difference between the value of labour-power and the value it creates as 'a piece of good luck for the buyer, but by no means an injury to the seller' (1, 194), and where he denies that 'the seller has been defrauded' (1, 585), must therefore be regarded as having a provisional and double-edged character. On the one hand, it is indeed the case that capitalist exploitation is not fundamentally based on the individual capitalist cheating his workers; according to all the laws of commodity production, the worker does get paid for the full value of the commodity he sells. On the other hand, these laws themselves entail an injury and a fraud much greater than individual cheating, the unconscious injury and defrauding of one class by another. The provisional character of the original statements is, therefore, made plain: 'The exchange of equivalents, the original operation with which we started, has now become turned round in such a way that there is only an apparent exchange . . . The relation of exchange subsisting between capitalist and labourer becomes a mere semblance appertaining to the process of circulation, a mere form, foreign to the real nature of the transaction, and only mystifying it' (I, 583).

Here, the analysis of the form which reveals the content, the penetration of the appearance which discloses the essence, *is* a journey from illusion to reality. The same goes for another of the appearances to which the wage form gives rise: namely, the appearance that the worker disposes of his labour-power according to his own free will. This is a mere appearance, an illusion, whose reality is that the worker is forced to sell his labour-power. Thus, the transition from the sphere of circulation, that 'very Eden of the innate rights of man [where] alone rule Freedom, Equality, Property and Bentham' (I, 176), to that of production which reveals 'that the time for which he is free to sell his labour-power is the time for which he is forced to sell it' (I, 302). This transition is one from illusion to reality: '. . . in essence it always remains forced labour—no matter how much it may seem to result from free contractual agreement' (III, 798).

However, two precisions are required at this point.

1. I have said that these analyses which refer us from the appearance (equal exchange, free labour) to the essence (unequal exchange, forced labour), are at the same time journeys from illusion to reality. They are also, it is clear from the above, transitions from the process of circulation to the process of production. But the circulation process is no illusion. What we are dealing with here are illusions arising *in* and *during* the circulation process by contrast with the realities uncovered by an analysis of the production process. This precision is important, because it is at all costs necessary to avoid dissolving the various 'levels' of the social totality, by regarding them all as mere forms of manifestation of one essential level, and thus depriving them of their specific efficacy. It is the attempt to theorize this necessity in the concept of 'overdetermination' that is Althusser's real contribution to contemporary Marxist discussion.[18] Nor is it simply a question here of the relation between the circulation and production processes. As Marx makes clear, from these semblances of the sphere of circulation there arises a whole ideological superstructure: 'This phenomenal form [the wage form], which makes the actual relation invisible, and, indeed, shows the direct

18. 'Contradiction and Overdetermination' in *For Marx*.

opposite of that relation, forms the basis of all the juridical notions of both labourer and capitalist, of all the mystifications of the capitalist mode of production, of all its illusions as to liberty, of all the apologetic shifts of the vulgar economists' (I, 540). The Marxist critique of the illusions pertaining to this superstructure equally does not deprive it of its positive reality.

2. The decisive factor, which makes possible the discovery in the production process of the essence of the false appearances of circulation, consists in this: that, in moving from circulation to production, the analysis moves from the consideration of relationships between individuals to that of the relations between classes, of which the former are a function. Only this change of terrain can demystify the appearances. Its importance will be dealt with at a later stage of the argument.

The wage form, then, unlike the value form, corresponds to no objective reality. Marx is quite unequivocal on this point and attempts to give it special emphasis: '. . . "value of labour" . . . is an expression as imaginary as the value of the earth' (I, 537). '. . . "price of labour" is just as irrational as a yellow logarithm' (III, 798).

And yet this illusory form is not one that is easily seen through or dissipated. Marx gave notice of this when he described as one of the three new elements of *Capital* his discovery of the irrationality of the wage form (Marx to Engels, 8 January 1868). But he also says it explicitly in *Capital*: 'These imaginary expressions arise, however, from the relations of production themselves' (I, 537). '. . . the price of labour-power . . . inevitably appears as the price of labour under the capitalist mode of production' (III, 801). 'If history took a long time to get at the bottom of the mystery of wages, nothing, on the other hand, is more easy to understand than the necessity, the raison d'être, of this phenomenon' (I, 540).

Like the illusions of fetishism discussed above, the illusion of the wage form is opaque and tenacious, because here as there it is a case of reality deceiving the subject rather than the subject deceiving himself. This is the way the value of labour-power *presents itself.* And Marx analyses some of the mechanisms of the process—for example, changes of wages corresponding with the changing length of the working day; 'price of labour' does not seem more irrational than 'price of cotton', exchange-value and use-value being intrinsically incommensurable magnitudes anyway

(1, 540–1). In this, as in the earlier case, what Marx tells us is that capitalist society itself is characterized by a quality of opacity, so that *it* creates the necessity of a methodology which will penetrate the appearance to uncover the reality, and then, by a reverse course, so to speak, demonstrate why this reality should take on such an appearance.

Science and Ideology: The Althusserian Disjunction

But, at all events, this opacity is a historically specific one. For Marx, different types of social relations are characterized by different degrees of opacity and transparency, and capitalism itself creates the historical possibility of a society where 'the practical relations of everyday life offer to man none but perfectly intelligible and reasonable relations with regard to his fellow men and to Nature' (1, 79). A socialist society would then be one where the social relations are not concealed or distorted by mystificatory ideologies. But here the notion that the distinction, essence/appearance, is a form of scientificity as such recurs in the shape of a problem. For, if the relations of a socialist society will be transparent, then surely this distinction will be unnecessary to the science of that society, and should be understood, like value and surplus-value, as part of that conceptual apparatus necessary to the analysis of capitalism; and not, like, say, forces and relations of production, as one of the concepts which Marxism brings to the analysis of any social formation. Marx's first specification of the theoretical status of the distinction is then further called into question.

In this connection it is not irrelevant to observe that, in much the same way as he de-historicizes the concept of alienation, Althusser obliterates the historical specificity of capitalist opacity in his thesis that, for Marx, even a communist society would not be without its ideology (and ideology in the Marxist sense, that is, involving false consciousness).[19] Again it is not only the interpretation of Marx that is in question. There are serious theoretical consequences. What becomes, for example, of the notion of the proletariat taking cognizance of its real situation in capitalist society in the act (process, praxis) of abolishing it; of its compre-

19. *For Marx*, p. 232; *Reading Capital*, p. 177.

hending the real mechanisms of capitalist exploitation, and revolting against them to create a society in which, among other things, it will be neither exploited nor mystified? What, in short, becomes of the notion of class consciousness? It has vanished literally without trace. In its place appears the radical disjunction (a new 'coupure', this) between the theory, the scientific knowledge, of socialist intellectuals and the ideology of the masses. Thus, Althusser speaks of categories appropriate for the ideological struggle but deficient for the purposes of theory,[20] and of Marxism as a science which produces new forms of ideology in the masses.[21] The unity between the theory of the theoreticians and the practice of the class is broken and one is left with nothing other than a variant of hostile bourgeois caricatures of Leninism: the political leaders use their knowledge to manipulate the consciousness of the masses. Once again, there is a legitimate concern at the bottom of this false position: the concern to preserve the specificity of theoretical practice. There is, after all, some distance between the consciousness of even the most revolutionary worker and the science of Marx or Lenin. But it is a distance and not a rupture. Further, it is the distance of a dialectical relationship, because traversed in both directions. The scientific theory is brought to bear on the consciousness of the class, but the consciousness of the class also directs and provides orientation for the theory. If this unity is sundered, it becomes difficult to distinguish the Marxist theory of political struggle from a theory of manipulation.[22] Perhaps for this reason, Althusser has more recently permitted himself some more adequate formulations of the relation between theory and class, ones precisely which lay emphasis on the ability of the proletariat to comprehend its objective position, and thus liberate it from the postulated eternal subjection to ideology.[23] What is questionable is whether such formulations can be rendered coherent with the theoretical structure he had previously elaborated, or whether, on the other hand, to defend them and give them foundation, he will be forced to abandon his positions one after another.

The source of Althusser's error is that he read in *Capital* only a

20. *For Marx*, p. 199.
21. *Reading Capital*, p. 131.
22. J-C. Forquin, p. 31.
23. Louis Althusser, 'Avertissement aux lecteurs du livre I du *Capital*', in *Le Capital*, Livre I, Garnier-Flammarion, Paris, 1969, p. 25.

theory of the *raison d'être* of mystification, a theory which, to be sure, is there. But in this reading he failed to perceive what is also there, a theory of the conditions and possibility of demystification. The latter is, perhaps, less developed than the first, and this primarily because *Capital* terminates abruptly as Marx takes up the consideration of classes—'Vingt lignes, puis le silence'.[24] Yet it is plain enough. Speaking of the way in which exploitation is concealed by the circulation process, Marx goes on: 'To be sure, the matter looks quite different if we consider capitalist production in the uninterrupted flow of its renewal, and if, in place of the individual capitalist and the individual worker, we view them in their totality, the capitalist class and the working class confronting each other. But in so doing we should be applying standards entirely foreign to commodity production' (1, 586).

The matter looks quite different: the appearance of a relation of equality between individuals gives way to the reality of collective exploitation. And this is achieved by an analysis of the *essential* relations of capitalist society, that is, the class relations. But it is not only theoretical analysis which has this effect. The *political struggle of the working class* is an exact duplication. Here, not the analyst, but the organized working class applies 'standards entirely foreign to commodity production'. *It* ceases to consider the relation of individual capitalist to individual worker and views them 'in their totality' by actually confronting the capitalist class as a whole. By doing so it penetrates the false appearances of bourgeois ideology. This in no sense invalidates Marx's proposition that the workers are inevitably mystified so long as, and to the extent that, they remain trapped within bourgeois relations of production. For this is so. But the proletariat does not escape these relations of production only on the day of the socialist revolution. It begins to move outside them from the moment it engages in organized political struggle, since the latter involves the adoption of a class position, this criterion entirely foreign to commodity production, and the refusal any longer to think exclusively in terms of relations between individuals. For this reason, the 'structuralist' notions of the revolution as rupture (Althusser) or limit (Godelier) are less precise than the notion of revolution as praxis (with, to be sure, its ruptural point). And the full force of Rosa Luxemburg's insistence on the demystifying

24. *Reading Capital*, p. 193.

effects of mass political struggle becomes evident. At the same time, the Althusserian disjunction between the consciousness of the masses and that of the theoretician is shown to lack foundation. The integral relation between the two is based on the fact that the theoretician takes up, in analysis, the same positions as the masses adopt in political struggle; though, of course, this should not be understood as a reduction of the sort 'theory is practice'.

The above passage from Marx also introduces another dimension of the distinction, essence/appearance, one which has been emphasized, above all, by Herbert Marcuse.[25] As we have seen, all the concepts with which Marx specifies the essential relations of capitalist society have a basically cognitive function. They make possible a knowledge of reality in opposition to the false evidences of immediate appearances. But if, in order to do this, and in the process of doing it, they refer us to 'standards entirely foreign to commodity production', then they are at the same time critical concepts. Thus, the concept of surplus-value not only permits a comprehension of the mechanisms of capitalist exploitation. By laying bare the division of the working day into necessary and surplus labour-time, it envisages a state of affairs in which there is no exploitation. It contains 'an accusation and an imperative'.[26] However, this critical function of the concepts must not be understood as a mere taking up of positions, or moralizing. If they fail in their cognitive function, then they are useless in their critical one. When Marx clearly takes his distance from 'that kind of criticism which knows how to judge and condemn the present, but not how to comprehend it' (1, 505), he informs us that the essential concepts derive what validity they have not from their particular moral stance (relativism), but from the fact that they permit a coherent organization of appearances and an explanation of their source such as no other concepts can provide. This is, indeed, the criterion which validates these concepts. As Marcuse has expressed it: 'If the historical structure . . . postulated as "essential" for the explanation . . . makes it possible to comprehend causally the situation both in its individual phases as well as in terms of the tendencies effective within it, then it is really the

25. Herbert Marcuse, *Reason and Revolution*, New York, 1963, pp. 258, 295–6, and 321.

26. Herbert Marcuse, 'The Concept of Essence' in *Negations*, London, 1968, p. 86.

essential in that manifold of appearances. This determination of essence is true; it has held good within the theory.'[27]

It remains to make explicit that in *Capital* the distinction between essence and appearance is, as well as everything else, a distinction also between the totality and its parts. Each single relationship or fact is an appearance whose full meaning or reality is only articulated by integrating it theoretically within its total structure. This has already been seen with regard to the light thrown on individual relationships by a consideration of the relations between classes.

But it applies more generally. I confine myself to certain 'pairs' of facts, treated by Marx in his chapter on machinery and modern industry. Machinery is the most powerful instrument for lightening labour; its capitalist employment leads to greater exploitation and domination. Science and technology make huge and unprecedented strides under capitalism; but at the expense of the workers' physical and intellectual powers. Modern machinery shatters the petrified forms of the division of labour creating the need for variability of functions and, thus, for a less one-sided, more rounded, development of the worker; under the anarchic conditions of capitalism, however, the worker lives and experiences this tendency as insecurity of employment and suffering. These pairs of facts are actually contradictions. As such, they represent tendencies which are neither simply progressive, nor simply regressive, because *contradictory*. The essence which explains them, and deprives them of all appearance of contingency, is the central contradiction between forces of production, the increasing productive power of social labour, on the one hand, and relations of production, the continued private appropriation of surplus-value, on the other. They partake of this central contradiction and, as partial facts, are only properly comprehended in relation to the social totality which they and it inhabit.

27. Ibid., p. 74.

4.

Louis Althusser[1]
1982

In the early 1960s Louis Althusser, French communist and philosopher, put forward a view of Marx's work that soon became widely influential. With *For Marx* and *Reading Capital* it won an international audience. It originated as a challenge to humanist and Hegelian themes then much current in discussion of Marx and inspired by his early writings, and it proffered a novel conception of Marxist philosophy.

Althusser sought to impugn the pre-eminent status accorded by many to these early writings, arguing that whatever the superficial similarities between them and Marx's mature work, here were two radically distinct modes of thought. The *problematic* of each —that is, the theoretical framework or system determining the significance of each particular concept, the questions posed, central propositions and omissions—was fundamentally different: in the young Marx, an ideological drama of human alienation and self-realization, with humanity the author of its unfolding destiny much in the manner of the world spirit according to Hegel; thereafter, however, a science, historical materialism, theory of social formations and their history; and its concepts of structural explanation: the forces and relations of production, determination by the economy, superstructure, state, ideology. The two systems of thought were separated by an *epistemological break* (in which a new science emerges from its ideological pre-history), and that break was disclosed, according to Althusser, by a critical reading

1. Born 16 October 1918, Birmandreïs, Algeria.

of Marx's work, able to discern in his discourse, in its sounds and in its silences alike, the symptoms of its underlying problematic.

The notions deployed in this periodization of Marx's thought—the problematic and the epistemological break, the idea of a so-called *symptomatic reading*—were proposed by Althusser as themselves belonging to the revolutionary new philosophy inaugurated *by* Marx. This philosophy, dialectical materialism, was implicit in the foundation of the science, historical materialism—though, because only implicit, in need of articulation and development—and was in the first instance epistemology, a theory of knowledge or science. Its chief target was empiricism, a view of cognition in which the knowing subject confronts the real object and uncovers its essence by abstraction; and which seeks, from this assumption of thought's direct encounter with reality, of the subject's unmediated vision of the object, for external guarantees of knowledge's truth. To the conception of knowledge as vision dialectical materialism opposed a conception of it as production, as theoretical practice; and was itself, therefore, said to be the *theory of theoretical practice*.

This practice, Althusser maintained, takes place entirely within thought. It works upon a theoretical object, never coming face to face with the real object as such, though that is what it aims to know, but having to do rather with what he called *Generalities I, II* and *III* respectively: a theoretical raw material of ideas and abstractions; conceptual means of production (the problematic aforesaid) brought to bear upon these; and the product of this process, a transformed theoretical entity, knowledge. Theoretical practice needs no external guarantees of the latter's validity, since every science possesses internal modes of proof with which to validate its own products. Governed by the interior requirements of knowledge, not by extra-theoretical exigencies, interests of society or class; autonomous therefore, not part of the superstructure, but following its own developmental course some way removed from the vicissitudes of social history; theoretical or scientific practice is distinct from ideological practice, distinct too from political practice and economic practice. These are all, nevertheless, equally practices, types of production. They share a common formal structure, each with its own raw material, means of production, production process and product. That is the way the world is. Epistemology in the first place, dialectical materialism contains also its ontology, theory of the ultimate nature and constituents of being.

Reality, Althusser insisted, is irreducibly complex and manifold, subject to multiple causation, in a word *overdetermined*, and the scientific, Marxist concept of social totality is not to be confused, consequently, with the Hegelian, whose complexity is merely apparent. The different features of a historical epoch, Hegel thought—its economy, polity, art, religion—are all expressions of a single essence, itself only a stage in the development of the world spirit. With each successive totality conceived as *expressive* in this way, explanation of history becomes reductionist, simplifying towards a unique central origin. Even Marxism has been thus vitiated in some of its deviant forms: such as economism, in which the elements of the superstructure are seen as but passive effects of the economic base's pervasive determinism; and such as historicism, whose special fault is that, assimilating all practices within a common historical present, it relativizes knowledge, deprives science of its autonomy and treats Marxism itself, not as an objective science, but as the self-expression of the contemporary world, class consciousness or viewpoint of the proletariat. Correctly understood, however, a social formation has no essence or centre; is said, therefore, to be *decentred*. It is a hierarchy of practices or structures, genuinely distinct one from another, and although, amongst them, the economic is causally primary, the others are relatively autonomous, possessing a *specific effectivity* of their own and, in some degree, independent histories. In certain circumstances they can even play the dominant role. The economic level is only determining in the last instance.

All this—vital to Marxist politics: that society be grasped, and each historical conjuncture analysed, in its full complexity— Althusser encapsulated in terming the social formation a *structure in dominance*. Its causality, dubbed by him *structural*, governs historical development. Human beings are not the authors or subjects of this process which, decentred, has no motive subject. They are supports, effects, of the structures and relations of the social formation. Marx, according to Althusser, rejected the idea of a universal human essence or nature. He espoused thereby a theoretical anti-humanism.

Althusser's work has provoked strong reactions, both partisan and hostile. Calm judgement will be more balanced. Though couched at times in an overblown, pretentious rhetoric, some of what he said was important, especially when he said it. A new theory does emerge in Marx's writings from 1845 and this, the materialist conception of history, is superior, cognitively and politically, to his early work. To have insisted upon it, and in an anti-reductionist form; and on the relative autonomy of science; and that Marx himself believed in the possibility of objective scientific knowledge—which he unquestionably did, aspiring to contribute to the sum of it—these were merits. However, the problematic and related notions also had less salutary results. Apart from its theoretical absurdity, the claim, for example, that Marx rejected *all* concepts of human nature is textually insupportable. The same with Althusser's argument that even a communist society will have its ideology, imaginary representation of the real: rightly or wrongly, in maturity as in youth, Marx reckoned here on a society transparent to its members. Althusser, of course, was not obliged to agree with him about this or anything else. But to pretend to have read *in* Marx the opposite of what is there is a form of obscurantism.

The Althusserian system, moreover, for all its emphasis on materialist science, displayed many of the features of an idealism. It attenuated the relationship borne by Marxism, as a developing theory, to the contemporary history of class struggles. In the name of rejecting empiricism, it cloistered knowledge within a wholly circular, self-validating conceptual realm. Shut off from direct access to what is given in reality, theory was allowed, nevertheless, a more mysterious correspondence with it, whose secret, at least as regards social reality, was nothing other than the *unique common essence* shared by theory and the other social practices as, ultimately, modes of production. The analogy with material production enabled Althusser to make important points about the conditions of theoretical knowledge. Legislating, however, that all levels of social reality are intrinsically so structured created a metaphysic of dubious value: in the case of politics, for example, it was a mere assertion, yielding no comparable elaboration or insight. Partly to remedy some of these weaknesses, Althusser subsequently offered a new definition of philosophy, but this was no advance. Whatever its defects, his original definition had both substance and clarity. The new one was vacuous. Previously theory of theoretical practice, philosophy was now said to have no object: not to be a theory at all, and yet to represent theory, and be a theoretical intervention, within politics; and not to be politics (the class struggle), yet to represent politics, and be a political intervention, within theory. Philosophy was, in other words, nothing in its own right and, at the same time, practically everything.

It has to be said, finally, that the ideas he proposed as the basis for complex, concrete historical analysis were remarkably barren in that role in Althusser's own hands, one measure of this being that on Stalinism, by his own account of things a key issue, he had nothing worthwhile to say: on the one hand, declarations un-argued and cryptic, smacking of evasion or apologia; on the other, an astonishingly trivializing explanation of it in terms of econo-mism—and of humanism to boot.

5.

Althusser's Marxism:
An Account and Assessment
1971

In a body of work which has received considerable attention in France and elsewhere and become one of the focal points of contemporary Marxist controversy, Louis Althusser has registered the necessity for a reading of Marx at once critical and rigorous. *Critical*: the assimilation of Marx's important discoveries can only be the product of a major theoretical effort which, so far from taking for granted that the whole of Marx forms a coherent and valid unity, attempts to distinguish *in* Marx between theoretical deficiencies, terminological ambiguities and ideological 'survivals' on the one hand, and truly scientific concepts on the other. *Rigorous*: the condition for the fruitful application and further elaboration of these concepts is a strict and scrupulous regard for their definitions, their implications, their scope and their boundaries, for what they exclude as much as for what they include. Only by dint of this will Marxist research escape the pitfalls of taking these concepts for what they are not and of remaining satisfied with the inadequate substitutes which can masquerade in their place.

The insistence on this double requirement bears witness to the self-conscious intention of a Communist philosopher to avoid both the shackles of uncritical orthodoxy and the temptations of conceptual imprecision. At the same time, the exercise should not be regarded as a purely academic one in which the only stake is the scholarly interpretation and assessment of Marx. For, if Althusser has thought it necessary to challenge those tendencies (humanism, historicism, Hegelianism) which have haunted

Western Marxism since Lukács's early work and become power-fully influential in the last two decades, it is because he believes that, being theoretically deficient, they cannot but produce serious negative effects in the political practice of the class struggle. Unable to provide an adequate scientific knowledge of the real political problems thrown up by this struggle, and offering instead the imaginary comforts of merely ideological formulae, such tendencies cannot contribute to the solution of these problems and may indeed be impediments to their solution. The stakes, ultimately, are political. The precise counts on which the humanist and historicist themes of Hegelian Marxism are found to be theoretically deficient will be elaborated in due course. Here it is sufficient to observe that Althusser defines his work as an intervention against these tendencies within Marxism and that it is only by situating it in this context that its significance is properly understood.

The first part of this article is an exposition of the theoretical positions of *For Marx* (1965) and *Reading Capital* (1965), Althusser's major, and most systematic, works to date despite the reservations he has since expressed about them. In the second part, I attempt a critical assessment of these positions, and conclude with some remarks on the texts Althusser has written since 1965—texts which are collected in *Lenin and Philosophy and other essays*. All these works are now available to the English reader in Ben Brewster's excellent translations.[1]

I Exposition

The Althusserian project receives its unity from one central and overriding concern: 'the *investigation* of Marx's *philosophical* thought.'[2] Behind the diverse problems considered and the solutions proposed, there is always one question at issue, for Althusser the essential question, namely, '*What is Marxist philosophy? Has it any theoretical right to existence? And if it does exist in principle, how can its specificity be defined?*'[3] The approach to

1. Louis Althusser, *For Marx*, Allen Lane, 1969, and NLB, London, 1977; Louis Althusser and Etienne Balibar, *Reading Capital*, NLB, London, 1970; Louis Althusser, *Lenin and Philosophy and other essays*, NLB, London, 1971. Referred to hereinafter as FM, RC and LP respectively.

2. FM p. 21. All italics in the original except where otherwise stated.

3. FM p. 31.

Marx's *Capital* too is informed by this question. For all that it is primarily a work of political economy, it is seen by Althusser and his collaborators as the basic site of the philosophy which is the object of their search.[4] Thus their reading of that work is an explicitly philosophical one undertaken by philosophers[5] in order to be able to respond to one of the exigencies confronting contemporary Marxist theory: the need for 'a more rigorous and richer definition of *Marxist philosophy*'.[6]

What is the source of this exigency? In the first place, the nature of Marx's own achievement: 'By founding the theory of history (historical materialism), Marx simultaneously broke with his erstwhile ideological philosophy and established a new philosophy (dialectical materialism). I am deliberately using the traditionally accepted terminology (historical materialism, dialectical materialism) to designate this double foundation.'[7] It is an achievement involving two distinct disciplines, but it is marked by a certain unevenness, for historical materialism and dialectical materialism have received different degrees of theoretical elaboration. The former, the Marxist science of social formations and their history, was mapped out and developed in Marx's mature works, to be enriched subsequently by theoreticians such as Lenin engaged in the practice of the class struggle. On the other hand, 'Marxist philosophy, founded by Marx in the very act of founding his theory of history, has still largely to be constituted, since, as Lenin said, only the corner-stones have been laid down.'[8] Dialectical materialism, that is to say, represents a philosophical revolution 'carried in' Marx's scientific discoveries;[9] at work in them, it exists in an untheorized practical state;[10] its mode of existence is merely 'implicit'.[11] Whence the need to give it proper theoretical articulation, resisting the temptation offered by its implicitness simply to confuse it with historical materialism.

For if the latter has been able to develop up to a point in the

4. RC pp. 30–1, 74.
5. RC pp. 14–5.
6. RC p. 77.
7. FM p. 33.
8. FM pp. 30–1
9. RC pp. 75–6.
10. FM pp. 173–5; RC p. 185.
11. FM pp. 33, 229.

absence of an explicit and thorough formulation of the principles of Marxist philosophy, this absence has not been without serious consequences and to continue to tolerate it would be to incur further risks. Anticipating somewhat the further course of this exposition, I will simply indicate here that, for Althusser, Marxist philosophy is a 'theory of the differential nature of theoretical formations and their history, that is, a theory of epistemological history',[12] or, what comes to the same thing, 'the theory of the history of the production of knowledge'.[13] It is, in short, 'the theory of science and of the history of science.'[14] As such, a well-founded Marxist philosophy is indispensable to the science of historical materialism, in order to identify its fragile points, to pose clearly its problems so that they may be capable of solution, to give it the concepts adequate to its tasks, and to facilitate its path in those areas of study where it has only just begun, or has yet to begin, to make its way. As the vigilant guardian of its scientificity, dialectical materialism can assist in consolidating and defending historical materialism against the ideologies which threaten it both at its weak points and at its frontiers. But without this philosophical attention, the scientific activity, left to develop spontaneously, will be helpless in the face of these threats and open to the invasions of ideology. This has happened in the past and will continue to happen so long as the science lacks the explicit theory of its own practice.[15] This is why 'the theoretical future of historical materialism depends today on deepening dialectical materialism.'[16]

Enough has been said, then, to establish that what we can expect to find in Althusser's work is primarily an elaboration of this Marxist philosophy, dialectical materialism, a provisional specification of its precise character and content. In aiming for a clear presentation of this Althusserian construction, I shall avail

12. FM p. 38.

13. RC pp. 56, 44, 75, 89, 157.

14. RC pp. 145, 86, 153. Cf. Macherey who gives this conception of philosophy its most acute formulation: 'La philosophie n'est rien d'autre alors que la connaissance de l'histoire des sciences. Philosophes sont aujourd'hui ceux qui font l'histoire des théories, et *en même temps* la théorie de cette histoire . . . philosopher c'est étudier *dans quelles conditions*, et *à quelles conditions* sont posés des problèmes scientifiques.' L. Althusser, J. Rancière, P. Macherey, E. Balibar and R. Establet, *Lire le Capital*, 2 vols., Paris, 1965, vol. I, p. 216.

15. FM pp. 169–73; RC pp. 29–30, 89–90 n. 5, 145–6.

16. RC p. 77.

myself of the following distinction. As theory of science and of its history, Althusser's dialectical materialism contains a series of concepts pertaining to the nature and process of theoretical knowledge, in other words, a set of *epistemological* concepts. In addition, to the extent that it functions as the theory of the particular science of historical materialism by reflecting on its concepts and problems, it incorporates a set of *historical* concepts. The two areas defined by this distinction (which is merely an expository convenience: as will be seen, the epistemological and historical concepts are integrally related) are, however, founded on one and the same first principle, which is the principle of intelligibility for both. This principle is the central Althusserian concept of *practice* or *production*. The exposition will therefore proceed as follows: from i) a preliminary discussion of the concept of practice/production, to a consideration of ii) the epistemological concepts and iii) the historical concepts which are based upon it.

1. Practice/Production

The '*primacy of practice*' is established for Althusser 'by showing that all the levels of social existence are the sites of distinct practices',[17] and Marx's double achievement, scientific and philosophical, can be summed up precisely in this, that, in breaking with the inadequate, ideological concepts which governed the thinking of his youth, he founded 'a historico-dialectical materialism of *praxis*: that is, . . . a theory of the different specific *levels of human practice* (economic practice, political practice, ideological practice, scientific practice)'.[18] This concern to emphasize that each level (or instance)[19] of the social totality is a practice must not be permitted to obscure Althusser's insistence, equally forceful, that the various practices are nonetheless really distinct, and should not be collapsed into one undifferentiated notion of practice in general. For we shall see in due course that most of the theoretical errors and deviations, within, and outside, Marxism, which constitute the objects of his criticism, are put down in the

17. RC p. 58.
18. FM p. 229.
19. See e.g. RC p. 97.

last analysis to an incorrect understanding of the concept of practice, and, in particular, to a tendency to reduce or negate the distance between the practices. The concept has thus a polemical or negative function which complements its positive function of foundation-stone of the Althusserian system, and its performance of both functions is importantly determined by the distinctions inscribed within it: 'we must recognize that there is no practice in general, but only *distinct practices*', for 'there can be no scientific conception of practice without a precise distinction between the distinct practices.'[20] I shall return in a moment to the principle of distinction.

The General Essence of Practice

It is necessary, first of all, to investigate the principle of unity, referred to by Althusser as 'the general essence of practice',[21] which makes possible a 'general definition of practice'[22] such that the different levels of social existence, whatever their concrete differences, are all equally practices. This principle of unity Althusser expresses as follows: 'By *practice* in general I shall mean any process of *transformation* of a determinate given raw material into a determinate *product*, a transformation effected by a determinate human labour, using determinate means (of "production"). In any practice thus conceived, the *determinant* moment (or element) is neither the raw material nor the product, but the practice in the narrow sense: the moment of the *labour of transformation* itself, which sets to work, in a specific structure, men, means and a technical method of utilizing the means.'[23]

Given this definition, politics, ideology and science (or theory), as well as economic production in the narrow sense, can all be regarded as forms of practice, to the extent that they all entail a transformation of a given raw material or object into a specific product by means of a labour process involving labourers and means of production—to the extent, that is to say, that each exemplifies 'the structure of a production',[24] that, as one of

20. RC p. 58.
21. FM pp. 188, n.26, 169.
22. FM p. 167.
23. FM p. 166-7.
24. RC p. 58.

Althusser's critics has put it, they all share this 'homologous form'.[25] Thus in Althusser we find reference not only to the economic mode of production, combining in specific relations of production the elements of the material production process,[26] but also, for example, to 'the *mode* of theoretical production' or '*mode of production* of knowledges,'[27] and to the 'mode of production of ideology'.[28] The same applies in Balibar's more extended treatment of this concept. The economic mode of production in every social formation is said to consist of a combination of the same few elements, namely, labourer, object of labour, means of labour, and non-labourer, in specific relations of production.[29] And, by extension, 'all the levels of the social structure have the structure of a "mode" in the sense in which I have analysed the mode of production strictly speaking.'[30] For, every level of the social structure, as the site of a distinct practice, is constituted by a set of similar elements, which are combined in specific social relations. Hence the scattered references to 'political social relations' and 'ideological social relations', as distinct from the economic relations of production.[31] These other relations represent combinations of the elements of political and ideological practice respectively.

We have, then, a general definition covering a number of particular practices by virtue of the formal similarities just discussed. But within this formal similarity there is a real dissimilarity of content separating the four major practices identified by Althusser. The dissimilarity of content consists in the fact that each practice has a different type of initial object or raw material which is transformed into a different type of product, by means, in each case, of a different type of 'labour' with different instruments of labour. Thus, where economic practice involves putting to work labour power and means of material production to transform natural or already worked-up materials into socially useful products, theoretical or scientific practice brings together

25. See A. Glucksmann, 'A Ventriloquist Structuralism', in *Western Marxism: A Critical Reader*, NLB/Verso 1977, p. 283.

26. RC pp. 170–77.

27. RC pp. 27, n.9, 41.

28. RC p. 52.

29. RC pp. 212–16.

30. RC p. 220.

31. RC pp. 140, 180, 220.

'thought power' and means of theoretical labour (the concepts of a theory and its method) to produce from concepts, representations, intuitions, a specific product: knowledges.[32] Political practice works on its own type of raw materials, given social relations, to produce its own type of product, new social relations. Ideological practice transforms the forms of representation and perception in which the agents of a social formation 'live' their relations with their world.[33] A respect for these real differences is the fundamental precondition for understanding the distinctive processes of the practices, their peculiar mechanisms and rhythms of development. For they all develop on their own sites, which are really distinct levels or instances of social reality: 'It is perfectly legitimate to say that the production of knowledge which is peculiar to theoretical practice constitutes a process that takes place *entirely in thought*, just as we can say, *mutatis mutandis*, that the process of economic production takes place entirely in the economy, even though it implies, and precisely in the specific determinations of its structure, necessary relations with nature and the other structures (legal-political and ideological) which, taken together, constitute the global structure of a social formation belonging to a determinate mode of production.'[34] The science of historical materialism, which is a theoretical practice, has precisely to study the different practices in their specificity, and their relations to one another in the complex unity of social practice which is the social formation.

What then of dialectical materialism? Within this, its own, conceptual universe it defines itself as the theory 'in which is theoretically expressed the essence of theoretical practice in general, through it the essence of practice in general, and through it the essence of the transformations, of the "development" of things in general.' As such, it is the materialist dialectic in person.[35] But if, in its generality, it is simply theory of practice, it has what might be called a principal aspect, thrown into relief by the primary Althusserian definition: dialectical materialism is, as already indicated, the theory of science or, as we are now in a position to say, 'the Theory of theoretical practice'.[36] In this

32. FM pp. 167, 173; RC pp. 42, 59.
33. FM pp. 167, 175–76, 233.
34. RC p. 42.
35. FM pp. 168–69.
36. FM pp. 171, 173, 256; RC p. 8.

guise, it embodies an epistemology.

2. Epistemological Concepts

'To conceive Marx's philosophy in its specificity is... to conceive knowledge as *production*.'[37] This much should already be clear. Althusser's own epistemology is simply an attempted elaboration of this 'new *conception of knowledge*'[38] disclosed to him by a critical reading of Marx. Its negative reference point, that which has to be rejected and abandoned in favour of this new conception, is empiricism: the conception of knowledge as *vision*.[39] And it is Althusser's radical and unremitting criticism of this latter conception which I shall take here as my point of departure.

The structure of the empiricist conception of knowledge is defined, according to Althusser, by a small number of central concepts: those of subject and object, of abstract and concrete, and of the given. The starting point of the knowledge process is conceived as 'a purely objective "given"', that is, as something immediately visible and accessible to direct observation. But since what *is* so given is supposed to be the real (object) itself, the concrete, the starting point for knowledge must be concrete reality. The subject must perform on the latter an operation of abstraction in order to acquire thereby a knowledge of it.[40] This is empiricism's first mistake: it takes the initial object or raw material of theoretical practice to be reality itself. The function of the operation of abstraction which is performed by the subject is to disengage or extract from the real object its essence, to eliminate in the process everything inessential or incidental which obscures that essence. For, if the object itself is accessible to direct observation, its essence is not, and the act of abstraction has to render this visible, so that it may be seen, grasped and possessed. The sight and possession by the subject of the essence of the object is what constitutes knowledge. However, this conception of knowledge (and here is the crucial step in Althusser's argument), presupposing as it does a reality with two parts,

37. RC p. 34.
38. RC p. 35.
39. RC pp. 19, 24.
40. FM pp. 183–84, 190–91; RC pp. 43, 161, 183.

actually inscribes within the structure of the real object to be known, the knowledge of that object. It does so by equating knowledge with one part of the real object, the essential part. Thus, the knowledge of a reality is conceived as part of that reality, and its only difference from the reality of which it is the knowledge is that it is merely part of it and not the whole of it.[41] This is empiricism's second mistake: it takes the product of theoretical practice, namely, knowledge, to be part of the reality known. It 'confuse[s] thought with the real by reducing thought about the real to the real itself.'[42]

From this it should be clear why Althusser rejects, as a contemporary variant of empiricism, the epistemology of *models*. Here again the model is conceived as providing knowledge of a reality by abstracting its essential from its inessential features. Reality, or the concrete, is then said to be 'always-richer-and-more-living' than the theory which attempts to comprehend it.[43] And we are face to face with a third deficiency of empiricism which is perfectly coherent with the first two: abstract theory is, at best, only an approximation of concrete reality. Theoretical concepts by their very nature (that is, by virtue of being abstract) have a built-in inadequacy, an 'original weakness' which is their 'original sin'. In consequence, the possibility is lost of a knowledge fully adequate to the reality of which it is the knowledge. This deficiency, which marks both the philosophical efforts of Engels[44] and the writings of Feuerbach and the Young Marx,[45] must be banished, along with the other errors of empiricism, from the epistemology of dialectical materialism. We shall see in what follows that the basic concepts of empiricism, where Althusser retains them at all, are radically transformed and given a different content and role.

Thought and Reality

In the first place the distinction between abstract and concrete, representative for empiricism of the distinction between thought

41. RC pp. 35–40.
42. RC p. 87.
43. RC pp. 39, 117–18.
44. RC pp. 82, 113–15.
45. FM pp. 186–87.

and reality, is transposed by Althusser into the realm of thought itself, and abstract and concrete there become raw material and product respectively of the process of production of knowledge. The latter takes place '*entirely in thought*', that is to say, wholly *within* what the empiricist would regard as abstraction, so that it 'never, as empiricism desperately demands it should, confronts *a pure object* which is . . . identical to the *real object*.'[46] This can be elaborated by reference to the three kinds of 'Generalities' discussed by Althusser. He calls Generalities I the concepts and abstractions which constitute the raw material of theoretical practice. This raw material to be transformed is never just a given, it is never concrete reality; it is always an already worked-up material consisting of abstract concepts which are the products of a previous practice. These concepts are partly scientific, the products of past theoretical practice, and partly ideological, the products of an ideological practice. And the raw material of ideological practice, in turn, is never reality itself. It always consists of abstractions, ideas, intuitions, which are themselves the results both of previous ideological practice and other subsidiary practices (empirical, technical), which Althusser mentions in this connection without expatiating upon them. So the raw material from which theoretical practice 'begins' (the process cannot have an origin, strictly speaking)[47] is never reality as such, but always an abstraction of one sort or another. It is transformed by the application of means of theoretical production, Generalities II, into a product, Generalities III. The means of theoretical production are the basic concepts of a science at any given moment, more or less unified within a specific theoretical framework which will determine the problems capable of being posed and resolved by the science. And the Generalities III which are the product of theoretical practice are the scientific concepts embodying knowledge. Following Marx in the 1857 *Introduction* to *A Contribution to the Critique of Political Economy*, Althusser calls this product the *concrete-in-thought*: it is the synthesis of abstract concepts which provides knowledge of the *real-concrete*; but it is also, as a theoretical product, completely distinct from this real-concrete whose knowledge it provides. The process of knowledge 'ends' as it 'begins' entirely within thought.[48]

46. RC pp. 42–43.

47. RC pp. 62–64.

48. Essential references for this paragraph: FM pp. 183–93. Cf. also RC pp. 41, 87–88, 90, 189–90.

The distinction between thought and reality (between theoretical practice and the other practices) is, then, irreducible and, as such, it entails two theses which are essential to dialectical materialism: '(I) the materialist thesis of the primacy of the real over thought, since thought about the real presupposes the existence of the real, independent of that thought (the real *"survives in its independence, after as before, outside the head"—Grundisse*, p. 22); and (2) the materialist thesis of the specificity of thought and of the thought process, with respect to the real and the real process.'[49] This is not a reductionist materialism. The point can be reinforced by indicating a shift in the terms by which Althusser attempts to register the distinction between thought and reality. In *For Marx* a distinction is made between the concrete-in-thought and the real-concrete, and the latter is, as that which is known by theory, the *object of knowledge*.[50] In *Reading Capital* this is no longer the case. To be sufficiently sharp, the same distinction now seems to require that the object of knowledge should be not the real-concrete, not the real object, but a different object, itself completely distinct from these. The object of knowledge is now situated within the realm of theoretical practice, and is a theoretical object, a concept or complex of concepts. Thus, 'the *object* of knowledge . . . [is] in itself absolutely distinct and different from the *real object* . . . the *idea* of the circle, which is the *object* of knowledge must not be confused with the circle, which is the *real object*.'[51] What impels Althusser to sunder the identity between real object and object of knowledge is, once again, his concern to emphasize that theoretical practice has its own raw material and its own product, both of them distinct from the reality it aims to know. The object of knowledge in the strict sense, that is, in the sense of object worked upon and transformed in the process of production of knowledge, is this raw material and this product, which in turn becomes raw material. It cannot be the real object.[52]

There is, for all that, a 'relation between these two objects (the object of knowledge and the real object), a relation which consti-

49. RC p. 87. I have modified the English translation slightly since it does not accurately reproduce the French text at this point.

50. FM p. 186.

51. RC p. 40 and *passim*.

52. RC pp. 43, 156.

tutes the very existence of *knowledge*'.[53] This relation will be discussed more fully below. Suffice it to indicate here its essential implication: if the object of knowledge in the strict sense is *not* the real object, the object which is known finally, *via* the object of knowledge, *is* the real object. Theoretical practice achieves, through the object of knowledge, the cognitive appropriation of the real object called knowledge. More accurately, it ensures, by means of the continual transformations it effects in the object of knowledge, the 'incessant deepening' of the knowledge of the real object. The latter therefore remains 'the *absolute reference point* of the process of knowledge which is concerned with it'.[54] Is this to say, borrowing a phrase used by Althusser in a different context, that the real object is the object of knowledge, 'but only in the last instance'?

The Role of the Problematic

In any case we must now examine the process of knowledge from the angle of that complex of Generalities II which Althusser calls the *problematic* of a science (or ideology). The term designates the theoretical (or ideological) framework which puts into relation with one another the basic concepts, determines the nature of each concept by its place and function in this system of relationships, and thus confers on each concept its particular significance. Since the concepts are only properly understood in the context of their problematic, they should not be regarded as so many discrete elements which can be isolated by analysis and compared with apparently similar elements belonging to another problematic. For, if the problematics in question are fundamentally different, any similarities established at the level of their respective elements will be, at best, superficial and, at worst, not really similarities at all. So construed, the problematic of a science (or ideology) governs not merely the solutions it is capable of providing but the very problems it can pose and the form in which they must be posed. It is a 'system of *questions*'. However, this problematic rarely exists in explicit and conscious form in the theory which it governs, so 'cannot generally be read like an open

53. RC p. 52.
54. RC p. 156. The italics are mine. Cf. also pp. 41, 48, 64, 66, 87, 107.

book.' It is, on the contrary, the unconscious structure of the theory 'buried but active' in it in the way that, as we have seen, Marx's philosophy is said to be buried but active in his scientific work. To be grasped, it has therefore to be 'dragged up from the depths'.[55]

Buried but active: let us look at these two characteristics of the problematic in turn and elicit their implications.

The problematic, by determining what it includes within its field, thereby necessarily determines what is excluded therefrom. The concepts which are excluded (absences, lacunae), and the problems which are not posed adequately (semi-silences, lapses), or posed at all (silences), are therefore as much a part of the problematic as are the concepts and problems that are present. And it cannot for that very reason be grasped by a simple literal or immediate reading of the explicit discourse of a text. Rather it must be reached by a 'symptomatic' reading where the explicit discourse is read conjointly with the absences, lacunae and silences which, constituting a second 'silent discourse', are so many symptoms of the unconscious problematic buried in the text. Like all knowledge, reading, correctly understood and correctly practised, is not vision but theoretical labour and production.[56] This is the theoretical basis, if you like, of Althusser's insistence, alluded to in the introduction to this article, on the need for a critical reading of Marx. It is also the clue to the enigmatic Althusserian 'circle': the problematic of Marx's philosophy, buried in his mature scientific works, is only accessible if one knows how to read correctly, that is, if one knows that knowledge is production, which is itself a principle essential to the problematic of Marx's philosophy. The elaboration and refinement of Marxist philosophical principles therefore requires that one disposes of them already in at least provisional form and can apply them in the theoretical practice of elaboration and refinement.[57]

As regards the *activity* of the implicit, unconscious, problematic, it is intended in the strongest possible sense. In words which we are enjoined by Althusser to take 'literally', the problematic is assigned those functions which other epistemologies, such as empiricism, attribute to a human subject: 'The sighting is thus no longer the act of an individual subject, endowed with the faculty of "vision" which he exercises either attentively or distractedly;

55. FM pp. 32, 39, 45–47, 62, 66–70.
56. RC pp. 15–33, 50, 86, 143–44.
57. FM pp. 38–39, 165–66; RC pp. 34, 74.

the sighting is the act of its structural conditions, it is the relation of immanent reflection between the field of the problematic and *its* objects and *its* problems. . . . It is literally no longer the eye (the mind's eye) of a subject which *sees* what exists in the field defined by a theoretical problematic: it is this field itself which *sees itself* in the objects or problems it defines . . . the invisible is no more a function of *a subject's sighting* than is the visible: the invisible is the theoretical problematic's non-vision of its non-objects, the invisible is the darkness, the blinded eye of the theoretical problematic's self-reflection when it scans its non-objects, its non-problems without seeing them, *in order not to look at them.'*[58] This passage, in which a theoretical *structure*, the problematic, is represented as the determinant element in the process of production of knowledge, so that the human subject ceases to be the subject of the process in the strict sense, is no mere polemical excess on Althusser's part. It is typical. The Althusserian universe is governed by structures and the only subjects that populate it are those subject *to* this government, their places and functions marked out for them by its ubiquitous hegemony. The elaboration of this particular theme will be undertaken in connection with the historical concepts in Althusser's work.

The Epistemological Break

It was intimated above that the problematic is a category as applicable to ideological as it is to scientific practice. But we know that these are two distinct practices, and the distinction can be said, provisionally, to consist in this, that an ideological concept 'designates' an existing reality, but does not, like a scientific concept, 'provide us with a means of knowing' it.[59] For Althusser, this means that there must be a radical qualitative difference between the problematic of an ideology and that of a science, for all that one may be able to discover 'similar' elements by abstracting these illegitimately from their respective problematics. In other words, a science is founded only at the cost of a complete rupture with the ideological problematic which precedes it, a thoroughgoing mutation of its basic structure. This rupture or mutation which founds a science Althusser calls an

58. RC pp. 25–26.
59. FM p. 223.

epistemological break. The role of the human subject in it is, again, subordinate: 'In this process of real transformation of the means of production of knowledge, the claims of a "constitutive subject" are as vain as are the claims of the subject of vision in the production of the visible. . . . The whole process takes place in the dialectical crisis of the mutation of a theoretical structure in which the "subject" plays, not the part it believes it is playing, but the part which is assigned to it by the mechanism of the process.'[60] Be that as it may, it is just such an epistemological break which is said to separate Marx, founder of the science of historical materialism, not only from his predecessors (Hegel, Feuerbach, Smith, Ricardo, and so on) but also from the ideological conceptions of his own youth. The break, situated by Althusser in 1845, is not a 'clean' one: 'Indispensable theoretical concepts do not magically construct themselves on command',[61] and ideological concepts survive in the works of Marx's maturity. So we see, once again, the need for a critical reading, able properly to locate the epistemological break in Marx, by distinguishing between the scientific and the ideological *throughout* his writings.[62]

It remains to ask: if science produces knowledge, what are the criteria which guarantee that this knowledge is true, that it is indeed knowledge? The question, according to Althusser, is 'false', and the classical Problem of Knowledge is not a 'real problem'. Any epistemology that sees the relation between the object of knowledge and the real object as a problematic one, that is, that regards knowledge itself as a problem, is simply ideological and to be rejected for that reason.[63] Rejecting the problem, Althusser rejects the available solutions to it, including pragmatism: 'It has been possible to apply Marx's theory with success because it is "true"; it is not true because it has been applied with success.' The whole matter is a non-problem because '*Theoretical practice* is . . . its own criterion, and contains in itself definite protocols with which to *validate* the quality of its product.' The

60. RC p. 27.
61. RC p. 51.
62. On the epistemological break, see, apart from the references already given, FM pp. 32–37, 167–68, 185, 192–93, and RC pp. 44–46, 90, 131, 133, 140, 146–57. In this connection it should be said that Althusser, stressing Marx's '*blinding*' 'novelty' (RC p. 78), refuses the conception of continuity in discontinuity embodied in the Hegelian notion of supersession ('Aufhebung'). Reasons of space prevent me from going into this. See FM pp. 76–78, 82, 188–89, 198.
63. RC pp. 52–55; FM p. 186.

established sciences 'themselves provide the criterion of validity of their knowledges.'[64] These criteria of validation internal to the theoretical practice of a science are its 'forms of proof' which, unfolding in the ordered discourse of the science, have the specific effect (called by Althusser the 'knowledge effect') of providing a cognitive grasp of reality. And the *mechanism* which produces this effect is the overall conceptual system of the science, since it determines not only the meaning of the concepts but also the 'order of their appearance in the discourse of the proof.'[65] *That* the effect produced is knowledge is no problem; *how* it is produced is. In other words, the only real problem according to Althusser is to understand the precise nature of the aforesaid mechanism.[66] To this real problem he does not claim to give an answer.[67]

3. Historical Concepts

What is the nature of the social formations studied by historical materialism? What are societies? 'They present themselves as totalities whose unity is constituted by a certain specific type of *complexity,* which introduces instances, that, following Engels, we can, very schematically, reduce to three: the economy, politics and ideology.'[68] We know already that each of these instances (levels), being a practice, combines, in social relations specific to itself, a set of formally similar elements, and that the resultant combination exhibits, in each case, the structure of a (mode of) production. We know, in short, that the different instances are *structures*, so that what Althusser refers to as the 'global structure' of the social formation or social whole[69] is itself 'a structure of structures'.[70] We must now examine the complexity of this global structure as conceived by Althusser. I shall approach his conception of complexity via the conception of simplicity he rejects,

64. RC pp. 56–9.
65. RC pp. 67–68.
66. RC p. 56.
67. RC p. 61.
68. FM pp. 231–32. It should be noted that *science* is not counted here as an instance of the social formation. In other Althusserian formulations it is. The significance of this inconsistency is discussed in Part II of this article.
69. RC pp. 42, 180.
70. RC p. 17.

or—for it amounts to the same thing—I shall approach Althusser's Marx here by way of Althusser's Hegel.

The problematic of Hegelian idealism may be regarded as an 'inversion' of the empiricist problematic discussed earlier. It shares with empiricism a basic structural similarity in that it too 'confuse[s] thought and the real'; but it does so 'by *reducing* the real to thought, by *"conceiving the real as the result of thought"*'.[71] This reduction, evidently the exact inverse of that perpetrated by empiricism, is embodied in the Hegelian conceptions of history and of the epochs, or social totalities, into which it can be periodized. All the phenomena of any one epoch (its economy, its polity and law, its philosophy, art and religion, its ethics, its customs, and so forth) are merely the externalizations of one moment of the development of the Idea, that is, of one internal *spiritual* principle which is the *essence* of those phenomena, manifesting itself in each and all of them, and expressed by each and all of them. Thus, for example, the essence of Rome, pervading its whole history and its manifold institutions, is the principle of the 'abstract legal personality'; the essence of the modern world, equally pervasive, is 'subjectivity'. And Hegel conceives every social totality in this manner as having a unique internal spiritual principle to which all the diverse realities can be reduced, since each of them is only an expression of it. Althusser therefore calls the Hegelian totality a 'spiritual' or 'expressive' type of totality, aiming by these designations to underscore the following: its apparent complexity conceals an essential simplicity, in the sense that the complex of diverse phenomena (appearances) is reducible to a single and simple essence. A sort of cross-section through the historical process at any point—what Althusser terms an *essential section*—will always reveal such an essence, one particular moment of the development of the Idea, manifest and legible in the multitude of social phenomena coexisting at that point in time. For, the historical process is nothing but the linear time continuum in which the Idea unfolds its potentialities, its successive moments. And the several totalities which follow one another are merely the successive expressions of these successive moments. As such, they belong, in all their aspects and instances, in all their apparent richness and complexity, to the same unique continuum in which the Idea unfolds. Their history is reducible to its history,

71. RC pp. 46–47, 87; FM p. 188.

in other words to one all-embracing history, which shares the simplicity of the Hegelian social totality, and by virtue of the same reductions. The conception, which reflects this simplicity, of a unique linear time continuum, is one 'borrowed from the most vulgar empiricism' and 'representative of the crude ideological illusions of everyday practice'; the only difference being that where the empiricist sees a series of events deployed on this continuum, Hegel sees the several moments of the Idea. The difference is explained by the inverse nature of the reductions committed by empiricism and Hegel respectively.[72]

Marxism, according to Althusser, breaks once and for all with the reductionism of this idealist/empiricist problematic, and with its conception of the 'simple unity' of an 'original essence', and establishes complexity as its principle: 'Where reality is concerned, we are never dealing with the pure existence of simplicity, be it essence or category, but with the existence of "concretes", of complex and structured beings and processes.'[73] Accordingly, complexity is central to the Marxist conception of the social formation, and this by virtue of the principle, already enunciated, that the various structures (practices, instances) of which it is constituted are irreducibly distinct and different.[74] They cannot, as with Hegel, be regarded as the mere expressions of a single spiritual essence which is immanent in them all without being exclusive to any one of them. But nor should one of them be conceived as the essence to which the others, as its phenomena, can be reduced. Thus, when Marx distinguishes the different instances of the social formation into a structure (the economic base, comprising forces and relations of production), and superstructures (politics, law, ideology, and so on), and assigns to the former the primary determining role, this is not in order to make it an essence of which the superstructures would then be so many phenomena, the mere passive effects of its unique determinism. Such a conception, economism or mechanism,[75] is a 'deviation' foreign to scientific Marxism, simplifying the complexities of the social formation and hence incapable of understanding it.

---

72. FM pp. 101–104, 202–204; RC pp. 93–97, 103.

73. FM pp. 197–99.

74. For this and the following two paragraphs, see FM pp. 94–117, 176–80, 200–18, and RC pp. 97–99, 106–107, 177–78.

75. Cf. RC p. 111.

The Law of Overdetermination

The superstructures are realities which are distinct from the economic structure. Indeed, they are its conditions of existence just as it is theirs, since economic production never takes place in a void; it only ever exists within the matrix of a global social totality comprising instances other than the economic. These non-economic, superstructural instances have their *specific effectivity* which means, first, that they are determining as well as determined; second, and in consequence, that the economy is determined as well as determining; and, third, that every instance contributes in its own right to determining the nature of the overall configuration of which it is a part, as well as being determined by it in turn. By the same token there is not one simple economic contradiction, that between the forces and relations of production, which governs everything. There is rather a multiplicity of contradictions existing at all levels of the social formation and constituting a kind of hierarchy of effectivities within it. So, determination is never simple but always complex and multiple, and this Althusser encapsulates in the concept of *overdetermination*. Is this to replace historical materialism by a sort of methodological pluralism? No. The autonomy of the superstructures is relative and not absolute, and their specific effectivity does not eliminate the primacy of the economy which for Althusser, following Engels, is still determinant 'in the last instance': '[The] specific *relations* between structure and superstructure still deserve theoretical elaboration and investigation. However, Marx has at least given us the "two ends of the chain", and has told us to find out what goes on between them: on the one hand, *determination in the last instance by the (economic) mode of production*; on the other, *the relative autonomy of the superstructures and their specific effectivity*.'[76] We may consider briefly what Althusser himself offers by way of theoretical elaboration.

The different structures of the social formation are themselves related as the constituent elements of a global structure, said to be *decentred* since its elements do not derive from one original essence, their centre, as do those of the Hegelian totality. This global structure contains a dominant element, not to be confused with the element which is determinant in the last instance, namely,

76. FM p. 111.

the economy, since 'in real history determination in the last instance by the economy is exercised precisely in the permutations of the principal role between the economy, politics, theory, and so on.'[77] To dispel the apparent paradox of an economy determinant in the last instance, but not necessarily always dominant, determination in the last instance is defined as follows: the economy determines for the non-economic elements their respective degrees of autonomy/dependence in relation to itself and to one another, thus their differential degrees of specific effectivity. It can determine itself as dominant or non-dominant at any particular time, and in the latter case it determines which of the other elements is to be dominant.[78] In any case, while one element can displace another to assume the dominant role, such variations occur within a structure which is *invariant* to the extent that it always has a dominant element, and this is what Althusser intends by calling the social formation a *structure in dominance*. But, for a Marxist political practice which aims to transform this invariant structure in dominance by revolution, the knowledge of its invariance is not sufficient. It must, if it is to be successful, be based on the most exact knowledge of the variations and the specific situations which they successively produce. The precise relations of domination and subordination between the different levels of the structure, the complex of contradictions which it embodies, their relative importance and reciprocal influence—all this must be grasped as defining the current *conjuncture* in which political action is to occur. The one thing that can be said in general is that successful revolution is never the simple outcome of the economic contradiction between forces and relations of production.[79] It requires the fusion or condensation of a multiplicity of contradictions, since it too is subject to the overriding law: overdetermination.

It may here be added that, with this concept, dialectical materialism reaches the conception 'of the development of things' which is the Marxist or materialist dialectic.[80] The concept has further ramifications which must now be elaborated.

---

77. FM p. 213.

78. Cf. FM p. 255; and Balibar, RC pp. 220–24.

79. In this connection see Balibar's analysis of Marx's notion of the *tendencies* of the capitalist mode of production. RC pp. 283–93.

80. FM p. 217.

Differential Historical Time

If the simplicity of the Hegelian totality is rejected, then so too is the simplicity of Hegelian history. The different instances of the social formation not being reducible to an original essence, the histories of these instances cannot be subsumed under a unique, all-embracing history which is the mere succession of such essences. On the contrary, each relatively autonomous level of the whole has its own relatively autonomous history, marked by its own rhythms of development and its own continuities, and punctuated in its own specific way by those mutations, breaks or ruptures which constitute its revolutionary events. Thus, there is a history of the economic structure, a history of the political superstructure, a history of ideology, a history of science, and so on. These differential histories are said to be *dislocated* with respect to one another in order to stress their irreducibility, the real differences between their respective rhythms, continuities and discontinuities. For Althusser this means in addition that there cannot be a unique linear time continuum common to all these histories, and against which they can all be measured.[81] The ideology of a simple time falls with the ideology of a simple history, to be replaced by the notion of a complex historical time constituted by the 'differential times' of the different levels. However, one must not infer from the irreducibility of these histories and times their absolute independence in relation to one another. They are no more absolutely independent than are the levels of the social formation of which they are the histories and times. In other words, their independence is the *relative* independence compatible with, and complementary to, their determination in the last instance by the economy, that is, their relative dependence. The complexity of historical time is, thus, a function of the complexity (overdetermination) of the social formation, and it follows that a section through the historical process will reveal, not an original, omnipresent essence, but a particular overdetermined conjuncture of that complex formation. For the authentic Marxist conception of history, the essential section is impossible.[82]

Now we have seen that one form of ignorance of this authentic

81. RC pp. 104–105.
82. RC pp. 99–109.

Marxist conception is economism. Another, which has vitiated the theoretical efforts of many Marxists, from Lukács, Korsch, and Gramsci to Della Volpe, Colletti and Sartre, is historicism.[83] I shall not give an exhaustive account of the latter here, since it represents a sort of compendium of all the mistaken notions we have already encountered (which is not surprising, all of them being variants or effects of a common, reductionist sin): its basis is the empiricist reduction of the object of knowledge to the real object; it negates the differences between the practices; it has, in consequence, a Hegelian conception of the social totality, and regards historical time as a linear continuum susceptible to the essential section; and so forth. I shall therefore limit myself to indicating the element of the historicist interpretation of Marxism on which Althusser himself lays greatest emphasis, defining it as its 'symptomatic point': namely, its conception of scientific and philosophical knowledge, hence of Marxism itself.

The Irreducibility of Science

Because of the reductions it countenances, the historicist interpretation tends to deprive theoretical practice, or science, of its specificity, to assimilate it to the other practices, ideological, political and economic, and ultimately to dissolve them all in a single notion of practice in general: historical practice or, simply, praxis. The history of knowledge thus loses its relative autonomy to become one with the unique 'real history' of the social totality. Marxism itself can then be regarded, not as a specific scientific practice developing on its own site, but as 'the direct product . . . of the activity and experience of the masses',[84] of their political and ideological practice, or as the self-consciousness (class consciousness) of the proletariat. For Althusser this is a 'leftist' conception whose political effect is to legitimate spontaneism, and whose theoretical effect is to relate the content and history of science to class conflict as its criterion of explanation—Marxism becomes the 'proletarian science' which confronts and challenges 'bourgeois science'. Against this theoretical effect, which is also a

83. For the account of historicism which follows, see RC pp. 105–106, 119–43, and FM pp. 22–24, 31, 171 n.7.
84. RC p. 134.

'theoretical monstrosity', he insists that the criterion of class has its limits and cannot explain the relatively autonomous history of science. He therefore takes Gramsci to task for regarding science as a superstructure: 'This is to attribute to the concept "superstructure" a breadth Marx never allowed, for he only ranged within it: (1) the politico-legal superstructure, and (2) the ideological superstructure (the corresponding "forms of social consciousness"): except in his Early Works (especially the *1844 Manuscripts*), Marx *never included scientific knowledge in it*. Science can no more be ranged within the category "superstructure" than can language, which as Stalin showed escapes it . . . [one must therefore distinguish] between the relatively autonomous and peculiar history of scientific knowledge and the other modalities of historical existence (those of the ideological and politico-legal superstructures, and that of the economic structure).'[85] In view of this, there can be no direct equation between the science of Marxism and the ideology of the proletariat. And spontaneism is therefore rejected in favour of 'Kautsky's and Lenin's thesis that Marxist theory is produced by a specific theoretical practice, *outside* the proletariat, and . . . must be "*imported*" into the working class movement'.[86]

There is one other consequence of the historicist interpretation of Marxism which should be mentioned. By depriving theoretical practice of all specificity, it deprives of its rationale that discipline, Marxist philosophy, which takes theoretical practice as its object of study. The historicist interpretation does not therefore recognize the distinction between dialectical materialism, the theory of science, and historical materialism, the science of social formations. On the contrary, the former is absorbed by the latter which does adequate service as a comprehensive theory of history, and a distinction which is crucial for Althusser is lost.

It is time, however, to take up another distinction, equally crucial: that between science and ideology. If it has been with us throughout the course of this exposition—in the notion that ideology threatens science at its weak points, in the concept of the epistemological break, in the opposition postulated between Marxism and the ideology of the proletariat—this is because it is implicit in the definition of Marxism as a science. To be com-

85. RC p. 133.
86. RC p. 141. Translation modified.

plete, the distinction requires some account of the Althusserian definition of ideology, an account which may take as its point of departure what has already been indicated provisionally, namely, that, unlike a science, an ideology does not provide us with adequate instruments of *knowledge*.

It fails to do so because 'it is governed by "interests" beyond the necessity of knowledge alone', or, to put the same thing slightly differently, because it 'reflects many "interests" other than those of reason.'[87] These interests may be religious, ethical or political, but they are in all cases 'extra-theoretical instances and exigencies' which impose on an ideology both its solutions and its problems and, thus, constitute its real (practical) ends or objectives.[88] So, 'ideology, as a system of representations, is distinguished from science in that in it the practico-social function is more important than the theoretical function (function as knowledge).'[89] The precise nature of this practico-social function will of course depend upon the nature of the social formation in question. In particular, in a class society it will be such as to legitimate relations of exploitation by concealing them from exploiters and exploited alike. Nevertheless, whatever its nature, it is a function that must be fulfilled in every society, since men must be *'formed, transformed and equipped to respond to the demands of their conditions of existence'*. And this requires ideology, a system of ideas, beliefs and values by which men live and experience their world. Ideology is therefore an essential part of every society, not excluding a classless, communist society.[90] For Althusser, moreover, it should not be equated with the ambiguous and idealist category of 'consciousness', since this might tend to suggest that it is a purely subjective phenomenon, freely chosen. But ideology is neither. It is, on the contrary, an objective structure of the social formation, which is imposed on most men by a mechanism they do not understand, a mechanism which determines that structure as the *objective* mode of appearance of reality.[91] This is the mechanism

87. RC pp. 141, 58.
88. RC pp. 52–55, 183.
89. FM p. 231.
90. FM pp. 191, 231–36; RC p. 177. Althusser distinguishes different levels of ideology. Its 'reflected forms' (FM p. 233) are pre- or non-scientific 'philosophies'. But the distinction does not affect the basic definition of ideology as dominated by a practico-social, rather than theoretical function.
91. FM p. 233; RC pp. 17, 66, 191.

which Marx termed *fetishism* and which is embraced by the Althusserian notion of *structural causality*.

Structural Causality

The latter is meant to describe the determination of its regional structures (ideology being one of them) by the global structure in dominance of the social formation, as well as the determination by these regional structures of their own constituent elements. It describes, in short, the effect of a whole on its parts, 'the effectivity of a structure on its elements'. This is a new concept of causality, existing in Marx's scientific work 'in a practical state' and requiring theoretical elaboration from Marxist philosophy. Pre-Marxist philosophy had, according to Althusser, only two concepts of causality: linear or transitive causality, able to describe the effect of one element on another, but not of the whole on its parts; and expressive causality, which could describe the determination of the parts by the whole, but only by reducing it to an essence of which they would be the phenomena, that is, by simplifying the whole. The concept of structural causality is distinct from both. From the first, because the structure is a cause present or immanent in its elements/effects, rather than exterior to them. And from the second, because it exists only in the totality of these elements/effects and their relations; it is not completely present in any *one* of them but, as Althusser puts it, 'is only present there, as a structure, in its *determinate* absence.' The structure can, in this sense, be described as both present and absent in its effects.[92]

In any case, on the concept of structural causality is based the Althusserian definition of Marxism as a '*theoretical anti-humanism*', and of humanism as an ideology. It is not men that make history. They are not the subjects of the process. And a scientific knowledge of social reality cannot be founded on an anthropology embodying a concept of human nature or of the essence of man. Rather, the 'absolute precondition' of such knowledge is 'that the philosophical (theoretical) myth of man is reduced to ashes', and that 'we do completely without [its] *theoretical services*.'[93] So, though humanism may still have a role to play as an ideology, its rejection for scientific purposes is complete and unambiguous.

92. RC pp. 180–93.

93. FM pp. 36–7, 227–30, 243–44; RC p. 119. As part of the humanist problematic, the concept of *alienation* is also ideological. Cf. FM pp. 158–59, 214–15, 239.

Nor is this affected by the centrality of the notion of practice. For, as we know, each practice is a structure, and, as such, exercises its determination over the elements it combines or relates—men, objects of labour and instruments of labour. Men cannot therefore be regarded as the active subjects of the process. They are simply its 'supports': 'The structure of the relations of production determines the *places* and *functions* occupied and adopted by the agents of production, who are never anything more than the occupants of these places, insofar as they are the "supports" (*Träger*) of these functions. The true "subjects" (in the sense of constitutive subjects of the process) are therefore not these occupants or functionaries, are not, despite all appearances, the "obviousnesses" of the "given" of naive anthropology, "concrete individuals", "real men"—but *the definition and distribution of these places and functions. The true "subjects" are these definers and distributors: the relations of production* (and political and ideological social relations). But since these are "relations", they cannot be thought within the category *subject*.'[94] Balibar has expressed this by saying that 'individuals are merely the effects' of the different practices, and that 'each relatively autonomous practice...engenders forms of historical individuality which are peculiar to it.'[95]

Thus, the human subject is definitively abolished, and the exposition ends, as it began, with the 'primacy of practice': first and last principle of Althusserian Marxism.

II Assessment

The assessment which follows neither aims nor claims to be exhaustive. It concentrates on certain problems in Althusser's work at the expense of certain others. This calls for a few explanatory remarks.

In the first place, I do not propose to consider the reading of Marx Althusser offers us and to judge it *as a reading of Marx*, endorsing or challenging its various points by reference to some alternative reading of Marx. This is not because such an exercise is entirely fruitless. On the contrary, to the extent that some of the crucial weaknesses in Althusser's work relate, it seems to me, to points where he has seriously misread Marx (and Lenin for that

94. RC p. 180. Cf. pp. 139–40, 174–75.
95. RC pp. 251–53. Cf. Althusser p. 112.

matter), and where Marx (and Lenin) are right against Althusser, it is an exercise which may help to focus on these weaknesses and bring them thoroughly to light.[96] It remains the case, nevertheless, that if Althusser is wrong, it is not simply *because* he departs from Marx. His errors and deficiencies can therefore be exposed for themselves without specific recourse to the classical texts of the revolutionary Marxist tradition. The latter procedure steers clear of judging Althusser in the name of any dogma.[97]

What I do propose to consider are a number of problems relating to Althusser's conceptions of science and scientificity, and of the relations between scientific and the other practices. Since Althusser defines his project as philosophical, and philosophy as the theory of science, it is not surprising that many of the difficulties in his work are concentrated in these conceptions. In particular, I shall argue that he produces an account of science that is idealist, paradoxical as this may sound, and an account of the relation between Marxist theory and Marxist politics that is both theoretically incorrect and politically harmful.

Secondly: I will therefore add that the predominantly critical tone of this assessment should not be taken as an indication that I judge Althusser's work unworthy of serious attention, and, to forestall misunderstandings of this kind, I shall suggest, briefly, the areas in which his theoretical contribution seems to me to be important.

96. See, for example, Michael Löwy, 'L'Humanisme Historiciste de Marx ou Relire Le Capital', *L'Homme et la Société*, No. 17, July/Aug/Sept. 1970, pp. 111–25.

97. It has the additional advantage that it does not risk being brushed aside as the product of a merely uncritical (literal, immediate, etc.) reading of Marx. That the Althusserian *practice* of critical reading (the *theory*, as I shall argue, deserves serious consideration) leaves much to be desired is a point I do not propose to argue here. The following remarks must suffice: this practice has achieved its *reductio ad absurdum* with Althusser's recent assertion that Marx's only works 'totally and definitively exempt' from *any* trace of Hegelian influence' are . . . the *Critique of the Gotha Programme* and the *Marginal Notes on Wagner* (LP p. 90). Althusser is, of course, perfectly entitled to reject as much of Marx as he finds deficient, arguing the case as best he can. He can reject the whole of Marx if necessary. But to claim that it is *Marx* who definitively breaks with Hegel while admitting that Marx's work, almost in its entirety, is marked by Hegelian influences; more generally, to claim, against the explicit letter of Marx's texts, that Marx is not *really* saying what he manifestly *is* saying (example: Marx on the ahistorical categories of classical political economy, RC, pp. 91–92)—these are claims indeed. Do they not install behind a facade of anti-dogmatism what is in fact merely a very special kind of dogmatism—one which insists on claiming the authority of Marx for all it deems scientific?

The Positive Achievements

Althusser has tried to forge and refine the concepts which will separate Marxism once and for all from the forms of reductionism (economism, spontaneism, and so forth) which have compromised it since its inception. Such forms have always been unable to comprehend the realities confronting the revolutionary socialist movement, realities whose names are: fascism, imperialism, the national question, combined and uneven development, racism, 4 August 1914; but also permanent revolution, the bureaucratization of the Soviet state, the debacle of the Comintern; and they have been unable to do so because these realities are, in every case, complex ones, not adequately explicable by unique reference to a single origin, whether this be the development of the economy or other. In the concept of overdetermination and its related concepts (specific effectivity, relative autonomy, determination in the last instance, structure in dominance) Althusser has tried clearly to pose and to respond to the exigency according to which they must be thought in the complex combination of their economic, political, ideological and theoretical causes and effects if they are to be adequately grasped and adequately dealt with. Of course, these realities have been understood, and well understood, before Althusser produced his work—not only by those whom he reads (Marx, Engels, Lenin) but also by those whom he does not read (Trotsky: symptomatic Althusserian silence). The pages of their works accordingly bear witness to the most acute awareness of the exigency which Althusser has posed.[98] To say this, however, is not to detract from his own achievement, and two reasons may be offered as to why it does not.

The first is a reason adduced by Althusser himself. If Marxist theory is to be freed, and decisively freed, from all traces of reductionism, it is not enough that its most oustanding practitioners should have avoided, in the analyses of the concrete problems and concrete situations they faced, the practice of reductionism. The theory which sustained their practice is also

98. I cite only Trotsky, since Althusser takes care of the others: see, as a few examples among dozens from his work, *Results and Prospects*, London, 1962, pp. 194–200; *The First Five Years of the Communist International*, Vol. 1, New York, 1945, pp. 50–63; *Through What Stage Are We Passing?* London, 1965, pp. 3–19, 34–36; *The Third International After Lenin*, New York, 1957, pp. 81–82, 96; etc.

required. The classical texts do not always give us this theory in an explicit and rigorous form, lapsing occasionally, and even in some of their most famous formulations, into a simplistic conception of the social whole. Althusser has tried to provide it by posing, not only in relation to this or that concrete example, but for and of itself, the problem of the specificity of the different practices/instances and of their complex inter-relationship. If, as we shall see with his conception of science, he has not answered all the questions he has asked, this does not deprive him of the merit of having asked clearly, without prevarication, and at length, questions which are crucial to the development of Marxist theory.

The second reason relates to the need, signalled in the introduction to this article, to situate Althusser in that theoretical context which makes him define his work as an intervention against Hegelian and humanist Marxism. Measured now, not against the classics of revolutionary Marxism, but against some of the writers who are the specific objects of his criticism, Althusser's achievement is thrown more sharply into relief. Lukács and Korsch, for example, in their very reaction against the economism of the Second International, do not avoid reductionism themselves, offering a conception of the social whole which falls squarely under the Althusserian category of the expressive or spiritual totality.[99] It is also the case, even if one does not share Althusser's view of them, that the great themes at the core of this tradition, of humanism and alienation, are not, *taken by themselves*, adequate to grasping any of the diverse social realities enumerated above. Unless they are specified in the

---

99. But one should avoid oversimplification. Take Korsch: in *Marxism and Philosophy*, NLB, London, 1970, he espouses, and in a very explicit form, a conception of totality which is expressive (see, especially, pp. 41–42), and it is this conception which governs his thought. At the same time, and however contradictory this may be, what he denies in this conception he also tries to affirm by insisting on the reality and irreducibility, that is to say, the relative autonomy, of ideology (see, for example, pp. 62–64, 84–85). If the affirmation does not succeed in freeing itself from the weight of the denial, Korsch is still worth the kind of critical reading which may perform that liberation, worth more, in any case, than the off-hand remark with which Althusser dismisses him as one of those who 'were lost later' (RC, p. 120). Lost, in the first instance, to and from the Communist movement: this loss was not unrelated to the descent of that movement into Stalinism. It should also be said that being lost did not prevent Korsch from writing an excellent book on Marx—see his *Karl Marx*, New York, 1963.

concepts with which Marx thinks the complexity of the social formation, these themes can just as easily lead to interminable philosophical ruminations on, for example, the ethical bases of Marxism as they can to new knowledges of concrete problems— and since the discovery of Marx's Early Works they have done. Bearing in mind, then, that it is this tradition and these themes, unilaterally interpreted, that have come to exercise an almost hegemonic influence within Western Marxism, and that this is the context in which Althusser has produced his work, his theoretical efforts in the area under discussion must be given their due.

It is also my view that the concept of the problematic, as elaborated by Althusser, represents a substantial contribution to the Marxist theory of ideology and of science. As has been intimated above, I do not find tenable the particular reading of Marx that Althusser has, by his use of this and related concepts, proposed,[100] although, for the reasons given, this point will not be argued here. It is a concept, nevertheless, which forces us to regard theoretical and ideological ensembles in their unity, and not as arbitrary agglomerations of discrete and self-sufficient elements such that these elements might be torn from their context without this altering their significance. By doing so, it undermines such teleological approaches as are ready to find germs and anticipations of Marx's mature theory even in his most youthful, schoolboy essays, and the superficial argument that, because the term 'alienation' is common to the *1844 Manuscripts* and *Capital*, it is the same concept, with the same role and importance, that is present in those works. Althusser has been perfectly right to challenge notions such as these, to try to isolate the analytical assumptions which legitimate them, and to focus on the eclecticism which they involve. By theorizing, against them, the concept of the problematic, he has laid the basis for a more systematic approach to the study of theories, ideologies, and their histories.

The Contradictions of Althusserian Science

This said, we can proceed to the main point: science. Even here

---

100. I have given some indications as to why I do not in 'Essence and Appearance: Aspects of Fetishism in Marx's *Capital*' above.

some of the impulses which motivate Althusser's positions must be recognized as fundamentally correct, and these may be enumerated in the form of two, intimately related theses:

(1) Scientific knowledge *in its content* is universal and objective, not dependent for its *validity* on the values and perspectives of this social group or that historical epoch, not therefore merely a matter of opinion or of interest. By emphasizing this, Althusser reasserts knowledge's rights against all forms of relativism, which, 'proving' in their theories of knowledge, of ideology and utopia, that all knowledge is necessarily partial and subjective, cannot escape the contradiction and embarrassment of claiming to be the knowledge of the impossibility of knowledge.

(2) Scientific knowledge is not immediately and directly (that is, miraculously) *given* in the consciousness of an individual or class, but has its specific *conditions and processes of production*, which involve, among other things, the activity of theoretical labour. By emphasizing this, Althusser reminds us that scientific activity is a *reality* (as real as the realities it studies and on no account reducible to them): to identify its products with what is immediately given in consciousness is to deny its rationale and thereby its very reality.

The difficulties, however, begin from here. In the first place, some of the arguments by which Althusser attempts to sustain these theses lead us straight into the realms of mystery. He rejects, as empiricist, the idea that concrete reality might form part of the raw material of theoretical practice, insisting that the process of production of knowledge takes place entirely in thought: this does not prevent him from arguing that the science of political economy investigates 'a raw material provided *in the last resort* by the practices of real concrete history'.[101] He rejects, as empiricist, the idea that the real object known by science is the object of knowledge, insisting that the object of knowledge is internal to thought: the real object is, nevertheless, the 'absolute reference point' because it is the object known via the object of knowledge; it becomes object of knowledge of the object of knowledge or object of knowledge *in the last resort*.[102] He rejects, as ideological, the theories in which classical epistemology tries to

101. RC pp. 109–10. My italics.

102. Cf. on this point Glucksmann, 'A Ventriloquist Structuralism', *Western Marxism*, pp. 286–90.

formulate the criteria of validity of knowledge, rejecting their very question, and replacing it by that of the 'mechanism' of production of the knowledge effect: but his failure to answer what is for him the real question gives his rejection the mere status of a gesture.

But, in the second place—and here we reach the main point—Althusser's attempt to give the first thesis all the weight he can leads him to an elaboration of the second thesis which is indistinguishable from idealism. For, if he begins by affirming the universality of knowledge *in its content*, he ends by denying the historicity of its *conditions and processes of production*;[103] their autonomy has become, quite simply, absolute. These assertions will be justified in a moment. Let it first be said that this represents a very substantial failure on Althusser's part. For the account of science he thus produces is not the one he wants to produce. He knows that the conditions of production of knowledge, though they do not affect its validity, are social and historical conditions and not, as idealism supposes, absolutely independent of social formations and their history. He knows it because he says it: science is *relatively* independent, organically related to the other social practices, its development crucially affected by that relationship.[104] But that is all he says. The nature of the relationship is not spelt out, so that we have once again the gesture of an intention but hardly a substantive theory. At the same time what emerges time and again in Althusser's text, in its ambiguities and silences as well as in its sounds, is a view of science which negates his intention. Lapses of rigour? Perhaps. But the rigour of a text counts for more than the intentions of its subject-author.[105]

I shall therefore examine four of Althusser's more ambiguous arguments before proceeding to his view of the relation between Marxist science and revolutionary politics, for that is the real site

103. This denial is most explicit in Rancière, who attributes to Marx 'une conception qui fonde la science dans une rupture radicale avec les conditions d'existence des agents historiques' (*Lire le Capital*, Vol. I, p. 209). In Althusser it never takes quite this form except perhaps once, when he seems to fault historicism for defining 'as historical the conditions for all knowledge concerning a historical object' (RC p. 122).

104. FM pp. 167, 229; RC pp. 41–42, 58, 60, 99–100, 133.

105. For Althusser's emphasis on rigour, see FM pp. 37, 116, 164, 193; RC pp. 74, 77, 90, 144; LP pp. 23–25, 76.

of his idealism.

(i) Science is not a superstructure. It is outside the structure-superstructure complex. In these propositions Althusser may be taken to be asserting the first of the two theses set out above. But he asserts something else as well. For he follows Marx in definining the social formation as constituted by the structure-superstructure complex.[106] He therefore excludes science from the social formation.[107] And he continues to do so in some of his more recent texts,[108] although in other respects he has modified his positions substantially.

(ii) Dialectical materialism is 'the theory of science and of the history of science'. Historical materialism is the theory of social formations and of their history. The distinction must be respected. But it is impossible to find, in Althusser's work, a precise justification for the third of these propositions: one can only construct it. He tells us, it is true, that scientific practice is a specific and irreducible practice. But then so too is every other practice. And this does not prevent Althusser from integrating the theories of ideology, politics and political economy *within* historical materialism as so many component sub-disciplines. For example, he repeatedly insists that the Marxist theory of political economy, since it considers one relatively autonomous region (level or instance) of the social formation, is simply one region of the Marxist theory of history, which considers the social formation as a whole.[109] If the Marxist theory of the history of science is different in this respect, distinct from, rather than a region of, the Marxist theory of history, this can only be because the history of science is absolutely autonomous, outside the history of social formations—because, once again, science is not an instance of the social formation.

(iii) 'Ideology . . . is distinguished from science in that in it the practico-social function is more important than the theoretical function (function as knowledge).'

106. FM p. 111.

107. Cf. above n. 68. Ben Brewster's Glossary (FM pp. 249–58; RC pp. 309–24), faithful in almost every detail to Althusser's thought, reproduces this exclusion at several points: see the entries for 'Formation, Social', 'Practice, Economic, Political, Ideological and Theoretical', and 'Superstructure/Structure'. Althusser has himself 'gone over the text of the glossary line by line'.

108. LP pp. 47, 129–130.

109. RC pp. 109, 113, 117, 145, 183.

(iv) Ideology is 'governed by "interests" beyond the necessity of knowledge alone'.

I take these two arguments in conjunction because it may be that they are simply the same argument and that what they both state is that the (class) interests and values expressed in ideology actually deform the content of the 'knowledge' it claims to provide and deprive it of the status of valid knowledge. They may, in other words, simply be reformulations of the science/ideology distinction. But they are ambiguous formulations to say the least. The first, because the very terms in which the distinction is drawn suggest that the theoretical function is not *itself* a practico-social one, and that to function as knowledge is not *itself* to function socially. The second, because it suggests that the only interests at work in the development of knowledge are interests internal to knowledge (the desire for knowledge, the search for truth: knowledge for its own sake), and not also the political and social interests which, if they cannot give knowledge its theoretical solutions, certainly assist in defining its problems. Thus, the ambiguities of these arguments lead in one and the same direction, the direction we are already acquainted with: towards the absolute autonomy in which science celebrates its 'escape'[110] from social formations and their history.

The Final Idealism

But we may leave these ambiguities as they stand, since they are only ambiguities, to take up the investigation of a silence whose meaning is, this time, unambiguous. This silence has a precise location: in his concern to stress the scientificity of Marxism, Althusser fails to provide any account of what distinguishes this particular science from the other sciences. The very recognition that there might be such a distinction only rarely marks his text—once in the following form: 'Hobbes said it long ago: men tear out their hair or their lives over politics, but they are as thick as thieves over the hypotenuse or falling bodies.'[111] It occurs a second time, in almost identical terms, elsewhere.[112] For the rest,

110. Cf. *Lire le Capital*, Vol. II, p. 93.
111. FM p. 122.
112. RC p. 185.

his constant emphasis on what Marxism as a science shares with the mathematical and physical sciences,[113] and his simultaneous failure to elaborate the difference which he barely takes the time to register in this Hobbesian aphorism, suggest that it is a difference of little importance.

It is, on the contrary, crucial, as is the problem it poses for any theory claiming to be the theory of science and of its history. This problem is one of the *differential* relations which the *different* sciences entertain with the other practices in the social formation, of their *differential* relationship to the class interests in confrontation there, hence, of their *differential* conditions and processes of production. Althusser never tackles this problem because he never tackles the problem of the relationship between scientific and the other practices in anything but the most gestural form. When he does not, as in some of the formulations discussed above, actually deny that relationship, he merely asserts it, but he does not theorize its nature. Hence, the purely programmatic character of his utterances on the epistemological break which separates the science of Marxism from its ideological past: the conditions and mechanisms of its occurrence are taken 'for a fact', not analysed, though such an analysis is declared to be an indispensable project.[114] For all, therefore, that we are assured that ideological, political and economic practices can and do contribute decisively to the occurrence of these kinds of theoretical event, Althusser's *effective* practice is to abstract from the precise character of this contribution, and, by concentrating exclusively on the conceptual shifts and restructurations involved, to treat the process as a purely intellectual one, that is, idealistically. It is only because he does so that he can submerge the difference between Marxism on the one hand, and the mathematical and physical sciences on the other. Considered independently of the other instances in the social formation, and of the class interests inscribed therein, they are all indifferently valid knowledges. Althusser's silence about the difference is thus part of a deeper silence: an idealist silence about science's mode of dependence in the social formation.

Let us track down this idealism in its last hideout, for there it is neither ambiguous nor silent, but quite explicit. Althusser thinks the relation between Marxist theory and the working class move-

---

113. See e.g. RC pp. 59, 150–3.
114. FM p. 168; RC pp. 27, 45–46, 50–51, 153.

ment as one of exteriority: the former is produced *outside* the latter, and must be *imported* into it, failing which this movement can only arrive at conceptions which are ideological, and bourgeois-ideological at that. These theses, however 'Leninist' one may care to think them,[115] are erroneous. For, where finally is this 'outside' if not on the inside of a purely intellectual process without historical conditions and determinants? To reduce the whole process by which Marxist theory was produced to a theoretical activity *autonomous* of the political practice of the working class, *autonomous* of the class and political conditions which were *its* indispensable, if not sufficient, conditions of production, is to perpetrate a reduction as grave as any of those castigated by Althusser himself. Its final effect is to make the relation between Marxist theory and the working class a unilateral and purely pedagogic one: the intellectuals 'give' the class the knowledge it needs. This is only the final consequence of every idealism: elitism. When knowledge celebrates its autonomy, the philosophers celebrate their dominance.

Marxism and the Working Class

These arguments will now be elaborated and the threads of this assessment drawn together. Marxist theory was not produced *outside* the working class movement. It was produced *inside* the working class movement. True, it was produced by intellectuals, and these intellectuals were most often of bourgeois or petty-bourgeois origin. But that is another matter. For these were not just any bourgeois intellectuals. They were precisely those who linked their fate with that of the working class, formed organizations to institutionalize that union, and participated in the class struggle for socialism. What they brought to the working class movement was not a well-formed science elaborated elsewhere, but the theoretical training and the elements of scientific culture essential to the production of such a science, things which their position as intellectuals had enabled them to acquire and which cannot emerge spontaneously from experience on the factory floor, or

---

115. They are Leninist in the sense that Lenin put them forward in *What is to be done?* However, the conceptions developed in his subsequent works are not the same. Cf. on this Lenin's 1907 Preface to the collection: 'Twelve Years' in *Collected Works*, Vol. 13, pp. 100–108.

from participation in strikes and demonstrations. At the same time, what they gained from the working class were a number of experiences not readily available to most bourgeois intellectuals and which do not emerge spontaneously from the activity of theoretical work: the experience of exploitation and repression, the experience of the struggle against these realities, the experience of the successes and failures of that struggle. The theoretical practice by which Marxist theory, as such, was founded and developed, and by which these experiences could be transformed into knowledges, was the theoretical practice of intellectuals of *this* type: a theoretical practice interior to the working class movement, and which could only teach the masses something because it also knew how to learn from them.

Marx learned, from the initiatives of the Communards, of the need for the proletariat to smash the bourgeois state. Lenin learned, from the self-organizing initiatives of the Russian proletariat in 1905 and 1917, of the significance of the soviets and of the possibilities of dual power. He learned, through years of experience of party organization, both the indispensability and the limitations of party organization. Rosa Luxemburg learned, in the experience of 1905, the importance of the mass strike. Marx learned, in the failure of 1848, and Trotsky learned, in the failure of 1905, the necessity of permanent revolution. In all these cases, of course, they did not just learn. They explained these lessons, theorized these experiences, brought all their theoretical training and abilities to the task of producing new knowledge. Doing so, they founded and developed the corpus of Marxist theory. But they did so as intellectuals engaged in the struggle and the organizations of the working class. It could not be otherwise.

For Marxism is not a science just like any other. Men tear out their lives over it. If it can claim for the knowledges it produces the same validity and objectivity claimed by the other sciences for theirs, it cannot claim for them the same universal recognition. These knowledges are anathema to the bourgeoisie and its ideologues (some of whom are also scientists): by disclosing the mechanisms and contradictions of its power, they call into question the permanence of that power. Since it is precisely permanent power that the bourgeoisie wishes and thinks for itself in one ideological form or another, it cannot but refuse to look at this question and the theory which contains it. The proletariat, on the other hand, can look at this question because it has a direct interest in looking at it. It does so *in its own way* whenever it challenges the foundations of bourgeois power, whenever it proves that its spontaneous political practice is not always and inevitably trade-unionist or reformist. This is not to deny either the fact or the indispensability of the arduous process of theoretical labour and research by which certain intellectuals produced a rigorous knowledge of this question, theorizing its bases and all its ramifications. But it is to say that this was only possible for them because they had ceased to be bourgeois intellectuals, abandoned their class origins and interests, and risked all the refusals and ridicule of official culture to espouse the interests, perspectives and struggles of the working class. It is to point to the political conditions of their theoretical work.

The First Rule of Revolutionary Politics

Lest the meaning of what has been said be misconstrued, a couple of cautions are necessary. First: it is not simply the proletariat's 'point of view' that it is exploited and oppressed. It is exploited and oppressed. But it is only from its 'point of view' that that exploitation and oppression can be comprehended, that is, known. Second: this is not by virtue of any *logical* necessity. Since it is not *simply* a class point of view that is embodied in Marxist theory, there is no reason in logic which could prove that that theory could not have been founded and developed by intellectuals in complete isolation and detachment from the struggles of the working class. But 'history is not a text in which a voice (the Logos) speaks':[116] it is not Reason which holds sway there. Powerful realities, in the shape of hegemonic interests and the ideologies that universalize them, make this logical possibility historically impossible.

I shall also take the liberty of saying at this stage, that all this has the most direct bearing on the particular way in which Althusser chooses to read Marx. For if Marx's work embodies the knowledge of history produced by his theoretical practice, if it is not *simply* an expression of the interests of the proletariat, it is that *as well*. Once again, this is not by virtue of any logical necessity. In logic, Marx could have produced a work that was

116. RC p. 17.

value-free. In fact, he did not. Thus, he not only analysed the modalities of exploitation, he also protested against it in the name of those who suffered it. A reading of *Capital* which fails to see this is a guilty reading indeed—guilty of an oversight of inexplicable proportions. No doubt, one could, by a fairly intricate analytical operation, purge Marx's concept of exploitation of its ethical and critical content (one would have, in the first place, to change its name), leaving it only its cognitive function. But then it would no longer be *Marx's concept* of exploitation. The use Marx himself makes of it is a critical as well as a cognitive one, because he expresses in his work the interests of the exploited. Althusser is right to insist that *Capital* should not be reduced 'to an ethical inspiration'.[117] He is wrong to pretend that it contains no values of any kind whatever. Doing so, he merely echoes Hilferding who, with a logic that was flawless and a historical understanding that was limited, believed one could accept the whole of Marxist science without the least commitment to socialism.

To come to the final consequence of Althusser's idealism: the knowledge which Marxism provides and which intellectuals import into the working class movement has, for him, a very specific kind of directive role. It tries to produce 'a *new* form of ideology in the masses'[118] by supporting and using, or transforming and combating the ideologies in which the masses live.[119] But Althusser also tells us, in at least a hundred passages, that ideology is a realm of mystification and deformation, of illusion, falsehood and myth, of confusion, prejudice and arbitrariness, of the imaginary and non-knowledge.[120] He thus cuts off the masses, by a necessity he never explains, from the knowledge of their situation which the intellectuals have produced. How then can the intellectuals brandish what they know to be an ideology without violating the first principle of revolutionary politics—to tell it as it is?

It would not be in order to conclude this article without indicating that Althusser's writings since 1965 represent a 'break', in at least certain respects, with the positions which have been

117. RC p. 139.
118. RC p. 131.
119. FM pp. 231, 232, 241.
120. FM pp. 66 n.29, 67 n.30, 74, 76, 79–82, 84, 126, 144, 186, 190; RC pp. 39 n.18, 47, 57, 62–63, 90, 97, 103, 105, 110, 111–12, 117, 172, 179.

dealt with here, and that the fundamental direction of this break at times seems similar to that of the assessment offered above. The changes in question are signalled in the 'self-criticisms' which Althusser appends to the English translations of *For Marx* and *Reading Capital*.[121] He there suggests a different view of the spontaneity of the masses ('*the most precious* aspect of the workers' movement') and the elements of a new definition of philosophy. He acknowledges his failure to specify the relationship between Marxist theory and the working class movement (though what has been identified above as idealism, he chooses to call 'theoreticism'). His subsequent texts return again and again to the nature of this relationship and in terms which appear to be similar to those I have used.[122] Equally, the new conception of philosophy they offer has the precise function of focusing on this same relationship.[123] Of all this readers of Althusser can satisfy themselves. On the other hand, while it undoubtedly constitutes an attempt to correct some of the major weaknesses in his original positions, whether the new positions reached can be taken for a genuine step forward is to be doubted. Whatever the errors and lacunae of *For Marx* and *Reading Capital*, they embody a systematicity, coherence, and substance, which are lacking in the revised formulations, and this lack is most visible where, perhaps, it matters most given the nature of Althusser's project, namely, in the new definition of philosophy: *not* a science or theory, but representing the class struggle *in* theory; *not* a political practice, but representing science *in* political practice; an 'original instance' representing the one alongside the other; and so forth. Within these mysterious, negative formulae, an empty space is enclosed.

121. FM pp. 14–15, 254, 256, 258; RC pp. 7–8, 318–19, 321, 324.
122. See e.g. LP pp. 7–9, 16–17, 23, 37, 53–54, 73–74, 95–96, 119.
123. LP pp. 21–25, 29–67, 105–106.

6.

Marxism and Proletarian Self-Emancipation[1]
1972

I claim no novelty for these ideas. Some of them are discussed in a recent article by Hal Draper.[2] They are treated at greater length, and in greater depth, in Michael Löwy's book on Marx's theory of revolution.[3] Going back to Marx himself, in 1864, in the preamble to the rules of the First International, he formulates the principle of self-emancipation in the following terms: 'The emancipation of the working classes must be conquered by the working classes themselves.' On a number of occasions after this, he and Engels explicitly reaffirm the principle,[4] and in the subsequent history of Marxist controversy it is espoused and defended, in one context or another, by Lenin, by Luxemburg and by Trotsky,[5] to name only these.

So the principle is old and has been discussed many times. I present it again for discussion here because its implications are far-reaching. They go beyond the simple affirmation of a democratic commitment to dimensions of Marxist thought which are at once epistemological, political and sociological. In other words,

1. This is the text of a talk given in London on 23 April 1972 at the first Radical Philosophy conference.

2. 'The Principle of Self-Emancipation in Marx and Engels', in R. Miliband and J. Saville (eds.), *The Socialist Register 1971*, London, pp. 81–109.

3. *La théorie de la révolution chez le jeune Marx*, Paris 1970.

4. K. Marx and F. Engels, *Selected Works*, 3 vols., Moscow 1969–70, Vol. 1, p. 104, Vol. 2, p. 19, Vol. 3, pp. 20, 94.

5. V. I. Lenin, *Collected Works*, Moscow 1960–1970, Vol. 9, p. 29; R. Luxemburg, *Selected Political Writings* (ed. R. Looker), London 1972, pp. 159, 272, 278; L. Trotsky, *Their Morals and Ours*, New York 1966, p. 42.

the principle of self-emancipation is central, not incidental, to historical materialism. As such, it provides a useful focus for the consideration of problems germane to a body of thought which I take to be of interest to radical philosophers.

If we subsume under the heading of radical philosophy such thinkers as have envisaged a fundamental transformation of the social order, then we find that one of radical philosophy's traditional concerns has been the project to transform men themselves. Without the transformation of men, of their attitudes, abilities and habits, the radical alteration of social relations and political institutions must prove unviable—an empty or dangerous utopia beyond human nature's eternal constraints. Projects of social transformation, then, rest on a contrast between human actualities and human potentialities, and they generally offer a conception, however minimal, of the *process* by which the potentialities are to be actualized. Everything hinges on the manner in which this process is conceived.

I take Rousseau as an example. No need to labour the point that for him what men are and what they could be are two different things. The entire difficulty resides in the attempt to bridge the gap between the two. A passage from *The Social Contract* testifies to this difficulty: 'For a new-born people to relish wise maxims of policy and to pursue the fundamental rules of statecraft, it would be necessary that the effect should become the cause; that the social mind, which should be the product of such institution, should prevail even at the institution of society; and that men should be, before the formation of laws, what those laws alone can make them.'[6] Translating freely: men are the products of their social circumstances, unfit to found society anew so long as they are corrupted by imperfect institutions; they can only recognize the need for, and acquire the ability to sustain, social change if they have already benefited from the influences of such change. They are caught in a vicious circle which closes to them the prospect of self-emancipation. Rousseau's solution to this problem is the Legislator who, putting his wisdom at the service of ordinary mortals, creates the framework of institutions and rules they need and teaches them what they can and should be. But he can only do this because he is wise. And he is only wise because he escapes the determinism of corrupting social circum-

6. *The Social Contract*, Book II, Ch. 7.

stances, that is, comes from *outside* the circle of ignorance which binds other men, as an *external* agent of transformation.

I shall give two more examples. Buonarroti: 'The experience of the French Revolution . . . [has] sufficiently demonstrated that a people whose opinions have been formed by a regime of inequality and despotism is hardly suitable, at the beginning of a regenerative revolution, to elect those who will direct it and carry it to completion. This difficult task can only be borne by wise and courageous citizens who, consumed by love of country and love for humanity, have long pondered on the causes of public evils, have rid themselves of common prejudice and vice, have advanced the enlightenment of their contemporaries, and, despising gold and worldly grandeur, have sought their happiness . . . in assuring the triumph of equality.'[7] Weitling: 'To want to wait, as it is usually suggested one should, until all are suitably enlightened, would mean to abandon the thing altogether; because never does an entire people achieve the same level of enlightenment, at least not so long as inequality and the struggle of private interests within society continue to exist.' And Weitling goes on to compare the dictator who organizes the workers with a duke who commands his army.[8]

I leave aside here the traditional ethical objection concerning the pursuit of liberatory ends by authoritarian means. There are other, more powerful objections to this sort of view. One may be called sociological/political: social reality is held to be inert, having the power to shape its human agents into acceptance or submission; yet against this immense power, the power of a Legislator, of a few 'wise and courageous citizens', is held to be effective. Another is epistemological: the conditions for a critical perspective on reality are denied, but some, again a few, find their way to the truth for all that. In fact, this sort of view combines the most mechanistic materialism and determinism (men are the mere effects of their circumstances) with the purest idealism and voluntarism (a few escape this potent conditioning to transform human circumstances at a stroke). To introduce here the distinction between leaders and masses: the masses are always passive and acted upon—in one case, by the society which shapes them, in the other, by the leaders who enlighten and liberate them.

7. Cited in Löwy, *La théorie* . . . p. 85.
8. Ibid., pp. 90–91.

In one of his more equivocal pronouncements, Althusser has told us that 'the whole Marxist tradition has refused to say that it is "*man*" who makes history.'[9] Well, one can quarrel about what is and what is not the Marxist 'tradition'. But the assertion of this truth by Althusser conceals another, no less significant, and theoretically indigestible for the Althusserians; and that is that all of the greatest Marxist *thinkers and revolutionary militants* from Marx to the present day *have* said, more or less explicitly, that it is *men* who make history albeit on the basis of objective conditions which they have to take as given.[10] The thought, admittedly general and abstract in this form, is nevertheless decisive, for it represents Marx's break with the whole problematic I have just surveyed, and it informs all of his more concrete and specific theoretical constructions. I shall make only brief reference to the *Theses on Feuerbach* since they are well known. Men are neither passive effects nor omnipotent wills, but at once the subjects and objects of a practice which generates and transforms social and ideological structures, and transforms men themselves in the process. In Marx's words: 'The coincidence of the changing of circumstances and of human activity or self-changing can be conceived and rationally understood only as *revolutionary practice.*'[11] The same thought is expressed in *The German Ideology.*[12] In any case, this breaks the circle which cuts men off from the possibility of self-transformation and, doing so, liberates them from the need for liberators.

But for Marx the agent of social transformation in the current epoch, the vehicle of socialist revolution, is not, abstractly, man-in-general, but the proletarian masses. If there is any validity in Althusserian anti-humanism, this seems to me to be it and to exhaust it. The problem of the transformation and emancipation of man is, in the first instance, the problem of the transformation

9. L. Althusser, *Lenin and Philosophy and other essays*, NLB, London 1971, p. 24.

10. See K. Marx, *Capital*, Moscow 1961–2, Vol. 1, p. 372; Marx and Engels, *Selected Works*, Vol. 1, p. 398, Vol. 3, p. 487; Lenin, *Collected Works*, Vol. 21, p. 57; Luxemburg, *Selected Political Writings*, p.194; L. Trotsky, *The History of the Russian Revolution*, Ann Arbor n.d., Vol 3, p. 166, and *My Life*, New York 1960, pp. 396–7; *Venceremos: The Speeches and Writings of Ernesto Che Guevara* (ed. J. Gerassi), London 1968, p. 293; etc.

11. The third of the *Theses*, in K. Marx and F. Engels, *The German Ideology*, London 1965, p. 646.

12. Ibid., pp. 229–30.

and emancipation of the proletariat. This process involves, beyond the capture of political power (the dictatorship of the proletariat) and all that follows from it, what broadly speaking we might call the *education* of the proletariat itself. Education in several senses: the throwing off of all habits of deference acquired by virtue of its subordinate position in capitalist society and reinforced by the dominant ideology of that society; liberation from all traces of that ideology, recognition of its real class interests and of the means necessary for the realization of those interests; the acquisition of confidence in its own ability to organize and rule, of experience in organization and in the making of political decisions—such confidence and experience being more or less denied to the proletariat by the political apparatus of the bourgeois state. In other words, what I have called the education of the proletariat is simply the process by which it acquires an autonomous class consciousness and through which it forms autonomous class organizations up to and including the institutions of dual power and of the future proletarian state. And this education is part and parcel of the socialist revolution which would be unthinkable without it. How is such education acquired?

I shall quote at length from Marx. The first passage is from *The German Ideology*: 'Both for the production on a mass scale of this communist consciousness, and for the success of the cause itself, the alteration of men on a mass scale is necessary, an alteration which can only take place in a practical movement, a *revolution*; this revolution is necessary, therefore, not only because the *ruling* class cannot be overthrown in any other way, but also because the class *overthrowing* it can only in a revolution succeed in ridding itself of all the muck of ages and become fitted to found society anew.'[13] The second is from *The Civil War in France*: 'The working class . . . know that in order to work out their own emancipation, and along with it that higher form to which present society is irresistibly tending by its own economical agencies, they will have to pass through long struggles, through a series of historic processes, transforming circumstances and men.'[14] The proletariat transforms and educates itself in the process of its revolutionary struggle to overthrow capitalist society. The

13. Ibid., p. 86.
14. Marx and Engels, *Selected Works*, Vol. 2, p. 224.

education of the proletariat is essentially a *self*-education. Lest this should provoke the old and facile charge of spontaneism I shall make some necessary qualifications.

The truth contained in so-called spontaneist versions of Marxism seems to me to be this: the spontaneous disposition of the working class to struggle, at least periodically, not merely for this or that partial gain, but against the very roots of its exploitation and oppression, against capitalist society itself, is the necessary but not sufficient condition of socialism. It is merely another way of saying that capitalist society embodies the objective contradictions which create the historical possibility (and I say no more than 'possibility') of socialism. If it is denied, then socialism becomes simply one ethical ideal amongst others, or the theoretical project of Marxist intellectuals, with no purchase on reality and as powerless against it as Rousseau's Legislator and its variants. Of course, just such a view of socialism has been and is widely held, from Eduard Bernstein to the countless contemporary opponents of revolutionary Marxism. I limit myself to saying here that if that view is correct, then Marxism is false. It is not surprising, therefore, that Lenin's thesis in *What is to be done?* (that the spontaneous movement of the working class creates trade unionism and *only* trade unionism which is 'precisely working-class bourgeois politics'),[15] used as a polemical weapon against the Economists, is a thesis he soon abandoned.[16]

At the same time, the emphasis that the education and emancipation of the proletariat are essentially processes of self-education and self-emancipation in no way contradicts the Marxist and Leninist theory of the party. For Marx and Lenin, the party is nothing other than the instrument *of* the working class, its own organization for struggle; it is not, for them, yet another *external* agent of liberation above or superior to the masses. It takes its rationale from various needs: the need for a combat organization to co-ordinate and lead the struggles of a class whose spontaneous and fragmented initiatives are necessary but not, by themselves, sufficient for revolutionary success; the need to assemble and prepare politically the most advanced sections of that class, the latter not being a homogeneous entity with regard to conscious-

15. Lenin, *Collected Works*, Vol. 5, pp. 437, 375.

16. See for example, *Collected Works*, Vol. 9, pp. 17–18, 113, Vol. 10, p. 32, and Vol. 13, pp. 100–108.

ness and organization, and such prior preparation being indispensable if truly mass upsurges, when they occur, are not to be wasted, dissipated and defeated; the need to centralize and consolidate the historical experience, lessons and knowledge gained by the working class from its previous struggles. But even the relationship between the party and the non-party masses should not be thought as purely unilateral, such that the former educates and emancipates the latter. For, the party can only have an effective influence over the masses outside it, if these masses are themselves drawn into political struggle and learn through their *own* experience the lessons conveyed to them in propaganda and agitation. And this is to say nothing of what the party itself must learn from them in order to demonstrate its capacity for successful leadership. In any case, the relationship is reciprocal and political rather than unilateral and pedagogic.

A further important qualification: the emphasis on self-education does not of course mean, for Marx, that the working-class movement has no need of intellectuals, and of intellectuals in particular who come from other classes than the working class. There is, for example, a fairly well known passage in *The Communist Manifesto* where Marx and Engels explicitly speak of a section of the bourgeoisie, and of bourgeois ideologists, 'going over' to the proletariat, 'joining' the revolutionary class.[17] In a less well known text of 1879, they reiterate this point: 'It is an inevitable phenomenon, rooted in the course of development, that people from what have hitherto been the ruling classes should also join the militant proletariat and supply it with educative elements. We clearly stated this in the *Manifesto*. But . . . if people of this kind from other classes join the proletarian movement, the first condition must be that they should not bring any remnants of bourgeois, petty-bourgeois, or other such prejudices with them but should whole-heartedly adopt the proletarian outlook.'[18]

So I have no intention here of trying to spirit away the massive theoretical labour by which Marx and subsequent Marxists produced a body knowledge which might orient and guide the stuggle of the working class. It would be simple naivety to imagine that workers could acquire that knowledge out of the

17. Marx and Engels, *Selected Works*, Vol 1, p. 117.
18. Ibid., Vol. 3, pp. 92–3.

experience of political struggle alone. However, it is this same body of knowledge that Marx refers to when he talks in the last quotation of the 'proletarian outlook'; it is this same body of knowledge that is said (in the afterword to the second German edition of *Capital*) to 'represent' the proletariat;[19] and it is this same body of knowledge that is said (in *The Poverty of Philosophy*) to be a 'product' of the historical movement of the proletariat.[20] By which I take Marx to mean the following: the political struggles of the proletariat which aim at the destruction of capitalist society are the condition of possibility of the science of Marxism which comprehends and explains capitalist society as one social formation amongst others, having a historical origin and a historical term. Without those political struggles, without the class interests which they aim to realize, without the commitment of revolutionary intellectuals to those interests and their participation in those struggles, without the contradictions of capitalism, Marxism would not have been produced. In that sense Marxism *is* a class science.[21] Only those who fail to make the necessary logical distinction between the sociological question of the genesis of a thought and the epistemological question of its truth will take this last assertion for an endorsement of relativism, which it is not.

To sum up on this point: Marx claimed to have elaborated a science. Whether that claim is accepted or not, it is important to note that he did not claim to have elaborated it outside, or independently of, the working-class movement and to have brought it to this movement in a unilateral way. This claim was made for him by others, by Kautsky and by Lenin (though in Lenin's case it was, again, a polemical weapon against Economism and not typical of his thought).[22] The claim seems to me to be idealist and incompatible with historical materialism. I make one more point and then conclude.

The above arguments notwithstanding, it is true that, within Marxist thought, the view of the masses as the total objects of their circumstances recurs. Two examples. The first is Althusser:

19. *Capital*, Vol. 1, p. 16.
20. K. Marx, *The Poverty of Philosophy*, Moscow 1966, p. 109.
21. Cf. Lenin, *Collected Works*, Vol. 1, pp. 327–8, Vol. 19, p. 23.
22. Cf., for example: 'Correct revolutionary theory . . . assumes final shape only in close connection with the practical activity of a truly mass and truly revolutionary movement.' Lenin, *Collected Works*, Vol. 31, p. 25.

for whom men are nothing more than the supports/effects of their social, political and ideological relations. But if they are nothing more than this, how can they possibly destroy and transform these relations? The answer is, as it has to be, by the power of a knowledge (Theoretical Practice) brought to them from elsewhere. The second is Marcuse: the working class integrated, manipulated, indoctrinated, its revolutionary potential contained, submitting to exploitation and oppression willingly, and failing to perceive, because unable to perceive, where its real interests lie. It is no accident that Marcuse keeps returning to the notion of 'educational dictatorship', only to reject it each time as unacceptable.[23]

I conclude with a quotation from Marx and Engels, from the 'Circular Letter' of 1879: 'When the International was formed we expressly formulated the battle cry: The emancipation of the working class must be the work of the working class itself. We cannot, therefore, co-operate with people who openly state that the workers are too uneducated to emancipate themselves and must first be freed from above by philanthropic big bourgeois and petty bourgeois.'[24]

23. H. Marcuse, *Eros and Civilization*, New York, 1961, p. 206, and *One-Dimensional Man*, London 1964, pp. 6, 39–41.
24. Marx and Engels, *Selected Works*, Vol 3, p. 94.

II

Mainly Trotsky

7.

Leon Trotsky[1]
1979

Born Lev Davidovich Bronstein into a moderately prosperous Jewish farming family in the southern Ukraine, Trotsky early became active in the Russian workers' movement and embraced Marxism. He was arrested in 1898 for political activity in the town of Nikolayev, imprisoned, and deported to Siberia. Escaping in 1902, he travelled to London where he met Lenin for the first time and he began, with Lenin's encouragement, to write for the journal *Iskra* and to argue for its political standpoint—the building of a centralized Russian workers' party—in lectures and debates within Russian émigré circles in Europe. From the first he displayed a powerful literary and oratorical talent.

Present in 1903 at the Second Congress of the Russian Social-Democratic Party, at which the historic schism between Bolsheviks and Mensheviks occurred, Trotsky sided with the Mensheviks against Lenin. Though he would soon distance himself from them to stand outside both factions for more than a decade, on this issue he felt, and wrote, that Lenin's theory of organization was undemocratic, aiming to substitute the efforts of a revolutionary elite for the initiative of the workers themselves.

Trotsky returned to Russia in 1905 to play a prominent part in the revolution of that year as a leader of the St. Petersburg Soviet of Workers' Deputies. The lessons he drew from this experience included reflections on the nature of workers' democracy and the theory, identified with his name, of permanent revolution: he

1. Born 7 November 1879; died 21 August 1940.

formulated this now in the argument that the Russian proletariat, contrary to an orthodox Marxist expectation held by Bolsheviks and Mensheviks alike, might embark upon socialist revolution before the workers of the more advanced capitalist countries.

For his part in the work of the Soviet, Trotsky was again imprisoned and condemned to exile in Siberia. In 1907, making another escape whilst under escort into exile, he returned to Europe to settle in Vienna until the First World War. During that conflict, which he spent in Paris and, briefly, New York, his was a leading voice in the revolutionary opposition to the war by the internationalist wing of European socialism.

After the February revolution of 1917, Trotsky again returned to Russia and at once made common cause with Lenin, eventually joining the Bolshevik Party. This had now, following a change of political position by Lenin, adopted a perspective essentially identical with Trotsky's own conception of permanent revolution. Trotsky became one of the Russian revolution's main leaders: brilliant orator, publicist, organizer, political strategist, President of the Petrograd Soviet. He prepared and led the October insurrection which delivered power into the Bolsheviks' hands. As Commissar of Foreign Affairs in the first Soviet government, he conducted the peace negotiations with Germany at Brest-Litovsk; as Commissar of War, supervised the construction of the Red Army through civil war and hostile foreign intervention; played a key role in the foundation and early congresses of the Communist International. Throughout these post-revolutionary years, he spoke and wrote on all important political issues, domestic and international, as also on literary, cultural and scientific topics.

From 1923 onwards, and especially after Lenin's death, Trotsky bent his efforts towards opposing the increasingly bureaucratic and authoritarian regime in the Communist Party, the rising power of Stalin, the latter's internal and foreign policies and the doctrine of 'socialism in one country' which he had begun to put forth. In this connection, Trotsky now developed and generalized the theory of permanent revolution. Defeated by Stalin, he was expelled from the Party in 1927, sent into remote exile near the Chinese border, and in 1929 deported from Russia altogether. During the next decade he would inhabit one brief and insecure refuge after another, in Turkey, then France, then Norway, finally Mexico. Isolated, beset by difficulties, bereft by family tragedies, he continued to write, prodigiously: history, autobiography, diagnosis and warning concerning the danger of Nazism, analysis of the nature of Soviet society, defence of the authentic Leninist heritage as he construed this, against its Stalinist despoliation, argument for the formation of a new revolutionary International. At work on a biography of Stalin, he was murdered in his home by one of Stalin's agents.

As political thinker and writer, Trotsky's importance is threefold. First, his work is one of the best examples of the creative application of Marxism in the area of political and historical analysis; between the time of Lenin's death and his own, Trotsky was in this respect without peer. Second, his best writing, a clear, compelling and imaginative prose combining objectivity with the deepest commitment, achieved a standard of literary excellence first set by Marx himself and matched since by Marx's followers too rarely. Finally, in what was a dark period for the revolutionary socialist idea, he came to stand—against the currents dominant in the European workers' movement, gradualist and reformist on the one hand, Stalinist, authoritarian, on the other— for a socialism in which proletarian revolution and workers' democracy must sit side by side.

Trotsky's early analysis of the configuration of Russian society, and his prognosis about the character of the revolution that would emerge from it, provide one of the most striking instances to date of a Marxist theoretical projection confirmed in its broad outline by the ensuing course of events. From 1905 onwards, he challenged the prevalent Russian Marxist belief that, in a backward country with a huge peasant majority, revolution could only mean bourgeois revolution, with its issue the extension of capitalist economy and the establishment of bourgeois-democratic political rule. In *Results and Prospects* (St. Petersburg 1906) and then *1905* (Dresden 1910), Trotsky argued that, owing to the specific features of Russia's history in which capitalist development was fostered by the state and based largely on foreign capital, the indigenous forces of the Russian bourgeoisie were too weak, and Russian liberalism insufficiently bold, to lead a revolutionary assault against Tsarism. The Russian working class was small but highly concentrated. Like the compact, relatively advanced capitalist sector which had produced it, it was an expression of what Trotsky was later to call the 'law of combined and uneven development': as capitalism from its heartlands projected its consequences over the globe, heedless of traditional and national boundaries, so the features of modes of production that were, in the classical Marxist schema, distinct, would be found fused together within one social reality; so Russia now combined a modern industrial proletariat with pre-capitalist agrarian and political structures. A successful revolution here, Trotsky asserted, would have to be led by this small, militant proletariat, carrying behind it the land-hungry peasants, and because of this it could not remain a bourgeois revolution. The Russian workers once in power would not be able or willing to leave capitalist property relations intact. Establishing the first dictatorship of the proletariat, they would initiate the transition to socialism. But they could not complete this on their own without linking up with successful socialist revolutions in the West. Confined to a backward country, the enterprise would be doomed to defeat.

The main tenets of this conception were part also of the outlook of Bolshevism by the time it led the Russian proletariat to power in 1917. Later, when revolutions to the west had failed, leaving the young Soviet state isolated, Stalin asserted first the possibility, then the reality, of a socialism constructed in Russia alone. In *The Permanent Revolution* (Berlin 1930) and other writings, Trotsky reaffirmed and developed his original conception. He insisted that the fate of Russian socialism still depended on the outcome of the revolutionary process elsewhere. He extended to the analysis of this process in other backward societies the framework first applied in his treatment of Russia; arguing, in anticipation of much subsequent discussion of 'underdevelopment', that such societies could not reproduce the path followed by the first capitalist nations.

The geographical reach of Trotsky's writings on these and related themes was long, covering Britain and China, Germany, France and Spain, the Soviet Union itself. So extensive an output could not be wholly even in strength. Two of its notable achievements, however, were his analyses of fascism and of the character of the Soviet state, historically novel phenomena still to be assimilated within Marxist understanding. With growing urgency Trotsky warned against the Comintern's complacency towards the Nazi threat in Germany. Nazism triumphant, he predicted, would install not just one reactionary variant of capitalist rule amongst others, but a qualitatively distinct form catastrophic for the working class, predicated on the destruction of its organizations and its means of political self-defence through the mass mobilization against it of petty-bourgeois strata. The Soviet Union, he proposed in *The Revolution Betrayed* (Paris 1936), was neither socialist, as Stalin and his apologists claimed, nor some new type of class, or even capitalist, society, as some critics averred. It was a transitional formation in which the chief economic conquest of the October revolution, socialized property relations, was still extant despite the fact that a privileged bureaucracy had fashioned for itself a monopoly of political functions. To advance to socialism the workers would have to overturn this bureaucratic group by a political revolution. On both these issues Trotsky's contribution was original, level-headed and penetrating, and it remains a starting point for contemporary discussion.

Trotsky was one of the great writers of his time. Keenly interested in literary and cultural subjects, to which he devoted a significant part of his output and in particular the theoretical study *Literature and Revolution* (Moscow 1923), his own literary achievement was considerable. It was built upon a lucid and incisive style and the ability to present ideas, persons, events, in a complex and vivid way. It encompassed pages of cogent political argument, historical and literary interpretation finely integrating abstract theory with concrete perception, sketches of contemporaries acutely observed; and an impressive account of the year 1905, an autobiographical work, *My Life* (Berlin 1930), unusual in the Marxist canon and remarkable by any standards, and an outstanding work of Marxist historiography, *The History of the Russian Revolution* (Berlin 1931). This was his masterpiece: an epic, in which individuals and masses moved against the vast back-drop of Russia's history to transform the destiny of the whole world.

On questions of socialist democracy and organization, Trotsky's record over forty years was neither uniform nor unblemished. He opposed at first the Leninist party concept, representing it in *Our Political Tasks* (Geneva 1904) as an attempt to hold the working class in tutelage. After 1917 he rejected out of hand all such interpretations of it, upheld it consistently against the charge of having begot the crimes of Stalin. His strictures of Lenin he came to see as unjust and mistaken. *Our Political Tasks* spoke in the name of a democratic socialism open to the struggle between different tendencies; *1905* depicted the soviet form, the workers' council, as the very embodiment of this democratic principle, born of direct proletarian action and expressing as directly as possible the diverse voices within the working class. Though he would share in the necessities, the expediencies and the errors of the Bolsheviks in power, Trotsky was later to return to and develop these themes in his struggle against Stalinism, arguing for the right of tendencies inside revolutionary organizations and, beyond, for a united front within which different currents in the workers' movement could openly compete. Taken all in all, across the inconsistencies, Trotsky's final record was clear: for a socialism both revolutionary and democratic in an atmosphere uncogenial to this synthesis, thus in lonely, but for this very reason vital, continuity with the best traditions of Marxism and of Leninism.

There have been obscurantist and ugly responses to Trotsky's intellectual and political achievement, chief of them the prejudice and obloquy he has suffered in widespread quarters, but also a sectarian involution to which some of his would-be disciples have succumbed. His work stands out, however, as an important source and inspiration of contemporary Marxist research, and the Fourth International which he founded has members and supporters in many countries.[2]

2. English translations of Trotsky's works directly referred to here: *The Permanent Revolution & Results and Prospects*, London 1962; *1905*, London 1972; *The Revolution Betrayed*, New York 1965; *The Struggle Against Fascism in Germany*, New York 1971; *Literature and Revolution*, Ann Arbor 1960; *My Life*, New York 1960; *The History of the Russian Revolution*, London 1965; *Our Political Tasks*, London, 1980. On Trotsky: Isaac Deutscher, *The Prophet Armed, The Prophet Unarmed* and *The Prophet Outcast*, London 1954, 1959 and 1963; Louis Sinclair, *Leon Trotsky: A Bibliography*, Stanford 1972; Baruch Knei-Paz, *The Social and Political Thought of Leon Trotsky*, Oxford 1978; Irving Howe, *Trotsky*, London 1978; Ernest Mandel, *Trotsky: A Study in the Dynamic of his Thought*, London 1979.

8.

Rosa Luxemburg[1]
1982

The youngest of five children in a fairly well-to-do and cultured middle-class Jewish family, Rosa Luxemburg grew up in Warsaw. She was an intelligent and academically successful girl of independent spirit and, rebelling against the restrictive regime then prevalent in the schools of Russian Poland, she became involved in socialist political activity from early youth. In 1889 she had in consequence to leave Poland to avoid arrest and went to Zurich. Here she enrolled in the university, studying first mathematics and natural sciences, then political economy; and at length completed a doctoral dissertation on Poland's industrial development. Active at the same time in the political life of the revolutionary émigrés from the Russian Empire and opposing the nationalism of the Polish Socialist Party, in 1894 she took the lead with Leo Jogiches, a comrade similarly engaged, in creating the Social Democracy of the Kingdom of Poland: he was its main organizer, she its ablest intellect and voice. The two of them had formed what was to be a long and intense relationship, the close political tie between them surviving a later personal estrangement. In 1896, wanting a wider political stage for her energies, Rosa Luxemburg moved to Germany.

Henceforth she was prominent in the important debates within European socialism. She made her mark at once during the revisionist controversy with her *Social Reform or Revolution*, still perhaps the best general Marxist riposte to reformism. While

1. Born 5 March 1871, Zamość, Poland; died 15 January 1919, Berlin.

capitalism endured, she contended, its crises and contradictions could not be subdued and to suggest otherwise, as Bernstein had, was to cut the very heart out of Marxism, denying the objective foundations of the socialist project and turning it into an abstract ethical utopia. The workers' movement had indeed to struggle for reforms through trade union and parliamentary activity. But as these would never suffice to abolish capitalist relations of production, it must not lose sight of its ultimate goal: the conquest of power for revolution. In 1904, in *Organizational Questions of Russian Social Democracy*, Luxemburg intervened in the dispute between Lenin and the Mensheviks, criticizing the former for his conception of a tightly centralized vanguard party; an attempt, as she saw it, to play guardian to the working class. Her themes here—characteristic of all her work—were the independent initiative, the self-activity, of the workers, their capacity to learn through their own experience and their own mistakes, the need accordingly for a broadly based democratic organization. She had other disagreements with Lenin in these years. Although she deplored national as every other kind of oppression, she did not support, as he did, either the independence of Poland or, more generally, the slogan of a *right* of nations to self-determination.

However, their common response to the 1905 revolution drew them closer; they both envisaged for Russia a bourgeois revolution, to be carried through under the leadership, and by the methods of struggle, of the proletariat. In the mass actions of the Russian workers Luxemburg thought to have discovered, in addition, a strategic idea of international relevance and began to urge it upon German Social Democracy, speaking in this as in other things for the left of the organization. In her *Mass Strike, Party and Trade Unions*, she proposed the mass strike as the form *par excellence* of proletarian revolution. Spontaneous expression of the creative power of the broadest masses and antidote to bureaucratic inertia, it linked political with economic struggles, and immediate with more far-reaching demands, in what was potentially a global challenge to the capitalist order. In 1910 this view led to her break with Kautsky, when he rallied to the cautious, purely electoralist policy of the party leadership. Another of her preoccupations was imperialism, with its threat of war, and in 1913 in her major theoretical work, *The Accumulation of Capital*, she set out to explain its underlying cause. A closed capitalist economy, she argued, without access to non-capitalist social formations, must break down through inability to absorb all the surplus-value produced by it. Imperialism was a competitive struggle between capitalist nations for what remained of the non-capitalist environment but, by eroding the latter, it led towards the universal sway of capitalist relations and inevitable collapse of the system.

Luxemburg led the opposition to the First World War in Germany. Intellectual standard-bearer of the revolutionary inter-nationalists gathered in the Spartacus League, in her *Junius Pamphlet* and other writings she denounced Social Democracy's patriotic stance as a betrayal. She had to spend most of the war in prison and there she wrote *The Russian Revolution*, in solidarity and sympathy with Lenin, Trotsky and the Bolsheviks, endorsing their attempt at socialist revolution; yet critical of their land and nationalities policy, above all of their curtailment of socialist democracy, and of their tendency in this connection to make a virtue out of unfortunate necessities. Freed in late 1918 to participate in the German revolution, she was brutally murdered by right-wing officers after the crushing of an abortive rising in Berlin.

Rosa Luxemburg's work has sometimes been interpreted as a species of political fatalism, on account of her theory of inevitable capitalist breakdown; and as displaying a boundless faith in the spontaneity of the masses. However this is to misunderstand or caricature her. The collapse of capitalism presented the prolet-ariat with alternatives: on the one side, crisis, reaction, war, finally catastrophe and barbarism; on the other side, socialism. Active struggle for socialism was therefore necessary and urgent. For her, true to a central Marxist theme, the substance of this struggle was indeed provided by the spontaneous, self-emancipatory efforts of the working class. But she did not deny the need for organization, nor the importance of Marxist theory and able leadership. The division between her and Lenin has often been exaggerated. They were united by as much. Luxemburg's lifelong concern for democracy and liberty was unambiguously that of a revolutionary Marxist and should not be confused with the criticisms of this tradition by other traditions— liberal, reformist or anarchist—completely alien to her.[2]

2. For Luxemburg's works directly referred to here, see Mary-Alice Waters (ed.), *Rosa Luxemburg Speaks*, New York 1970, and Rosa Luxemburg, *The Accumulation of Capital*, London 1963.

9.

Political Participation in the Revolutionary Thought of Leon Trotsky

1970

My aim in this essay is to consider the role played by the concept of political participation in a theory unambiguously oriented towards the revolutionary transformation of the existing order, in the hope that this might provide some perspectives on that concept which are absent from, or only marginal to, its consideration in other contexts. While I am concerned primarily with the thought of Trotsky, it is helpful to discuss the latter in relation to two other revolutionary thinkers with whom he had, in different ways, a close intellectual affinity, namely, Lenin and Rosa Luxemburg. Furthermore, the themes and emphases which characterize Trotsky's thought develop within a framework of assumptions that is specifically Marxist, so that their consideration may be expected to have a bearing on revolutionary Marxism in general, if only by implication.

The following passage may serve as the point of departure: 'The most indubitable feature of a revolution is the direct interference of the masses in historic events. In ordinary times the state, be it monarchical or democratic, elevates itself above the nation, and history is made by specialists in that line of business—kings, ministers, bureaucrats, parliamentarians, journalists. But at those crucial moments when the old order becomes no longer endurable to the masses, they break over the barriers excluding them from the political arena, sweep aside their traditional representatives, and create by their own interference the initial groundwork for a new regime . . . . The history of a revolution is for us first of all a history of the forcible entrance of the masses into the realm of rulership over their own destiny.'[1]

We may note for the moment that, as the historian of a revolution in which he himself had played so important a role, Trotsky characterized revolution as, first and foremost, an act of mass political participation, in which the old political structures are broken and the masses, hitherto excluded from meaningful participation in the political arena, begin to take control of their own 'destiny'. This suffices to establish that in so far as the problem of revolution was always at the centre of Trotsky's thought, the concept of political participation too is bound to make its appearance there. Nor did he limit himself to such general characterizations as the above. As an active revolutionary throughout more than forty years of political life, thus with a perspective on revolution that was active and strategic, rather than that of the detached observer, he also defined the precise modalities and purposes of political participation as he understood it. This more complex definition may be said, broadly, to cover three different areas, areas constituted by Trotsky's conceptions about (i) the forms and purposes of participation in political struggle by the masses of the working class, (ii) the forms and purposes of participation in the party of that class, and (iii) the relationship between this wider and narrower participation, between the class and its party. I shall not, in my exposition, attempt artificially to maintain a rigid distinction between these three areas of discussion, but, bearing all of them in mind, will try to show their combinations, in tracing the evolution of Trotsky's thought from the time he first entered the political arena at the turn of the century, to the moment in 1940 when he was struck down by an assassin of the GPU.

In the historic split in the RSDLP which occurred at its Second Congress in 1903, Trotsky sided with the Mensheviks against Lenin, an act he was later to regret as a serious political error. According to his own testimony, recorded shortly after the congress, the split was for him like a bolt from the blue.[2] That he should describe it thus will not be surprising if it is recalled that, prior to and even during the Congress, all the members of the Party grouped around *Iskra* had stood for a centralized party, the creation of which was to be one of the fundamental tasks of the

1. Leon Trotsky, *The History of the Russian Revolution*, Ann Arbor n.d., p. xvii.

2. Leon Trotsky, *Rapport de la délégation sibérienne*, Paris 1970, p. 60.

congress. And the burden of the charges levelled against Lenin by the Mensheviks, apart from those relating to his personal political conduct, was not the principle of centralism as such, so much as that of 'ultra-centralism', or 'pitiless centralism', to invoke the terms used by Rosa Luxemburg in her intervention in the dispute.[3] With regard specifically to Trotsky, he had himself, in Siberian exile in 1901, written an essay in which he argued the need for a centralized party able to co-ordinate the activities of local Social-Democratic organizations, and for a central committee with the power and the right to expel dissident groups in exceptional circumstances. And he had arrived at this position independently, before the publication of *What is to be Done?*, and before he knew anything of *Iskra*.[4] The line which now separated him from Lenin, a line which he himself did not hesitate to draw in an active and vigorous polemic, consisted, in principle at least, neither in the rejection of the need for a centralized party, nor even in any denial that such a party had a leading role to play in the struggle for power of the working class. He did not, that is to say, adopt a frankly spontaneist conception of the revolutionary overthrow of capitalism, according to which the working class might, without political organization and without political leadership, take power in a kind of elemental and undisciplined upsurge.

The issue, as he saw it, was this: was the centralized party to be created from above and on the narrow basis of a small but compact group of Marxist intellectuals, or from below and on the basis of an ever growing participation of the working class in the struggle against Tsarism? To opt for the former course, as he charged Lenin with doing, was to build a party which represented the working class only formally. While Lenin's formulations in *What is to be Done?* tended to make mass revolutionary struggle dependent on the existence of the vanguard party, Trotsky was more inclined to see the growth of the former and the activity of the latter as mutually conditioned phenomena. The growing participation of the working class in political struggle would create a real base for a centralized working-class party, and give it a weight

3. See her 'Organizational Questions of Russian Social Democracy', in Mary-Alice Waters (ed.), *Rosa Luxemburg Speaks*, New York 1970, pp. 122, 116.
4. *Rapport . . .*, pp. 87–88; and Leon Trotsky, *My Life*, New York 1960, p. 132. See also Isaac Deutscher, *The Prophet Armed*, London 1954, pp. 44–46.

and political influence which would enable it in turn to draw wider masses into its ranks, and so on. This position contained also the explicit rejection of a thesis which has come to be regarded as the hallmark of Leninism, but which Lenin in fact borrowed from Kautsky[5] in his struggle against economism, and which is not, in my view, at all representative of Lenin's thought considered as a whole. This is the thesis that, left to itself, the proletariat is incapable of arriving at a revolutionary socialist consciousness, and that the latter can only be brought to it from without by bourgeois intellectuals. For the young Trotsky, neither the principle of a centralized party nor a Marxist political consciousness could be unilaterally introduced into the working-class movement from without. On the contrary, both should be the product of an interaction between the independent initiative of the masses, on the one hand, and the party's attempt to win them for socialism, on the other.[6] Trotsky saw Lenin's one-sided conception of the relation between party and class as an attempt to 'substitute' the former for the latter and, in playing on the theme of 'substitutionism', envisaged a process in which 'the party organization . . . at first substitutes itself for the party as a whole; then the Central Committee substitutes itself for the organization; and finally, a single "dictator" substitutes himself for the Central Committee.'[7]

In thus placing greater emphasis on the independent initiative of the working class, Trotsky's critique of Lenin was strikingly similar to that made by Rosa Luxemburg, both in its general approach and on many points of detail.[8] Still, like hers, it did not simply invoke the spontaneous participation of the masses in political struggle as a sufficient condition of the overthrow of the old order. It did, in principle, envisage for the party a leading role in the assault on that order. It is more than doubtful, however, that this principle was an organic part of Trotsky's political thought and make-up in the years that followed. The evidence to the contrary is in fact overwhelming, and can be gleaned both from his writings after 1905 and from his entire political conduct

5. V. I. Lenin, *Collected Works*, Moscow 1960–1970, Vol. 5, pp. 383–4.

6. For the position summarized here, see Leon Trotsky *Nos tâches politiques*, Paris 1970, pp. 73–74, 92–93, 101–3, 123–9, 147–50, 161, and *Rapport . . .* pp. 61–62, 64–66, 78, 81.

7. *Nos tâches politiques*, p. 128; cf. Deutscher, *The Prophet Armed*, p. 90.

8. See *Rosa Luxemburg Speaks*, pp. 115–119, 126–7 and *passim*.

up to 1917.

Only a year after the 1903 split Trotsky broke his organizational affiliation with Menshevism, and henceforth he stood outside both factions of the Party. In addition to personal animosities, important theoretical differences accounted for this stance, the most crucial among them being Trotsky's theory of permanent revolution, which received its first systematic formulation immediately after the revolution of 1905. At this stage, the keynote of that theory was that the Russian revolution would bring the proletariat to power, and, by virtue of that fact alone, initiate a process which would go beyond the solution of purely bourgeois democratic tasks to the implementation of measures of a socialist character. *Despite* her relative backwardness, Russia would be the first country to see the liquidation of capitalism and the initial steps of construction of a socialist society.[9] Both Bolsheviks and Mensheviks, for all their other differences on the question of the nature of the Russian revolution, were agreed on one fundamental point, which separated them from Trotsky's perspective: it could only be a bourgeois revolution. According to Lenin, to deny this was, among other things, 'absurd'.[10] Trotsky, for his part, saw in this common opposition to his views a kind of unity in error, and, on that basis, began to regard the split in the Party as no longer having any principled foundation. In the years that followed, consequently, all his efforts were bent towards reconciling the two wings of the Party.

What is interesting, for the purposes of the present essay, is the conception of the dynamic of (permanent) revolution which seemed to lie behind Trotsky's 'conciliationist' stance. In later years, and on more than one occasion, he himself explained it in the following way: 'My conciliationism flowed from a sort of social-revolutionary fatalism. I believed that the logic of the class struggle would compel both factions to pursue the same revolutionary line.'[11] Returning to the same theme towards the end of his life, he wrote: 'The policy of conciliation thrived on the hope that the course of events itself would prompt the necessary tactic. But that fatalistic optimism meant in practice not only repudiation of factional struggle but of the very idea of a party,

9. Leon Trotsky, *Results and Prospects*, London 1962, pp. 194–213.
10. Lenin, *Collected Works*, Vol. 9, p. 29.
11. Leon Trotsky, *The Permanent Revolution*, London 1962, p. 49.

because, if "the course of events" is capable of directly dictating to the masses the correct policy, what is the use of any special unification of the proletarian vanguard, the working out of a programme, the choice of leaders, the training in a spirit of discipline?'[12] According to these *ex post facto* explanations of Trotsky's political position from 1905, the conception of revolution entertained by him did effectively obliterate the independent role of a revolutionary party. The proletariat would of its own accord, and through its own independent activity, successfully carry out its revolution. Responding to its pressure, the party might fall into line; on the other hand, it might, resisting that pressure, be swept aside. In neither case would the revolution *depend* upon the conduct of the party, upon its political leadership or its tactical positions. A look at Trotsky's writings of this period confirms that this was indeed the conception of revolution that had taken shape in his mind in 1905.

Two considerations may be adduced to explain his adoption of such a conception. The first is that the 1905 revolution, far from being led by either Bolsheviks or Mensheviks, had taken both groups by surprise. The second is the emergence during that year of the soviets, in which Trotsky played an important role from the beginning, and which he saw as organizations generated by the workers themselves in the process of making a revolution. As he wrote of them shortly afterwards: 'These were not previously-prepared conspirative organizations for the purpose of seizure of power by the workers at the moment of revolt. No, these were organs created in a planned way by the masses themselves for the purpose of co-ordinating their revolutionary struggle.'[13] Whatever the force of these considerations, it is any case clear that, in his earliest exposition of the theory of permanent revolution, Trotsky found little room for a leading role for the party. Thus, in unfolding the perspective of the Russian revolution's leading to the implementation of socialist measures, he argued that: 'The point at which the proletariat will be held up in its advance in this direction depends upon the relation of forces, but in no way upon the original intentions of the proletarian party.'[14] The same

12. Leon Trotsky, *Stalin*, London 1947, p. 112; and see also *My Life*, pp. 165, 224, and the 1919 preface to *Results and Prospects*, p. 163.

13. *Results and Prospects*, p. 192.

14. Ibid., p. 212.

confidence in the efficacy of independent mass political action reveals itself in a theme, which now appeared in Trotsky's thought, and was to remain there up to his death: the theme, namely, that socialist parties, to the extent that they generate their own officialdom, bureaucratic procedures, and traditions, tend to become conservative, and might, in a situation of acute social crisis, act as obstacles to, rather than agents of, revolutionary transformation. Here, once again, Trotsky's thought meets that of Rosa Luxemburg. One of the points in her indictment of Lenin's conception of the party had been that the vanguard of professionals he envisaged would tend to obstruct the revolutionary movement, rather than guarantee its revolutionary character.[15] And in a pamphlet written in 1906, and directly inspired by the Russian events of the previous year, she invoked the mass strike as at once the surest method of overcoming the growing conservatism of the European Social-Democratic parties, and the prototype of proletarian revolution itself.[16] Trotsky expressed a similar perception in the following way: 'The function of the socialist parties was and is to revolutionize the consciousness of the working class. . . . But the work of agitation and organization among the ranks of the proletariat has an internal inertia. The European Socialist Parties, particularly the largest of them, the German Social-Democratic Party, have developed their conservatism in proportion as the great masses have embraced socialism and the more these masses have become organized and disciplined. As a consequence of this, Social Democracy . . . may at a certain moment become a direct obstacle to open conflict between the workers and bourgeois reaction. . . . The tremendous influence of the Russian revolution [of 1905] indicates that it will destroy party routine and conservatism, and place the question of an open trial of strength between the proletariat and capitalist reaction on the order of the day.'[17]

Trotsky's sensitivity in this period, less keen, it is true, than that of Rosa Luxemburg, to the possibility that the European parties might prove inadequate as instruments of revolution, notwithstanding their own ideological pronouncements, could not but reinforce his tendency to deny to the party any important

15. *Rosa Luxemburg Speaks*, p. 121.
16. 'The Mass Strike, Party and Trade Unions', Ibid., pp. 182, 202–5, 214–8 and *passim*.
17. *Results and Prospects*, p. 246.

role, and to place his confidence exclusively in other forms of working-class participation in revolutionary struggle. In particular, he espoused such forms as would involve wider masses of the working class than those already organized within the socialist parties, forms like the soviets and the general strike.[18] As late as 1915, he was still arguing that socialists should 'cease relying on less stable and less trustworthy elements such as the slogans and tactics of a party, and . . . refer to more stable historical factors: to the social structure of the nation, to the relation of class forces and the tendencies of development.'[19] In Trotsky's writings after 1917 such formulations are nowhere to be found. They are henceforth replaced by a conception of the revolutionary process in which 'the slogans and tactics of a party', not to say its whole conduct, assume an exceptional importance.[20]

One can only account for this changed assessment of the importance of the party if one takes it in conjunction with the fact that Trotsky now rallied to Bolshevism, formally joining the Party at the end of July 1917, though his political solidarity with it was quite clear soon after his arrival in Petrograd in early May. Two factors probably determined this decision. In the first place, since Lenin's return to Russia, and the change of orientation embodied in his *April Theses*, the political position of the Bolshevik Party was now, in all essential respects, identical to Trotsky's own perspective of permanent revolution. Secondly, Trotsky's hypothesis that a new revolutionary crisis would bring Bolsheviks and Mensheviks closer together, the hypothesis on which he had based his attempts to reconcile the two factions, was now refuted. Precisely the opposite had occurred. With the *April Theses*, the common ground there had been between them disappeared for good. No longer able to cling to the idea that 'the course of events' or the spontaneous pressure of the working class would, of their own accord, unite the two factions and impel them on the path of socialist revolution, he ceased to regard the latter as

18. On the latter, see Deutscher, *The Prophet Armed*, pp. 110–111.

19. 'The Struggle for Power', appendix to *Results and Prospects*, p. 250.

20. Nicolas Krassó's article, 'Trotsky's Marxism', *New Left Review*, No. 44, July/August 1967, pp. 64–86, so construes the 'characteristic unity' (pp. 85–86) of Trotsky's thought as to deny this change, although it constitutes *the major change* in his thinking, and one which is quite clear in virtually all his political writings after 1917. The article contains, in addition, a number of other errors and inaccuracies.

a predetermined outcome and began to see it as a possibility, the realization of which would depend upon correct political leadership, a strategy oriented towards the capture of power, and the willingness at the opportune moment to deliver the decisive blow. Since the Bolshevik Party seemed to him to possess these qualities, Trotsky now joined that party. Parallel to this process of drawing closer to and eventually joining the Bolshevik Party, a different conception, broadly Leninist, of the relation between party and class began to emerge in Trotsky's writings. It did not emerge full-blown. In fact, it was only in the years 1923–40 that Trotsky gave it extensive elaboration. Nevertheless, his articles of 1917 already bear the unmistakable signs of a growing belief that the successful outcome of revolution would depend on the leadership of a revolutionary party.[21]

For the brief period from 1919 to 1921, however, the idea of leadership became one of tutelage, as Trotsky took up authoritarian positions which amounted to an explicit violation of the principles of socialist democracy he had hitherto defended, and was shortly to return to, to defend till the end of his life. This was the period of War Communism, of civil war and foreign intervention, and, in the face of the almost complete collapse of the Soviet economy, Trotsky now became the foremost spokesman for solutions such as the militarization of labour, the stifling of the autonomy of the trade unions, and their incorporation into the administrative machinery of the Soviet State.[22] It is not unlikely that Trotsky's role at this time as organizer and leader of the Red Army directed his thoughts towards such measures. Be that as it may, on the question of the role of the party in relation to those it was supposed to represent, he gave expression to sentiments whose character was unequivocally 'substitutionist' to employ his own phrase of an earlier period. A couple of examples of this will suffice. In July 1920, at the Second Congress of the Communist International, Trotsky had this to say: 'Today we have received a proposal from the Polish Government to conclude peace. Who decides such questions? We have the Council of People's Commissars but it too must be subject to certain control. Whose

21. See e.g. Leon Trotsky, *The Struggle for State Power 1917*, Colombo 1966, pp. 33–34, 43–45, and *After the July Days, What Next?*, Colombo 1967, pp. 31–33, 37, 41–42.

22. See Leon Trotsky, *Terrorism and Communism*, Ann Arbor 1961, pp. 107–11, 128–76.

control? The control of the working class as a formless, chaotic mass? No. The Central Committee of the party is convened in order to discuss the proposal and to decide whether it ought to be answered. And when we have to conduct war, organize new divisions and find the best elements for them—where do we turn? We turn to the party. To the Central Committee.'[23] And at the Tenth Congress of the Party in March 1921, he took the Workers' Opposition to task for having 'placed the workers' right to elect representatives above the party, as it were, as if the party were not entitled to assert is dictatorship even if that dictatorship temporarily clashed with the passing moods of the workers' democracy'.[24]

It was at this same congress that the ban on organized factions within the Party was imposed, and Trotsky did not dissent from the measure. Later on, in the 1930s, he was to argue that this and the prohibition of the other Soviet parties had been intended as temporary measures, adopted in the heat of civil war and its aftermath in defence of the new regime.[25] But, as the above passages make clear, Trotsky did not at the time justify the curtailment of Soviet democracy as simply a regrettable necessity. On the contrary, he made a virtue of that necessity[26] and, doing so, played his part in erecting the absence of democracy into the principle it was to become under Stalin. Trotsky himself recoiled from the process well before its consummation. Gradually during the course of 1922 he began to move away from the positions he had recently occupied, and in the following year he opened his attack on the internal regime in the Party. Pointing to the danger that 'the apparatus manifests a growing tendency to counterpose a few thousand comrades, who form the leading cadres, to the rest

23. Leon Trotsky, *The First Five Years of the Communist International*, New York 1945, Vol. 1, pp. 99–100.

24. Deutscher, *The Prophet Armed*, pp. 508–9.

25. Leon Trotsky, *Stalinism and Bolshevism*, London 1956, p. 14, *The Revolution Betrayed*, New York 1965, pp. 95–96, 266–8, and *The Case of Leon Trotsky*, New York 1969, pp. 424–5.

26. This was one of the points made by Rosa Luxemburg in her sympathetic-critical assessment of the Russian revolution written in prison in 1918: 'The danger begins only when they make a virtue of necessity and want to freeze into a complete theoretical system all the tactics forced upon them by these fatal circumstances, and want to recommend them to the international proletariat as a model of socialist tactics.' See 'The Russian Revolution' in *Rosa Luxemburg Speaks*, p. 394.

of the mass whom they look upon only as an object of action', Trotsky called for 'a vibrant and active democracy' in the Party, which would allow all its members 'to participate actively and consciously in working out its views and in determining its course of action'.[27] But the fact that he had himself been a party to the measures initiating the process he was now attacking severely hampered him in the struggle within the Party. For example, on the question of the prohibition of factions, he recognized that: 'If factions are not wanted, there must not be any permanent groupings; if permanent groupings are not wanted, temporary groupings must be avoided; finally, in order that there be no temporary groupings, there must be no differences of opinion, for wherever there are two opinions, people inevitably group together.'[28] If this argument has a conclusion, it is that democracy could not be restored without lifting the ban on factions (and relaxing the Bolshevik monopoly of power). While Trotsky was later to draw just such conclusions,[29] he limited himself for the moment to expressing the conviction that a more prudent use of the ban would do the trick.[30] That he was forced by his opponents to fight on the terrain of Leninist orthodoxy, where dissent from anything Lenin had said or done counted as sufficient proof of error, may partly explain Trotsky's failure at this stage to push his thoughts through to the end. But his own arguments of the recent past also played their part, since his current objections to the authoritarian regime in the Party could now be represented as a hollow pretence.

At this point in the exposition, the form of presentation of Trotsky's thought which has been utilized hitherto is dropped. The somewhat schematic historical account was indispensable inasmuch as the task was to deal with a changing set of conceptions which had to be related to a changing political context. I also wanted to identify the path travelled by Trotsky before he arrived at anything like a stable theoretical position. I now abandon this procedure to take up a more conceptual approach and examine the internal pattern of Trotsky's views in the years after 1923,

27. Leon Trotsky, *The New Course*, Ann Arbor 1965, pp. 17, 25, 17.
28. Ibid., pp. 27–28.
29. *The Revolution Betrayed*, pp. 266–8, *The Case of Leon Trotsky*, p. 440.
30. *The New Course*, pp. 29–33.

drawing on all his writings between that year and his death. This may tend to overstate the fixity and coherence of his views in this period, but for the purposes of the present essay it is, I think, justified. For, throughout this time Trotsky took up a Leninist position, though one which incorporated some of the main themes of his earlier thought. With regard to the forms of political participation to be used by the working class in the struggle for socialism, Trotsky's basic assumptions from now on remained broadly the same. And it is these assumptions which I want to bring out.

It may be worth beginning by making explicit such assumptions as form the necessary basis for the espousal of forms of political participation not already provided for by the existing political machinery. These assumptions are not, of course, in any way peculiar to Trotsky's Marxism. The first is that the democratic political institutions of capitalist societies do not, where they exist, secure for the working class a participation that is effective or genuine. This assumption is clear enough in Trotsky's statement that 'bourgeois democracy is a system of institutions and measures by the aid of which the needs and demands of the working masses, reaching ever higher, are neutralized, distorted, rendered innocuous'; and in his corresponding denial 'that in Britain, France, the United States, and other democracies private ownership is maintained by the will of the people. No one ever asked the people about it.'[31] As such, parliamentary institutions are not an effective instrument for the overthrow of capitalism, there can be no purely parliamentary road to socialism, and Trotsky makes his own an idea which looms large in Lenin's *State and Revolution*: that the state in capitalist society is not a neutral weapon, that can be taken over by the working class and used for its own purposes; it must be smashed and replaced.[32] This is not to say, however, that for Trotsky the presence or absence of democratic institutions is irrelevant. If they are not sufficient as a means of revolutionary transformation, they are at

---

31. Leon Trotsky, *Where is Britain Going?*, London 1960, p. 49.

32. Leon Trotsky, *Whither France?*, Colombo 1961, p. 33, *The Living Thoughts of Karl Marx*, New York 1963, p. 42, *The History of the Russian Revolution*, Vol. 3, p. 126. Cf. Lenin, *Collected Works*, Vol. 25, pp. 388, 406, 414, 483–91. For a discussion of this idea in connection with Marx, see Michael Evans, 'Karl Marx and the Concept of Political Participation', in Geraint Parry (ed.), *Participation in Politics*, Manchester 1972, ch. 6.

all events an inestimable advantage to the working class, enabling it to make certain concrete gains within the limits of the existing society, to organize in the open, and to conduct its political education and propaganda at large.

Reference to Trotsky's writings on Germany in the period 1929–33 is enough to establish this, for he there took issue with the 'theory', if such it can be called, and tactics of the Comintern during the so-called Third Period, some basic features of which were the view that there was no objective difference between fascism and Social Democracy, and hence the designation of the latter as 'Social Fascism' and the refusal to combine with it in a struggle against Hitler; and the belief that Hitler's coming to power would not substantially change anything, nor be more than a brief episode should it in fact occur. Against this Trotsky repeatedly, and with increasing urgency, insisted that this position amounted to a simple failure to recognize the specific character of fascism; that a Nazi victory in Germany would mean the annihilation of all independent workers' organizations, Social-Democratic ones included, and the complete destruction of democratic institutions and political liberties; and that a united front between Communists and Social Democrats was the only hope of avoiding this. Without it, all prospects of socialism would, together with the existing democratic institutions, disappear for a long time to come.[33]

Now, if the democratic institutions of a capitalist society are not, by themselves, adequate for the abolition of that society, then this task can only be solved by revolutionary methods, and I want here to recall, by a further quotation, Trotsky's characterization of revolution as an act of mass political participation, beyond what is possible within capitalist society: 'Revolution crushes and demolishes the machinery of the old state. Therein is its essence. Crowds fill the arena. They decide, they act, they legislate in their own unprecedented way; they judge, they issue orders. The essence of the revolution is that the mass itself becomes its own executive organ.'[34] It follows from what has been said that this kind of political participation is, in the first place,

---

33. Leon Trotsky, *The Turn in the Communist International and the German Situation*, Colombo 1958, p. 20, *Germany, the Key to the International Situation*, Colombo 1958, pp. 11, 30, *What Next? Vital Questions for the German Proletariat*, New York 1932, pp. 12–13, 28–30, 60. Cf also *Whither France?*, pp. 4, 67.

34. *Stalin*, p. 404.

instrumental.[35] Its purpose is to achieve what cannot be achieved in any other way, namely, the overthrow of the existing order. And despite the great importance given by Trotsky after 1917 to the role of the vanguard party—something I shall deal with later at greater length—the forms of this mass political participation are the same ones as were singled out by him at a much earlier period: namely, the mass or general strike, as an act which breaks down the political and occupational divisions within the working class, assembles it as a collectivity, and makes it conscious of itself as such; and the soviets, as institutions expressing the demands of the workers in as direct a way as possible, and as the germinal organs of the future workers' state.[36] As the instrumental agencies of revolution, these forms are thereby also instrumental in breaking a possible obstacle in the path of the latter, the inertia of the revolutionary party itself.

We have already encountered the theme of the tendencies towards conservatism in any large socialist party. After the First World War, or more exactly, after August 4th 1914, Trotsky regarded his hypothesis of 1906 as confirmed, and never ceased to identify the Social-Democratic parties as a formidable obstruction in the way of socialist revolutions in Europe, given their continuing hold on large sections of the working class and their refusal to transgress the limits of legality.[37] In 1933, he renounced his allegiance to the Comintern, following what was on his analysis a capitulation, without struggle, of the German Communist Party before Nazism,[38] and thereafter regarded it as defunct as a revolutionary force. In Trotsky's writings of this period, the problem of preserving the revolutionary character of revolutionary parties is, accordingly, a major preoccupation: 'Each party, even the most revolutionary party, must inevitably produce its own organizational conservatism; for otherwise it would be lacking in necessary stability.'[39] What it gains in stability, it

35. See the distinction made by Geraint Parry in the Introduction to *Participation in Politics*.

36. On the mass strike, see *Whither France?*, pp. 74, 83–84, 149, 151–2, and *Where is Britain Going?*, p. xii; on soviets, see e.g. Leon Trotsky, *The Third International After Lenin*, New York 1957, pp. 201–4.

37. See Leon Trotsky, *The Lessons of October* in *The Essential Trotsky*, London 1963, pp. 113–77, at p. 171, and *The Third International After Lenin*, p. 261, *Whither France?*, p. 48, *The Revolution Betrayed*, pp. 8–9, 23, 59.

38. See Isaac Deutscher, *The Prophet Outcast*, London 1963, pp. 200–1.

39. *The Lessons of October*, p. 173.

may lose in flexibility, and flexibility—the 'aptitude to orient itself rapidly, to change tactics quickly . . . to carry out abrupt turns'—is, for Trotsky, one of the few traditions that a revolutionary party can safely afford to cultivate. The danger is always that, enmeshed in the politics of a period of normality, it will be unable or unwilling, when a revolutionary situation occurs, to change course rapidly enough and lead the working class towards the capture of power.[40] As for guarantees against this contingency, there are none, in the strict sense. So much so that Trotsky came to regard it as a 'law that a party crisis is inevitable in the transition from the preparatory revolutionary activity to the immediate struggle for power'.[41] There would always be substantial elements within it who would invoke the possibility of failure, recommend caution or postponement. As a paradigm of the crisis in the revolutionary party on the eve of revolution, Trotsky cited the history of the Bolshevik Party itself in 1917, both the resistance to Lenin's change of course in April, and the opposition led by Zinoviev and Kamenev to the October insurrection. And in his *History*, he expressed the view that, had Lenin not returned to Russia in 1917, the revolution would not have taken place.[42]

In the context of this assumption, that within even the most revolutionary party there will be an inner resistance to any attempt to take power, *one* of the functions of participation in revolutionary struggle by wider masses of the working class than are already organized within the party, is precisely to lessen that resistance and, if possible, to overcome it. This is not to say that Trotsky retains from the period 1905–17 the tendency to assign to the party a negligible role. As will be seen, without the revolutionary party there can be no revolution. With such a party there might be. But it depends as much on what the party can get from the revolutionary proletariat in the way of courage, initiative and freedom from bureaucratic routine as it does on what the party can give it in the way of ideological and tactical leadership. And in a revolutionary situation, according to Trotsky, it is just such qualities of determination which the masses are likely to possess to a greater degree than the party, and to bring to bear on the

---

40. *The New Course*, pp. 50–51; cf. *The Third International After Lenin*, pp. 91, 97.
41. *The Lessons of October*, pp. 118–9. Cf. *The History* . . ., Vol. 3, p. 165, and *The Third International After Lenin*, p. 98.
42. *The History* . . ., Vol. 1, pp. 330–1.

latter. All this may appear to contradict his assertion, recorded above, that the course of the Bolshevik Party in 1917 and the October revolution itself hinged on the presence of one man—Lenin. It needs, however, to be borne in mind that, while Trotsky was after 1917 unstinting in his admiration for Lenin's revolutionary genius,[43] his view of what that genius amounted to was different from one, fairly common, which stresses primarily Lenin's organizational abilities and inclinations. The following passage is typical: 'Lenin's strength did not lie so much in his ability to build a machine—he knew how to do that, too—as in his ability at all critical moments to utilize the living energy of the masses for overcoming the limitations and the conservatism characteristic of any political machine.'[44] The theme is recurrent. Lenin not only builds a revolutionary party, he also thinks and feels with the masses, knows how to sense their mood, and when that mood is revolutionary he brings its pressure to bear on the party itself to overcome its inertia. His importance as an individual does not, therefore, contradict the notion that the masses outside the party play their part in breaking the resistance within it. Their consonance is, on the contrary, explicit: 'Lenin exerted influence not so much as an individual, but because he embodied the influence of the class on the Party.'[45]

To say that Trotsky regards mass political participation in revolutionary struggle as instrumental, inasmuch as it is the only effective means for the overthrow of capitalism, is of course only to state one side of the matter. The negative task has its positive complement, namely, the creation of socialism, and I want to argue that this in itself means that the political participation envisaged cannot have a purely instrumental character but will combine instrumental and developmental[46] aspects in a particular way. This is because it is a fundamental assumption of socialist theory that human potentialities are not exhaused by any *given* activities of men, nor by their *present* attitudes and needs, level of education, and so on. So far from taking for granted that men remain the same, it adopts the contrary postulate, that they can and do transform themselves. And part of the content of the

43. See e.g. the sketches collected in Leon Trotsky, *Lenin*, New York 1962.
44. *Stalin*, pp. 141–2.
45. Ibid., p. 204, and cf. also pp. 63, 208; *The History* . . ., Vol. 1, p. 119, and *Trotsky's Diary in Exile 1935*, London 1958, p. 81.
46. See Parry in *Participation in Politics*.

concept of socialism is that it will be based on men of a different kind, and, in particular, men with the ability and the desire to take the most active part in determining the decisions which affect their lives. Now, unless it is supposed that the desired transformation will take place, in miraculous fashion, at a single point in time—which is derisory—then it must, at the very least, be suggested in what ways the instrumentalities espoused for the creation of socialism will themselves encourage the developmental effects deemed necessary and desirable. The content of the future must already be sketched in the activity of the present. If the means chosen are revolutionary ones, then revolution itself must be seen as a process of political education, in which its participants begin to acquire the abilities and attitudes indispensable to the new social order.

The thinker who most adequately represents this kind of perspective is Rosa Luxemburg. In her refusal to countenance anything smacking of tutelage over the working class, or to accept that socialism might be introduced on its behalf, in her profound faith in its independent initiative, and in her emphasis on the *value* of such mistakes as it would inevitably make in entering the arena of revolutionary politics, since those very mistakes would constitute an education[47]—in all this, a picture emerges of the revolutionary process as one of the self-education of the working class. This is, moreover, an education that can be acquired in no other way: while capitalism persists, social and economic conditions do not permit it; and if it is postponed pending a *prior* transformation of those conditions, then socialist democracy is reduced, for her, to a simple act of faith.[48] '. . . the proletariat require a high degree of political education, of class-consciousness and organization. All these conditions cannot be fulfilled by pamphlets and leaflets, but only by the living political school, by the fight and in the fight, in the continuous course of the revolution.'[49] 'Socialism will not be and cannot be inaugurated by decrees; it cannot be established by any government, however admirably socialistic. Socialism must be created by the masses, must be made by every proletarian.'[50] The above quotations may serve to convey the spirit of a work in which the transformation of

47. See *Rosa Luxemburg Speaks*, pp. 82–83, 130.
48. Ibid., pp. 393–4.
49. Ibid., p. 172.
50. Ibid., p. 419.

men takes place neither before, nor after, but during the revolution on the basis of maximum political participation.

The same theme of the instrumental/developmental character of revolutionary politics is present, if less evidently so, in Trotsky's political thought. It is clearest in a work of 1938, in which Trotsky rejects the attribution to Marxism of an ethical unscrupulousness with regard to the means employed in attempting to achieve socialism. If 'the end justifies the means', a principle Trotsky accepts, then at all events the means chosen must really be means to the end in view: 'Seeds of wheat must be sown in order to yield an ear of wheat.' Otherwise the end itself is distorted. 'Precisely from this it flows that *not* all means are permissible . . . the great revolutionary end spurns those base means and ways which set one part of the working class against other parts, or attempt to make the masses happy without their participation; or lower the faith of the masses in themselves and their organization, replacing it by worship for the "leaders".'[51]

Since the end must already be operative in the means employed, the liberation of the workers can only be their own work,[52] and it is in the very process of achieving it that they must develop those qualities which will sustain a socialist society. Thus, for Trotsky, mass participation in the political forms thrown up by a revolution is not only a manifestation of the widespread desire to assume more active control over political and economic life, it also promotes and consolidates that desire. Revolution is consistently seen by him as an educative process, in which the same mass actions which are necessary to destroy the existing economic and political structures, also have the effect of delivering the working class from the hold of bourgeois ideology, of making it conscious of its interests as a class, of raising its confidence in its own ability to organize and decide, and of providing it with the experience of those activities.[53] In this context, it may be worth mentioning the emphasis in Trotsky's writings on the need for honesty and truthfulness in revolutionary politics. This constitutes more than a personal defence against the vilification and slander directed against him and emanating from Moscow; it is also a vital political principle. Anything less than the truth is inconsistent with the

51. Leon Trotsky, *Their Morals and Ours*, New York 1966, pp. 40–42.
52. Ibid.
53. See e.g. *My Life*, p. 334, *The History* . . ., Vol. I, pp. 149–52, 221, 420, and *Whither France?*, pp. 143, 155.

notion of revolutionary transformation as also an educative process, and opens the way to cynical manipulation. The growing avalanche of Stalinist distortion and falsification therefore met with Trotsky's untiring criticism and outspoken contempt.[54]

It remains to consider the role Trotsky assigns to the party in this later period of his life. On the highest level of abstraction, the party represents the subjective factor in the historical process,[55] and the recognition of its importance bespeaks a rejection of the belief that revolutionary situations will automatically or inevitably produce successful revolutions, a belief we have seen to be implicit in Trotsky's thinking prior to 1917. Where revolutionary situations occur, the role of the party is to attempt to win the confidence of the class as a whole by offering political leadership, and when it judges that it has done so, to take the initiative in delivering the blow that will topple the existing regime. In the absence of the party, or where it fails to act correctly, the revolutionary energy of the masses will be dissipated in sporadic actions and they will suffer defeat.[56] The necessary, but not sufficient, condition of the party's being able successfully to fulfil this function in a revolutionary period, is a certain political preparation during periods of political stability. This will consist, among other things, of attempting to assemble within the party those elements of the working class already conscious of their interests as a class, the party being in principle the class for itself as opposed to the class in itself;[57] of attempting to preserve its theoretical positions, its accumulated experience, and thereby its revolutionary character, against the pressure of bourgeois ideology;[58] towards these ends, of undertaking political and educational work, utilizing to their fullest extent the institutions and channels open to it; and so on. To the extent that the party succeeds in all this, it represents, whatever its actual numbers, the objective interest of the working class, namely, socialism,

---

54. Leon Trotsky, *The Stalin School of Falsification*, New York 1962, pp. xxxi, 174–5 and *passim*, *The Third International After Lenin*, pp. 66–68, 118, *My Life*, p. 528, *Their Morals and Ours*, pp. 42–43, and *The Case of Leon Trotsky, passim*.

55. Leon Trotsky, *The First Five Years of the Communist International*, London 1953, Vol. 2, p. 308, *The Third International After Lenin*, p. 84.

56. *The Lessons of October*, p. 117, *The History* . . ., Vol. 1, p. xix, Vol. 3, pp. 167–75.

57. *What Next? Vital Questions* . . ., p. 41.

58. *Stalinism and Bolshevism*, p. 4, *Stalin*, pp. 403–4.

hence 'the very highest tasks and aims of mankind'.[59] This much is probably familiar and not in need of further elaboration.

What may be worth stressing is that, for Trotsky, there are no *guarantees* that the party does in fact represent what it claims to represent. This is a hypothesis which requires to be verified in practice: 'The identity, in principle, of the interests of the proletariat and of the aims of the . . . party does not mean either that the proletariat as a whole is, even today, conscious of its class interests, or that the party under all conditions formulates them *correctly*. The very need of the party originates in the . . . fact that the proletariat is not born with the innate understanding of its historical interests. The task of the party consists in *learning*, from experience derived from the struggle, how to demonstrate to the proletariat its right to leadership.'[60] The emphasis here is as much on the need for the party to learn from the class by direct participation in the struggles of that class, as it is on its role as leader or educator. The possibility of a consciousness adequate to the task of overthrowing capitalism is thus made dependent on the mutual interaction between party and class. While Trotsky thereby rules out the prospect of revolution in the absence of a revolutionary party, he equally rules out the idea that the party might be in possession of a ready-made truth which it injects unilaterally into the working-class movement, and which establishes beyond question its right to leadership. This reciprocity in the relations between the party and the working class is also clear in the following polemical formulation: 'Agitation is not only the means of communicating to the masses this or that slogan, calling the masses to action, and so on. For a party, agitation is also a means of lending an ear to the masses, of sounding out its moods and thoughts . . . only the Stalinists have transformed agitation into a noisy monologue. For the Marxists, the Leninists, *agitation is always a dialogue with the masses*.'[61] The party that abandons this dialogue risks degeneration and eventual death as a revolutionary force, and it then becomes necessary to build a new organization. Trotsky's foundation of the Fourth International should be seen in the context of these assumptions.

In the light of the above, it is probably unnecessary to spell out

59. *Their Morals and Ours*, p. 38.
60. *What Next? Vital Questions . . .*, pp. 44–45. Trotsky's emphasis.
61. *Whither France?*, pp. 76–77. Trotsky's emphasis.

that the Leninism Trotsky saw himself as defending and elaborating was not the Leninism of *What is to be Done?* On the eve of his assassination, Trotsky referred to the 'erroneousness' of some of the conceptions there set out, and to Lenin's own acknowledgement of it.[62]

62. *Stalin*, p. 58.

10.

Lenin, Trotsky
and the Party[1]
1977

Origins

To begin at the beginning: seventy-five years ago, Lenin wrote
What is to be done?. This was one year before the 1903 congress of
the Russian Social Democratic Labour Party in which the historic
split between Bolsheviks and Mensheviks took place. In connection with that split he wrote another work, *One Step Forward,
Two Steps Back*, and these two pamphlets contain the initial
formulation of the Leninist theory of party organization. As
everyone knows, two other outstanding revolutionaries of that
epoch, Rosa Luxemburg and Leon Trotsky, opposed and criticized Lenin in vigorous polemics: Luxemburg in the essay
Organizational Questions of Russian Social Democracy, Trotsky in
his book, *Our Political Tasks*. In 1918, on the eve of her murder,
the signs were that some of the differences between Luxemburg
and Lenin, which have in any case been exaggerated, were
diminishing. In Trotsky's case, he opposed Lenin on the question
of the party for nearly a decade and a half, then in 1917 was won
over and joined the Bolshevik Party, and henceforward defended
and fought for the revolutionary substance of the Leninist theory
of organization until his death. But in doing this, and in order to
do it, he had now to oppose the *cult* of Lenin that was part and
parcel of the emergence and triumph of Stalinism.

1. This is an edited transcript of a talk given in London on 11 September 1977
at the Marxist Symposium organized by the International Marxist Group.

Trotsky and Lenin

In his *History of the Russian Revolution*, Trotsky the historian, speaking in the third person of Trotsky the political actor, wrote that he 'came to Lenin as to a teacher whose power and significance he understood later than many others, but perhaps more fully than they.'[2] This was not, as many will doubtless want to say of it, immodesty or arrogance on Trotsky's part. It was, I think, a sober appraisal of his own relationship to the political legacy of Lenin. For, consider. On one side, there is a whole army of bourgeois ideologues, social democrats, libertarians and others, for whom Lenin's work represents the ruthless drive for power of a totalitarian elite. On the other side, you have Stalinists, Maoists, and a variety of other would-be Leninists, for whom Lenin is a sort of omniscient leader, practically a god. Trotsky's relationship was different. After 1917 he always acknowledged the lasting importance of Lenin's theory and practice of the party for the Russian and the international proletariat, and this has to remain central. But two points should be remembered. First, Trotsky's own past, his own previous opposition to Lenin, meant that he had a perspective on some of the earlier mistakes and weaknesses of Bolshevism that no other Bolshevik leader had. And second, there was the vigorous struggle he waged against the cult of Lenin, realizing that the usual function of gods is to reinforce some authority, and that the main function of the myth of the 'great leader' is to put a halo of infallibility around existing so-called great leaders. Trotsky fought against the cult and this, as well as his own earlier opposition to Bolshevism, established for him a certain critical distance within the overall continuity with Lenin.

Lenin and Trotskyism

Now, in order not to be misunderstood: I am not in turn wanting to suggest that it is Trotsky who was the great hero and leader who understood everything well and never went wrong; that obviously will not do. With regard, in particular, to the cult of

2. Leon Trotsky, *The History of the Russian Revolution*, Ann Arbor n.d., Vol. 2, p. 310.

Lenin, Trotsky made his own mistakes. But taken all in all, his relation to Lenin and Lenin's work was one neither of blind hostility nor of deification. It was a relationship of *critical* continuity and respect. And this creates a special opportunity, and at the same time a special obligation, for those belonging to the international movement which Trotsky founded and also for others who are influenced by his work. It is an opportunity – and I stress, *opportunity*, not guarantee, for nothing is guaranteed, it has to be fought for – and an obligation to seize the real substance, the revolutionary essence, of the Leninist theory of organization, whilst critically separating from it the incidental errors and blemishes, the excesses, in the history of Bolshevism; and also, as importantly, the numerous one-side caricatures and distortions which masquerade under the name of Leninism, be they of a bureaucratic-authoritarian, sectarian-elitist, propagandist or opportunist kind.

That is the theme I want to pursue. I shall begin by recalling briefly the general context and the main themes of Lenin's initial formulation of the theory of the party.

Context

Recall, then, that when Lenin wrote these works there was no revolutionary workers' party in Russia. A founding conference had taken place in March 1898 at Minsk, with some nine or ten delegates, but it had no effect since most of the participants were arrested immediately afterwards. Recall that the socialist movement, such as it was, consisted of scattered groups, mainly of intellectuals and only beginning to make contact with the Russian working class; that there was a complete local fragmentation of these groups, with no overall co-ordination between them; and that they had to operate clandestinely, in conditions of police repression, leaders constantly being imprisoned, exiled to Siberia, and so on. And recall, perhaps crucially, the fact that *What is to be done?* had a particular ideological target, that trend known as economism: which stressed the economic, trade-union struggle as against the need for political-revolutionary perspectives; which stressed day-to-day practical tasks – getting on with the job, so to speak – as against the need for broad revolutionary socialist propaganda and agitation; and which in order to reinforce these emphases made a kind of principle of the spontaneity of the working class, arguing along the lines: this is what the workers are doing in any case, so this is what we should support, rather than getting carried away with grand perspectives of revolutionary socialism and so forth.

Theory

Against this trend Lenin put forward the following well-known arguments. First, the importance of theory: in the most famous formulations, 'Without revolutionary theory there can be no revolutionary movement', and 'the role of vanguard fighter can be fulfilled only by a party that is guided by the most advanced theory'[3]—by which Lenin meant Marxism. Lenin referred to Engels' earlier formulations about the three 'sides' of the class struggle: not only the political and economic sides but the theoretical side as well.[4] In a language that everyone can understand, Lenin in other words made the point now dignified with other names (specificity of levels, relative autonomy of superstructures and so on) that the workers' movement *needs* knowledge, it *needs* science, to guide its political struggles; and this knowledge and science do not flow automatically from anything as if they were a gift of God, they have their own preconditions: theoretical production, study, ideological struggle, a many-sided battle of ideas. So any anti-intellectualism, any philistinism in relation to ideas and theory, mere 'getting on with the job', risks diverting the socialist movement by bringing it under the sway of false, bourgeois ideas. 'Bringing it under the sway' is not, actually, the right way of putting it. Obviously, the whole argument starts from the assumption, which goes back to Marx, that the dominant ideas of any epoch are the ideas of the ruling class. The workers' movement *will* be under the sway—more or less—of such ideas, and hence the need for this theoretical struggle.

Trade Union Politics and Socialist Politics

A second crucial theme: the distinction between trade union and

3. V. I. Lenin, *Collected Works* (henceforth CW), Moscow 1960–1970, Vol. 5, pp. 369, 370.
4. Ibid., pp. 370–372.

socialist politics. Now, it is formulated by Lenin in these terms because of the economist emphasis on trade unionism, but in fact what Lenin says goes for any struggle for immediate, day-to-day, partial demands, any struggle for reforms within capitalist society. Naturally, trade unionism and the struggle for reforms are a vital necessity, but the exclusive concentration on these does not represent an adequate socialist politics. It is equivalent to a self-limitation by the socialist movement within capitalism, to abandoning the field of battle to bourgeois ideas, because in practice it means you accept that within the structure of capitalism a satisfactory amelioration of the condition of the working class can be achieved. Lenin's essential thought here is: there is no automatic dynamic which leads from trade unionism, from immediate, everyday struggles, to revolutionary consciousness and thus to socialism. This is, if you like, the 'spontaneist illusion'; the idea that by struggling very vigorously for higher wages or better working conditions, that will somehow produce socialist consciousness.

To put the same thing slightly differently, perhaps, from the way in which he expresses it, you cannot achieve what Lenin calls socialist consciousness, revolutionary consciousness, from some partial, sectional perspective on society, whether it be that of a group of employees in relation to their employers or some other. Why not? Because what revolutionary consciousness consists of is precisely a *global* understanding—of *all* class relationships and at every level of society (economic, political, cultural, and so on) but particularly at the level of the state. That is why the indispensable precondition of socialist consciousness is an all-round propaganda and agitation which relates to *every* manifestation of exploitation and oppression, be it economic, political, cultural or other; and that is the basis too of Lenin's assertion that the model of a revolutionary is not the trade union secretary but the tribune of the people.[5] Only thus can socialist politics be carried on and socialist consciousness be achieved.

Spontaneity and Consciousness

This leads us to the very heart of Lenin's argument in *What is to*

5. Ibid., p. 423.

be done?, to the whole question of spontaneity and consciousness, and I want to say that here we encounter both the central proposition of his theory of the party, on the one hand; and on the other, two unilateral theses which, even though explicable in terms of the object of the polemic he was pursuing, are in need of correction nevertheless.

To begin with the unilateral theses, these are, in my opinion, first, that 'the working class, exclusively by its own effort, is able to develop only trade union consciousness'; or as Lenin also puts it, and perhaps more strongly: 'The spontaneous working-class movement is by itself able to create (and inevitably does create) only trade unionism.'[6] I say this is explicable in the light of the polemic he was engaged in, and it even has a sort of validity: for long periods of time in the history of capitalist societies. But it is in need of correction, because in what we call pre-revolutionary and revolutionary situations, the spontaneous working-class movement goes beyond mere trade unionism. The second unilateral thesis is contained, I think, in one of the senses Lenin gives to the well-known formula that socialist consciousness is brought to the working class *from without*. Now, everyone has their own idea of what this means and there are very sophisticated ways of explaining it and somehow showing it all to be fine. I am just interested in what Lenin himself actually says. The fact is that he uses this formula in two ways. One of them (and this I think is unilateral) follows Kautsky in proposing that socialist consciousness is 'introduced into the proletarian class struggle from without' by members of the bourgeois intelligentsia.[7] 'Outside' and 'inside' are understood in these terms: the inside the proletarian class struggle, the outside the bourgeois intelligentsia, which introduces socialist consciousness. Without making too much of a meal of it, I think that is wrong. It is another way, obviously, of trying to state the importance of theory. But what it also does is fail to state *which* bourgeois intelligentsia this is that elaborates socialist consciousness, under what conditions, and as part of what movement. This sense of the formula, 'from without', is wrong and needs correction.

6. Ibid., pp. 375, 437.

7. Ibid., pp. 383–384. And cf. this, at pp. 375–376: '. . . in Russia, the theoretical doctrine of Social Democracy arose altogether independently of the spontaneous growth of the working-class movement; it arose as a natural and inevitable outcome of the development of thought among the revolutionary socialist intelligentsia.'

There is, however, another meaning—the important meaning
—of the idea that proletarian socialist consciousness is introduced
from without and this contains what I would say is the central
proposition of Lenin's theory of the party. I think the following
passage sums it up: 'the basic error,' Lenin says, 'that all the
Economists commit [is] their conviction that it is possible to
develop the class political consciousness of the workers *from
within*, so to speak, from their economic struggle . . . . Class
political consciousness can be brought to the workers *only from
without*, that is, only from outside the economic struggle, from
outside the sphere of relations between workers and employers.
The sphere from which alone it is possible to obtain this knowledge is the sphere of relationships of *all* classes and strata to the
state and the government, the sphere of the interrelations between *all* classes.'[8] 'Inside' and 'outside' in this passage refer not,
now, to sociological groupings, as it were, workers and bourgeois
intellectuals, the latter the vehicle of socialist consciousness. They
refer, instead, respectively to the partial and the global. Socialist
consciousness is not generated out of any particular struggle. No
such struggle leads automatically towards an adequate understanding. This can come only from a global perspective on the
relations between all classes.

And I say this contains the central proposition in Lenin's
theory of the party, because what the theory states, in a nutshell,
is that the party is necessary as an instrument of political centralization. Without some such instrument, all the fragmentary struggles, sectional experiences and partial perspectives of different
layers of the masses cannot be combined into a successful revolutionary assault on capitalist society, which has its *own* organ of
centralization, its own organ of combat, in the bourgeois state.
The party is required as a politically centralizing instance, to
combine the partial struggles and link them up, in confrontation
ultimately with that state. A party with a *global* theory and
programme is needed, capable of unifying the many different
struggles.

Organization

Lastly, on the themes of Lenin's work in this period, a few words

8. Ibid., pp. 421–422.

about what he has to say concerning organizational issues in the narrowest sense. Here again I think there is a central point amongst some more circumstantial matters. The central point is contained in the difference he had with Martov over the definition of a party member, a difference which foreshadowed the Bolshevik-Menshevik split. In Lenin's conception, the party is not a loose, amorphous body of occasional sympathisers; it is a party of activists, or 'cadres', one which aims, in other words, to assemble a class-conscious proletarian vanguard and does not simply dissolve itself in the level of consciousness of the class as it is. But there are other organizational arguments in these works— concerning, for example, *professional* revolutionaries and strict secrecy, concerning limitations on democratic procedures— which Lenin justified by the circumstance of having to operate in conditions of political repression. For now I will say no more than that there are polemical exaggerations in them too, to which I shall return.

Luxemburg and the Young Trotsky

Leaving aside incidentals, what was the basis of Luxemburg and Trotsky's opposition to Lenin? It was the charge of Blanquism, as Luxemburg labelled it—substitutionism, in Trotsky's expression. In other words, like the Mensheviks with whom they were aligned in this matter, and like many other people since, Luxemburg and Trotsky accused Lenin of wanting to replace the struggle of the proletarian masses, to replace the *self-emancipation* of the working class, by the actions of a self-appointed elite. Was there any validity in this charge? No. In thinking to reject elitism, what Luxemburg and Trotsky were actually doing was rejecting the necessity for an organization of the proletarian vanguard, in favour of a social-democratic model of organization (in the current and not original sense of that political description). They were rejecting the sort of organization without which—the October Revolution showed positively and a string of failed revolutions has shown negatively—the revolutionary situations that recur periodically cannot be consummated in successful revolutions. So, because I am now going to make some more critical remarks and do not want to be misunderstood, I stress that *that* was Lenin's incomparable historical merit: that he conceived and fought for such an organization *tooth and nail*. Does this mean that Lenin's works in this period are a kind of compendium of pure truths and Luxemburg and Trotsky's opposition and criticism should be thrown in the dustbin? It is unfortunate, for example, that the Trotskyist movement has never republished *Our Political Tasks* although it is a very interesting book. Is that, then, the conclusion one draws—Lenin represents the truth and these other works are not worth reading? No, because the dialectic of truth and error, if I may so put it, is a bit more complicated than this.

Bureaucratization

One obvious reason why that should be so, first of all, is that it is possible to be right about some things, even about the main things, and wrong about others. Take, for example, the whole problem of the bureaucratization of workers' organizations. No-one in this epoch had an adequate grasp of it, and the merit of providing us with the basis of a theory here belongs to Trotsky, in coming to grips with Stalinism in the 1920s and 1930s. But in Lenin's work before 1914, in his constant emphasis on, and drive towards, the need for a centralized organization, there is no understanding, no inkling of a grasp of this problem: of the danger of the autonomy of an organizational apparatus, the danger of its developing its own interests, inertia and conservatism. Whereas there *is* the beginning of an understanding of it in Trotsky's writings and Luxemburg's writings before the First World War. As it has proved to be no small problem in the history of the workers' movement, Trotsky and Luxemburg should be given their due as contributors to what we would count *today* as an adequate, rounded out, Leninist theory of organization.

The Spontaneity of the Masses

There is a more tricky issue, however, in what I am calling the 'dialectic' of historical truth and error, which I will try to get at by returning to the issue of the spontaneity of the masses. Trotsky and Luxemburg, I repeat, were wrong in their opposition to

Lenin's central political project. But in their opposition and in being wrong, they also criticized—Trotsky explicitly, Luxemburg implicitly—those formulations regarding spontaneity and consciousness that I identified earlier as being one-sided: that spontaneity produces only trade unionism, that consciousness is introduced by bourgeois intellectuals. So, were they wrong in *these* particular criticisms? And if they were, was Lenin wrong when he too later acknowledged the polemical one-sidedness of *What is to be done?*[9] Was he wrong in 1905 when *he* spoke of the working class as 'instinctively' and 'spontaneously' social-democratic (that is, socialist, in the meaning of that time)?[10] Or was he wrong in 1905 to speak like this? '. . . any movement of the proletariat, however small, however modest it may be at the start, however slight its occasion, inevitably threatens to outgrow its immediate aims and to develop into a force irreconcilable to the *entire* old order and destructive of it. The movement of the proletariat, by reason of the essential peculiarities of the position of this class under capitalism, has a marked tendency to develop into a desperate *all-out* struggle, a struggle for complete victory over all the dark forces of exploitation and oppression'[11]—which could be the words of an unqualified 'spontaneist'.

Was he wrong in these things? No, he was not wrong, because what 1905 crystallized in Lenin's thinking—I do not say he had no idea of it before, just that 1905 brought it out in a very sharp way—was that beyond the necessity (a crucial necessity) of assembling, training and preparing a proletarian vanguard, successful revolution requires something else as well, the winning of the masses, and this is impossible without the explosion of vast, mass, *spontaneous* struggles, spontaneous at least vis-à-vis the revolutionary organization. From some point of view, of course, nothing is ever spontaneous. But with respect to what a revolutionary organization is capable of initiating and to the control it is capable of exercising over events as they unfold, the great struggles in the course of which the masses can be won—and institutions of dual power emerge, and a revolution be completed

9. See CW, Vol. 13, pp. 100–108.
10. CW, Vol. 10, p. 32.
11. CW, Vol. 8, p. 426.

—these are not things that can be neatly planned or controlled. They involve massive, spontaneous struggles, going well beyond trade unionism. This is complementary to what Lenin says about spontaneity in other types of situation. Luxemburg and Trotsky, in their mistaken opposition to him, grasped some of it earlier than he did. So, again, they must be given their due.

On Stick-Bending

And that brings me to the essential point I want to make in this connection. It concerns what you could call the art of stick-bending. Some people will say, indeed have said (if you want an example of what I am talking about, you can find it in Tony Cliff's book on the subject, in many ways a useful book),[12] that Lenin was not actually wrong about anything here, he was just 'bending the stick'. The origin of this lies in the fierce debates that took place over the split in the Russian party and a statement of Lenin's to the effect: the Economists had bent the stick one way—in order to straighten it out, I had to bend it back. He was admitting, in other words, to his own polemical exaggerations. Hence: Lenin was bending the stick. When it is necessary to emphasize organization, theory, and so on, you bend the stick against spontaneity. When it is necessary to emphasize the importance of the spontaneous struggles of the masses, you bend the stick another way. That, it is said, is all that he was doing; there were no actual mistakes.

Now, let us begin by conceding a certain truth in this, and that is the following: there is a kind of dialectic of political struggle, related to the aforementioned dialectic of historical truth and error, which means that inevitably a political argument, pamphlet or discourse is different—and this does have its fortunate side—from an academic discourse. It will not contain all the necessary qualifications. Precisely because the task at one moment is this and the opposition is that, exaggerations, certain kinds of one-sidedness, will occur. To stress that Lenin's work is bound to be marked by such things is obviously right. But a number of points should be borne in mind here.

12. Tony Cliff, *Lenin*, London 1975. See, in particular, Vol.1, p. 67.

First, even granting this without any sort of reservation, my central point still remains valid. Exactly for such reasons, you need to read the works of—in this case—Lenin, who in the global sense was right, so as to free what is right in them from certain exaggerations and plain mistakes surrounding it. And conversely, you need to adopt a serious attitude to the work of those who were wrong, to see whether it might not also contain some incidental insights. This already supports my main contention therefore. Secondly, however, very often in all the talk of stick-bending, it is simply hindsight that is at work. So, you have to read Lenin's *What is to be done?* in conjunction with what he wrote in 1905. But of course in 1903 his opponents were not able to read what he wrote in 1905. They had to read what he was writing then, in 1902 and 1903, and they reacted to what they saw as wrong or exaggerated in it. You must not overlook that. Thirdly, to admit the inevitability of some bending of the stick is not the same thing as having an 'anything goes' attitude towards it: so that, right, in order to win this political battle anything goes as to what may be said. What lurks behind this rather uncritical attitude is, again, the myth of the genius-leader: yes, Lenin exaggerated in 1902, but he was there in 1905 to correct any mistakes his followers had made; no need to worry consequently, he saw it all right in the end. But, of course, this will not always be true; and it carries certain dangers.

For instance, Lenin in *What is to be done?* tries to meet the criticism that his views on organization do not conform with full democratic procedures. What does he reply? He replies that full democratic procedures involve two things at least, complete publicity and elections to all offices. And he then offers two arguments, a main and a subordinate one. In the main argument he asks: can we, in Tsarist conditions, operate with full publicity and elections to all offices? And his reply is: no, it will simply facilitate the work of the police. Lenin's principal argument in other words is a circumstantial one, that such things are not possible under the conditions of Tsarism. This does not cast any doubt on the principle of internal democracy. However, in the subordinate argument he says: anyway, there will be something else operating, a strict selection of members, strict confidence amongst comrades, the greatest of dedication—and thus we will have 'something even more than "democratism"'.[13] Obviously,

13. CW, Vol. 5, pp.477–480.

that is bending the stick. Is it justified? It is not, because it suggests in a small way that, under certain circumstances perhaps, there is an adequate substitute for the principle of internal democracy. This is, I say, polemical overstatement and not Lenin's principal line of thought, but it is an example of stick-bending which is not justified.

What might be the danger? Well, in 1905, when Lenin wanted to open up the party, there being now masses of workers in struggle who were suitable candidates in his view for a much broader, more open party, he met opposition amongst Bolshevik cadres, committee men trained in the arguments of *What is to be done?*, who accused him of wanting to play at democracy. Another example from the same year: you may take the sectarian response of many Bolsheviks to those spontaneous, non-party institutions, the soviets, and ask whether that response might not have had something to do with certain of the one-sided formulations of the earlier period. And more importantly and more tragically than that, take the Stalinist use of some of these formulas to justify the crimes and horrors which everyone here knows about. I am *not* saying, in any form or shape, that there is a germ of Stalinism in the work of Lenin. What I am saying is that, in 1977, a kind of glorification of stick-bending will not do. Some qualification is required: yes, inevitably, there will be polemical exaggeration in any party or faction or tendency struggle, but it must be kept within careful limits.

The Older Trotsky

Some observations now on the older or mature Trotsky. Central to his political life and work was to build on and continue to fight for the Leninist theory and practice of organization, recognizing what I have called Lenin's *incomparable* historical merit in founding this theory and practice. But despite Trotsky's acknowledgement of his own fundamental misjudgement in the years before the Revolution, he still referred on the eve of his death to the erroneousness of some of Lenin's arguments in *What is to be done?*. This is not something you come across much: that Trotsky, in admitting his own mistakes, was not taking over lock, stock and barrel all the arguments of that work. He still referred to the erroneousness of some of the formulas about spontaneity and consciousness. And he did not totally disown his own book, *Our Political Tasks*. Though wrong in a key respect, unjust towards and misjudging Lenin, it contained, he thought, sound insights into the mentality of some of the Bolshevik committee men in that period.[14] Furthermore, I believe that Trotsky's own role after 1923 is not unrelated to the fact that he was the one outstanding revolutionary of that generation who had the independence and courage to oppose Lenin in the pre-revolutionary period. Of course, it was not only over the party but over other issues also and in which he turned out to be right. But I believe it was this very courage and independence, expressed in some ways misguidedly before 1917, that contributed after Lenin's death to the fact that it was Trotsky who came finally to recognize the mistakes which had been made, under Lenin's leadership and his own, by Lenin's party: the mistake of banning factions within the party and that of banning the legal soviet opposition at the end of the civil war—mistakes which played their part, albeit not the main one, in the demise of soviet democracy.

On the question of proletarian democracy, both internal to a revolutionary organization and within the workers' movement as a whole, Trotsky was *second to no-one*. What I have argued is that his own opposition to Bolshevism up to 1917 and then his opposition to the *cult* of Lenin after 1917 helped to determine this later trajectory of his: of laying the basis for a more rounded theory of democracy in the socialist movement.

Tendencies and Factions

I want to end with some reflections on this. So far I have stressed the need for political unification: the party as politically unifying and centralizing the various different struggles. But a vital ingredient of the Leninist theory of organization is also the most vibrant internal democracy in the party. Why? Well, you can refer back to what I have called, perhaps rather pretentiously, the dialectic of truth and error. It is because outside of Stalinist textbooks and Maoist fantasies there is no great leader who knows all the political answers. There is only one way of finding correct answers and that is through a fierce and vigorous battle of ideas,

14. See Leon Trotsky, *Stalin*, London 1947, pp. 58, 62.

lines, and so on. I shall quote Lenin to show that this is not something just put about by Trotskyists: 'there can be no mass party, no party of a class, without full clarity of essential shadings, without an open struggle between various tendencies, without informing the *masses* as to which leaders and which organizations of the Party are pursuing this or that line. Without this, a party worthy of the name cannot be built.'[15] Or look at the actual practice of the Bolshevik Party—not just in quiet periods but over matters of vital importance, matters of life and death for the revolution such as the Treaty of Brest-Litovsk—look at the vigorous battle then between different groupings and tendencies within it. It was not any over-enthusiastic militant of the Fourth International but a very sober historian, E. H. Carr, who wrote of the Bolshevik Party as manifesting 'a freedom and publicity of discussion rarely practised by any party on vital issues of public policy.'[16]

Today

So, in conclusion, the opportunity and the obligation which I say exists for those influenced by Trotsky's work is to fight for the substance of the Leninist theory of organization as *vital* to the self-emancipation of the working class; to reject contemptuously all those representations of Lenin as an unprincipled dictator who just wanted power; to reject them completely, but without any apologetics or cultism towards him.

I have spoken here of two broad ideological and political attitudes towards Lenin in this century, uncritical cultism and the portrayal of him as a totalitarian dictator. There is today a third approach, which I think one should look upon with caution and which I decline to label. Without always repudiating him explicitly, it purports to go beyond the Leninist theory of organization; but what this 'going beyond' actually consists of, its character in detail, is unspecified and rather mysterious. I will give three recent examples.

15. CW, Vol. 13, p. 159; and cf. Vol. 31, p. 427.
16. E. H. Carr, *The Bolshevik Revolution 1917–1923*, Harmondsworth 1966, Vol. 1, p. 195.

First, Ralph Miliband in an article entitled 'Moving On' writes of the need for a new organization of the left.[17] I cannot go into all his arguments but, in relation to our theme, he deals with the Communist Party and the sham of its claims to internal democracy (though already here there is the sign of something wrong in that he puts under the same heading the 'sacred cows' of democratic centralism and the ban on factions, as if they belonged together). He then speaks of the revolutionary left organizations, putting them under one umbrella and saying that their internal regimes make that of the Communist Party seem like a model of party democracy. Now, you do not have to be a genius to recognize that this refers to something real; but it is not true of all the organizations of the revolutionary left and, what is more, Miliband knows it, because I have heard him say as much in a public delivery of the same argument, in which his criticism of the British section of the Fourth International was interestingly different: this was written off on account of the large number of tendencies within it, at odds with one another. Whatever else he may want to say about it, that is something different from a rigid, undemocratic internal regime and so forth. However, this is not the main point. The main point is that Miliband speaks of 'moving on', suggesting the need for a new socialist formation after having discounted everybody else. What would its programme be? And what its structure? How would it differ from the 'out of date' Leninist vanguard? Silence! Not a word. Literally not one word. So, moving on here, this going beyond Leninism, is a complete mystery.

My second example is the French Marxist philosopher, Louis Althusser, in an interesting intervention in the recent debate within the French Communist Party over the dictatorship of the proletariat. He has a number of valid things to say about the need for real debate, but what is interesting is this: he says, differences, yes, these we must have; organized tendencies, no—though he does acknowledge, it is worth noting, that they existed in the Bolshevik Party. But no. Why? Because they are a threat to the unity of the organization. Then he goes on, 'if recognized and organized tendencies are rejected, it is not so as to fall *behind* that political practice [of the Bolshevik Party] towards less

17. Ralph Miliband and John Saville (eds.), *The Socialist Register 1976*, London, pp. 128–140.

freedom . . . it is to go *beyond* it. . . . Not organized tendencies, but'—what?—'real discussions', and 'new forms of expression', 'exchange of experience'.[18] Well, this is in some ways beyond belief. After a history of sixty years and given everything we know today about the evolution of workers' organizations, he says, differences yes, not organized tendencies but . . . real discussions. And how will you have these real discussions, how ensure them, if they cannot be organized? And if they are to be organized, how escape the absolute and vital necessity of tendencies, groupings, factions? Here you have another suggestion of going beyond the Leninist theory and practice of the party which is a sham.

My third example is from a booklet some of you may have seen, put out by the Communist University of London.[19] Gerry Leversha has an article there, 'Beyond Spontaneity', in which the Leninist type of organization is said to be unrealistic in the West. He refers to it as an elite party and then says, 'Reared in conditions of clandestinity, it relied far more upon unquestioned obedience than on equal debate.' As far as I am concerned, that is simply derisory. In speaking so, Leversha diplomatically refrains from mentioning that the party to which he belongs is actually *behind*, it falls short of, Leninist norms of internal democracy. Anyway, what does he argue for in order to transcend 'the Jacobin limitations of Leninism' in favour of 'the fullest flowering of debate . . . inner-party democracy . . . adequate channels of expression for dissenting viewpoints' and so on? How may one ensure this full flowering of debate? What mechanisms? How does the issue relate to tendencies and factions? Silence. So, again, it is a 'going beyond' which leads nowhere.

18. Louis Althusser, 'On the Twenty-Second Congress of the French Communist Party', *New Left Review*, No. 104, July/August 1977, particularly pp. 20–22.

19. Jon Bloomfield (ed.), *Class, Hegemony and Party*, London 1977, pp. 109–125.

11.

Classical Marxism and Proletarian Representation
1980

The names of Leon Trotsky and Rosa Luxemburg have often been linked, sometimes with good reason and sometimes also without. It has been said, wrongly, that they shared before 1917 a common view of revolutionary prospects in Russia, Luxemburg like Trotsky supporting the idea of permanent revolution. With better foundation it has been noted that there was, in their respective tactical inferences from the events of 1905, a shared and early awareness of the organizational inertia and conservatism then taking shape within European socialism and a like belief in the efficacy of mass struggle as the antidote to this. Partisans of the self-activity of the masses, they put their faith in it in face of the dangers of party bureaucracy.

Perhaps the most frequent association of the two revolutionaries has been by reference to the similar criticism they directed at Lenin—in the name precisely of proletarian self-activity—in 1904, following the Bolshevik-Menshevik split. That is the subject of the present essay. For, if the fact of this common criticism is widely known, the two works in which it was articulated are differentially so. The full measure and the details of their congruence have not been generally accessible because Trotsky's *Our Political Tasks* had to wait some three quarters of a century before it became available in translation in the major European languages. Until very recently what was known of it, save by a small number of scholars, was known second-hand: some of its ideas; a few quotations; one passage in particular on the logic of political 'substitutionism', oft-cited, usually from Isaac Deutscher's work.

Given the extent to which the diffusion of Trotsky's writings has depended on the efforts and resources of his own followers, the fate of *Our Political Tasks* is not really surprising. That its republication was accorded no priority stood in continuity with the reticence towards it of Trotsky himself. In fact, in the works of his later years there are only a couple of direct references to this youthful polemic. In one, he speaks of it as immature and mistaken in its criticism of Lenin, although he does allow that it justly characterized the mentality of some of the party activists of the day, for whom the principles of centralism had come to displace any need to rely upon the workers. In the other, his judgement is severe without qualification. On the question of organization *Our Political Tasks*, according to Trotsky, 'developed views very close to those of Rosa Luxemburg' and her views on organization are described by him as 'errors'.[1]

A comparison of his pamphlet with Luxemburg's *Organizational Questions of Russian Social Democracy* shows the resemblance between them to be close indeed. I shall not undertake a comprehensive account of it here but propose only to explore one important area of the common ground. My interest, however, is not in whether Trotsky and Luxemburg were in error or were justified in their criticisms, and these writings of theirs are searched neither for evidence of their shortcomings vis-à-vis Lenin nor for telling insights concerning the ulterior development of the Bolshevik Party. This is already well enough rehearsed. I want rather to identify in the positions they put forward, along with something of indubitable value, an ambiguity in the concept of party and, hence, a problem about the political representation of the working class; and to suggest that this problem, sometimes thought to be a specific feature of the Leninist idea of a revolutionary vanguard, was part of an older orthodoxy that Lenin shared with his Marxist critics. This is not, it should be said, an argument that revolutionary Marxism as such is irredeemably flawed, compromised, and so forth. It *is* an indication of matters left unsettled and incomplete in classical doctrine, even where it spoke most vehemently for socialist democracy and on behalf of

1. Leon Trotsky, *Stalin*, London 1947, p. 62; and '"Trotskyism" and the PSOP', in *Leon Trotsky On France*, New York 1979, pp. 233–34.

the self-emancipation of the working class.

We may begin from a passage of Luxemburg's *Organizational Questions*, setting out the 'contradictory' nature of the struggle for socialism: 'The world-historical advance of the proletariat to its victory is a process whose particularity lies in the fact that here, for the first time in history, the masses of the people themselves, against all ruling classes, are expressing their will. But this will can only be realized outside of and beyond the present society. On the other hand, this will can only develop in the daily struggle with the established order, thus, only within its framework. The unification of the great mass of the people with a goal that goes beyond the whole established order, of the daily struggle with the revolutionary overthrow—this is the dialectical contradiction of the Social-Democratic movement which must develop consistently between two obstacles: the loss of its mass character and the abandonment of its goal, becoming a sect and becoming a bourgeois reformist movement.'[2]

Rosa Luxemburg's use of these lines here was not her first. She reproduced them very nearly verbatim from her earlier *Social Reform or Revolution*, which was well known for its cogent statement of the anti-revisionist case.[3] We may assume that Trotsky was acquainted with them from one or both of these sources. In his own polemic against Lenin allusion is made to hers.[4] In any case, whether because, knowing them, he also had these lines consciously in mind during the composition of *Our Political Tasks*; or only because the thought they express is in effect a familiar part of the Marxist legacy, the proletariat constituting there at once offspring and grave-digger of capitalism, produced by and formed within it, but bearing the prospect of its replacement by socialism—the fact is that there is a striking parallelism in the manner whereby Luxemburg delineates the twin pitfalls of reformism and sectarianism and Trotsky puts back to back, as it were, the Russian 'economists' and those charged by him with 'substitutionism'.

2. 'Organizational Questions of Russian Social Democracy' (referred to henceforth as OQ), in Dick Howard (ed.), *Selected Political Writings of Rosa Luxemburg*, New York and London 1971, p. 304.

3. 'Social Reform or Revolution', Ibid., p. 131.

4. Leon Trotsky, *Our Political Tasks* (referred to henceforth as OPT), London n.d. (1980), p. 106. Page references are to this edition though all quotations are from an unpublished translation by Brian Pearce, for permission to use which I am grateful to NLB.

The Logic of 'Substitutionism'

He poses the issue in terms of the consciousness of the workers and their objective interest: 'Between these two factors—the objective fact of class interest and class awareness thereof—there lies a path filled with the jolts and blows of life, mistakes and disappointments, waverings and defeats. The problem of tactical wisdom for the Party of the proletariat is wholly enclosed between these two factors and consists in discovering how to shorten and make easier the path which lies between them. . . . The Party, basing itself upon *the given level of consciousness of the proletariat*, intervenes in every major political event, striving to bend the resultant in favour of the immediate interests of the proletariat and, what is even more important, striving to make its intervention a means of *raising* the level of the proletariat's consciousness. . . . The bigger the gap separating the objective and subjective factors . . . the more natural is the appearance in the party of "methods" which in one form or another represent *surrender* to the colossal difficulty of the task imposed upon us. Like the political self-denial of the "economists", the political "substitutionism" of their antipodes is nothing but an attempt by a young Social-Democratic Party to "play a trick" on history.'

Neither 'economists' nor 'politicals', according to Trotsky, really face the questions of political tactics entailed by the distance between the proletariat's consciousness and socialism. The 'economists' only register its subjective interests, leaving everything else to the natural course of events; thus, trail along behind it and march '*at history's tail*'. The 'politicals' begin from its objective interests and, confident in their knowledge of them, act in place of the class and attempt 'to transform history *into their own tail*'.[5]

Luxemburg for her part, it may be remarked, hard by the lines I have reproduced from her article, chides Lenin and his supporters in very similar terms, writing sarcastically, '. . . the "ego" of the Russian revolutionary . . . declares itself once again as the all-powerful director of history'; she speaks of it also as having 'played more than one trick' on the socialist movement in Russia.[6] However, more important than such incidental echoes is a deeper

5. OPT, pp. 74–77.
6. OQ, pp. 305–6.

thematic correspondence. In the contexts in which these passages from Luxemburg and Trotsky are respectively embedded they can be seen to be associated with the same theoretical message. It may be formulated in three linked pairs of oppositions purporting to contrast Lenin's with a more adequate standpoint.

The first and most obvious of them, no longer very interesting perhaps for having been gone over many times, is summed up in a slogan from *Our Political Tasks*: 'Long live the self-activity of the proletariat—and away with political substitutionism!'[7] About this let it suffice to say that Luxemburg and Trotsky alike accuse Lenin of a sectarian error. In the political space—defined by both of them in an idiom of forward movement—between the proletariat, its consciousness and its struggles, on the one hand, and the final socialist goal, on the other, they accuse him of being too remote from the former out of a certainty of standing for, and knowing how to reach, the latter. Thus where, for Luxemburg, the socialist movement is the first historically to count on 'the organization and the independent direct action of the masses' and 'there is no ready-made, pre-established, detailed set of tactics which a central committee can teach its Social-Democratic membership as if they were army recruits', Lenin's views, she suggests, do precisely presuppose an 'omniscient' and 'infallible' central committee.[8] For Trotsky, likewise, 'the guarantee of the stability of our Party must be sought in its basis, in an active and self-acting proletariat', and he protests against the 'utterly fantastic' and 'purely rationalist' conception according to which its development is to take place 'solely through the logical extraction, by a central committee. . . , of new tactical and organizational conclusions from certain theoretical premises.'[9]

The second contrast is but the institutional correlate of this first and opposes the requirements of socialist democracy to those of Leninist organizational centralism. The opinion of Lenin's critics about his centralism is, again, familiar enough not to have to be laboured here. The best-known lines of *Our Political Tasks*—envisaging the successive 'substitutions' of, first, the Party organization for the Party, then, the central committee for the Party organization, and finally, a dictator for the central

7. OPT, p. 72.
8. OQ, pp. 288–89, 305–6.
9. OPT, pp. 95, 2.

committee—follow immediately on the passage depicting political 'substitutionism' and 'economism' as twins.[10] Rosa Luxemburg's thoughts about what she calls 'ultra-centralism' are no different, its spirit being according to her a 'sterile', policing one: to control the Party; to narrow the movement rather than develop it.[11] As to the appeal to norms of socialist democracy which both she and Trotsky make against Lenin, it is, familiar as it may also be, the problematic area forming the main concern of this article and will be examined once we have at our disposal further argument which is germane to it.

For it is best approached in fact by way of the third and last of the aforesaid oppositions, one that has received much less attention than the others as far as I know. We may speak of it as contrasting a *historical* with a *formalist* political conception. I take the terms of the antithesis from Trotsky, but let us see first how it is expressed by Luxemburg. She attacks the notion that opportunism can be regarded simply as an alien presence within the labour movement, introduced there by forces that are representative of the bourgeoisie. She does concur with a definition of it according to which opportunism undermines the class independence of the proletarian movement, serving to subordinate it to bourgeois interests and ambitions. She concedes also that one of its sources is the large number of non-proletarians that gravitate to Social Democracy in a decomposing capitalist society, though she goes on to add that Social Democracy must not turn them away but learn how properly to integrate them and their dissatisfactions within a revolutionary socialist politics. However, she insists that opportunism has an additional source in the very nature of the struggle for socialism, as it is set out by her in the passage we have taken as our point of departure. If, in Marxist terms, the irreplaceable foundation of that struggle is the 'will' of the working class, a political will that is only formed and can only develop in the framework and the conflicts of bourgeois society, then this is bound to leave its mark, negatively as well as positively, on the course of the struggle itself. Imposed or merely encouraged by the initial, capitalist framework, there will be both misconceptions and mistakes. The socialist movement has to learn through hard experience.

10. OPT, p. 77.
11. OQ, p. 295.

Lenin's Subjectivism

This is, if you want, a 'dialectical' thought, and where it occurs in *Social Reform or Revolution*, it is supported by the passage from Marx's *Eighteenth Brumaire* on the relentless self-criticism integral to the proletarian revolution. In any event, on the basis of it Rosa Luxemburg reproaches Lenin for the 'totally ahistorical illusion' that opportunist errors can be averted once and for all. Although Marxist theory certainly furnishes powerful weapons against them, they arise 'from social conditions', those surrounding a mass movement. Seen in this light 'opportunism appears as a product of the labour movement itself, as an unavoidable moment in its historical development.' In Russia it is very much a result of the 'tactical groping and experimentation' inevitable in difficult political conditions. It is therefore astonishing, says Luxemburg, 'to think that . . . one could prevent the appearance of the opportunist current through this or that paragraph of the party constitution', exorcise it 'by means of a scrap of paper'.[12]

The same theme is to be found in the young Trotsky more fully elaborated. Already in 1903, before the appearance of Luxemburg's and his own texts here being compared, his report on the Second Congress of the Russian Party at which the Bolshevik-Menshevik schism had occurred made reference to Lenin's 'sterile formalism'. In part, what Trotsky meant by the term was the sort of thing we have just seen Rosa Luxemburg deploring: the 'bureaucratic dream' of achieving through the Party rules a 'statutory remedy for opportunism'.[13] But more generally he had in mind a whole sectarian posture which too one-sided a reaction to 'economism' had tended to produce. Responding to 'economism', in particular to its closeness to the day-to-day concerns of the workers, as to a pure and simple error, Lenin's supporters had been led, he thought, to espouse only the forms and not the substance of revolutionary politics and organization. As he put it, 'for many comrades, both "politics" and "centralism" still have only *formal significance*, as the mere antitheses of "economism" and "amateurism".' Political agitation dealt largely in conventional formulas 'too little linked with the

---

12. OQ, pp. 301–5; and see 'Social Reform or Revolution', p. 132.
13. Leon Trotsky, *Report of the Siberian Delegation*, London n.d. (1980), p. 21. See the remarks in note 4 above which apply here too.

actual life and everyday demands of the working masses'; centralism also was seen by these comrades abstractly, as a self-sufficient form instead of as the 'synthesis of local and general organizational tasks'. Suggesting that amongst the Bolsheviks was to be found a number of former 'economists', who had thus merely exchanged their original mistaken abstraction for its inverse, Trotsky summed up this line of reasoning in the following way: 'Whereas previously, in the period of "economism", these comrades could not or would not link the trade-union and group interests they served with the general tasks of class politics, which they ignored, now, in the era of "politics", they are showing themselves incapable of linking the tasks of revolutionary political struggle, to which they give formal recognition, with the immediate, everyday demands and, in particular, with trade-union and sectional needs. Whereas previously, in the era of "amateurism", they could not or would not link in their minds the detailed tasks of local work with the need to create a fighting central apparatus for the Party as a whole, now, in the full flood of "centralism", they completely leave out, in their discussions and decisions concerning this apparatus, all the *practical complexity and concreteness for the Party* of the tasks to which this apparatus must adapt itself, the tasks for the sake of which it is created. And this is why . . . the rectilinear, that is, purely formal, "centralism" of Lenin found among its most decided supporters . . . some of yesterday's "economists".'[14]

The Historical Roots of Opportunism

There should be no need to emphasize the homogeneity between the foregoing arguments from Trotsky's report and the manner in which we have already seen him talk in *Our Political Tasks* about 'substitutionism'. For, he characterizes this similarly as an attempt to bring forward 'the abstract force of the class interests of the proletariat' in lieu of 'the real force of a proletariat conscious of its class interests'; outlining, by contrast, a conception in which political development takes place 'only through the reciprocal action of "will" and "consciousness"' as he puts it—that is, 'when, on the basis of the level of consciousness achieved, we

14. Ibid., pp. 18–20.

organize, by appropriate tactical methods, the political will of the class.'[15] What may, however, be worth digressing to point out is the line that runs between this particular preoccupation of two of his earliest political writings and a central theme in the programmatic document written by him more than thirty years later for the founding conference of the Fourth International.[16] Because in the first case Trotsky writes against Lenin, whereas in the second he writes as a convinced Leninist, it is easy and has been a common practice, especially amongst his own followers, to overlook the continuities between these anti-Leninist texts of the earlier period and some of his later ideas. This is a mistake. Here, for example, there is a strong continuity in both the content and the terms of the reasoning as, in youth and maturity alike, he urges the indispensability of seeking the links between revolutionary programme and organization, on the one hand, and the immediate demands and popular consciousness of the working class, on the other.

Focusing again now on the third of our oppositions, between formalist and historical conceptions, a good part of the burden of *Our Political Tasks* is that Lenin and his supporters neglect this, the supremely difficult tactical problem, believing, in sectarian spirit, that political wisdom and success are vouchsafed to them by their Marxist doctrine. Trotsky, needless to say, does not challenge the merits of the latter. But he does impugn any claim to their exclusive possession and, like Luxemburg, he questions above all the idea that Marxism might constitute a full and permanent defence against political error. Indeed, some of the most cogent passages of his text, relevant and resonant beyond their own immediate historical context, touch on these matters. In its internal conflicts to date, he contends, the different groupings in Russian Social Democracy have all appealed to the class interests of the proletariat as their legitimating criterion—the tribute paid by a section of the revolutionary intelligentsia to Marxism—and the recurrent theme has been condemnation of adversaries for an 'unconscious betrayal of the proletariat' in favour of bourgeois interests. Whilst, according to Trotsky, such common appeal to one recognized value has had a certain posi-

15. OPT, pp. 77, 47.

16. See Leon Trotsky, *The Transitional Program for Socialist Revolution*, New York 1973, pp. 75, 108–9.

tive, regulative function, enabling the existence and overcoming of difference without division, nevertheless the precise method of mutual criticism is a 'primitive' one. One tendency 'anathematizes' another; each sees its predecessor as 'nothing but a gross deviation from the correct path . . . a bundle of errors'. It is in this connection, against the habit of simply sweeping aside whole political trends, that he commends what he calls 'a *historical* standpoint' in questions of internal party development.[17]

It is not that Trotsky, for his part, denies there have been mistaken political trends. We have seen the reproofs he directs at both 'economists' and Bolsheviks. But he identifies the conditions for their mistakes in the historical experience of the Russian movement, thus defines a sense in which they were necessary mistakes, and, as well as warning where misguided trends, unchecked, might terminate, he indicates such valuable features of that experience as they express—the arousal by the 'economists' of 'broad strata of the proletariat' and their work amongst the masses, even if it was not yet socialist political work; *Iskra*'s determined fight, which in time spawned the exaggerations of Bolshevism, to win a part of the intelligentsia for Marxism and the interests of the proletariat, even if this work was not yet directly aimed at the proletariat itself. The calls simply to 'liquidate' one or another recent tendency must, Trotsky says, be rejected as jeopardizing a political culture painfully acquired. On the other hand, 'Every period develops its own inertia and tries to foist its own tendency upon the movement as a whole.' This is where diversions and mistakes must occur, and the movement be endangered if it is not alert to the problem: a worthwhile but limited political quality is improperly accentuated or prolonged, exceeds its legitimate sphere or outlives its usefulness. In Trotsky's words, '. . . every *partial process* in the general class struggle of the proletariat . . . produces its own immanent tendencies: its methods of thinking, its tactical procedures, its specific slogans and its specific psychology. . . . Every partial process strives to go beyond the limits set by its nature and to impose its tactics, its way of thinking, its slogans and its morality upon the entire historical movement which has called forth this partial process. The means is turned against the end, the form against the content...'[18]

17. OPT, pp. 8–12.
18. OPT, pp. 16, 30–31, 38, 94 and *passim*.

Now, this whole dialectic, of experience, experiment and error, of critical adjustment and correction in the light of them, of misconceptions generated by the social environment and mistakes that are due to the inertia of the movement itself, our two authors champion against Lenin in the name of a more historical sensibility than he allegedly displays and as though, bent on control of Russian Social Democracy, he was ignorant of or, perhaps, just wilfully blind to it. There are many who will agree that so he was. There are, equally, those who will doubt or deny it. Irrespective, however, of whether he was an appropriate object of this censure, there is a point in the stance adopted by Trotsky and Luxemburg that bears close scrutiny, a point at once valuable to any contemporary Marxist reflection on socialist democracy and seriously limited by an orthodoxy of its own time.

In contrasting their own with Lenin's attitude to, respectively, 'economism' and opportunism, Trotsky and Luxemburg are speaking of reformist tendencies deeply antipathetic to their natures and which they reject categorically as misconceived. By their own theoretical lights, these are political tendencies that, pressed to the end, must lead their proponents to break with the proletarian cause or the proletariat itself into bourgeois paths and away from socialism.[19] Yet criticizing as one-sided and ahistorical any characterization of the currents in question that stops at this, the two unite in refusing to regard them as just a foreign or treacherous element in the workers' movement. Mistaken they are, but they are its own mistakes; a part of its own experience and not just something alien, some illegitimate intrusion. Mistakes are the movement's right and its destiny also, since it is set about by obstacles of every kind, material, political and ideological, and its path cannot but reflect their presence. We may put this in another way. Such tendencies may be wrong, diversionary, unwarranted exaggerations of a partial truth or what have you when tested against criteria of Marxist theory, and in so far as they are not only theoretical abstractions but also actual currents of political opinion, be simultaneously a legitimate part of the workers' movement. In this sense, the order of theoretical knowledge and the order of political belief and alignment are distinct. Differences in the second must be resolved through processes of debate and competition and by practical political experience.

19. OPT, p. 9, OQ, p. 301; and see also 'Social Reform or Revolution', p. 130.

They cannot be settled by the authority of a profounder knowledge, be it real or only claimed, by bureaucratic regulation from above, be this ever so scientifically informed. The only truly authoritative resolution is democratic.

Marxist Pluralism

I extrapolate here, in other words, a pluralist principle. This is a Marxist conception of working-class democracy allowing for points of view other than one's own and even though they may be thought either tendentially or actually to compromise the very goal of socialism. I shall not argue for the pluralist principle, but simply lean on the record of 'actually existing socialism' which speaks eloquently enough in its behalf as a negative example, and on a considerable literature in moral and political philosophy which supports it more directly. That such support has frequently been associated with defences of private property does not invalidate the principle nor devalue it where, as in the present case, the perspective it belongs to is clearly socialist. It is distinguishable from any vindication of capitalism; no worthwhile form of democracy is possible if it is not respected. What I want to explore is the institutional embodiment envisaged by Trotsky and Luxemburg for this democratic and pluralist principle both of them invoke in their criticism of Lenin. What actual institutional norms, if any, do they propose—concerning the organization and representation of the working class, accountability of political leaders, and so on—which might help to lend a more discernible shape to their broad commitment?

In the first place, and predictably given the polemical context, both put forward what they consider to be a healthier concept of Social-Democratic centralism than Lenin's, arguing that it must be founded on the will and initiative of the party's rank-and-file membership and not on mere dictates sent down from some leading body. Luxemburg says it can be based neither 'on blind obedience, nor on the mechanical subordination of the party militants to a central power'; that it 'is, so to speak, a "self-centralism"', the 'rule of the majority within its own party organization'; that it has 'a co-ordinating, synthetic character and not a regulative and exclusive one'.[20] Trotsky deprecates the kind

20. OQ, pp. 289, 290, 295.

of thinking in which the 'summit' of the organization 'becomes the centre of Social-Democratic consciousness, with, under this centre, disciplined executants of technical functions', and maintains against it that any non-autocratic centralism 'presupposes *active participation by all members of the Party in general Party life*'.[21]

Then also, in the second place, Trotsky has something schematic to say about the nature of proletarian democracy in the period of socialist transformation. Referring to the experience of the Paris Commune, he talks of the political power of the working class as involving a cultivation of 'the habit of exercising constant, active control over all the executive personnel of the revolution'. He is explicit here, moreover, about the pluralist requirement. In connection with protesting against Blanquist organizational concepts and a Jacobin notion of dictatorship, he comments on the 'colossal' social, economic and political problems that will be thrown up by the dictatorship of the proletariat and continues: 'The tasks of the new regime will be so complex that they cannot be fulfilled otherwise than by competition between different methods of economic and political construction, by prolonged "controversies", by systematic struggle—not only between the socialist world and the capitalist world but also between different tendencies within socialism, tendencies which will inevitably appear as soon as the dictatorship of the proletariat gives rise to tens and hundreds of new problems for which no-one has ready made solutions.'[22] In Luxemburg's essay there are no comparable remarks on the physiognomy of proletarian rule, though these do, as it happens, anticipate sentiments that she was to express in 1918 and, by an irony the historical reasons for which are well enough known, address to Trotsky himself, as well as to Lenin, as follows: 'The tacit assumption underlying the Lenin-Trotsky theory of the dictatorship is this: that the socialist transformation is something for which a ready-made formula lies completed in the pocket of the revolutionary party. . . . This is, unfortunately— or perhaps fortunately—not the case. . . . New territory. A thousand problems. Only experience is capable of correcting and opening new ways. Only unobstructed, effervescing life falls into

21. OPT, pp. 87, 112.
22. This section of Trotsky's pamphlet is omitted from the English edition. See L. Trotsky, *Nos tâches politiques*, Paris 1970, pp. 198–202.

a thousand new forms and improvisations . . . corrects all mistaken attempts.'[23]

The Party: Two Ideas

However, if we leave aside what our protagonists were to write later and dwell upon 1904, then it has to be said that, beyond the above very general indications, the only institutional provision they make can be encapsulated in a phrase: namely, '*the* Party of the proletariat'. I emphasize the article because that is how Trotsky and Luxemburg think of the matter; despite the pluralist commitment, singularly, *a* proletarian party as representative of the interests of the working class. It is a way of thinking and a diction that has been endemic in Marxism since its inception. It runs from Marx and Engels into intellectual habits of the present day, even ones quite free of any suspicion of a Stalinist influence. As I mean to put it in question, I had better delimit in advance the exact scope of my intention and so avoid any confusion of it with another sort of criticism.

My point is not to suggest that classical Marxism entailed a monolithic view of proletarian rule, that Marx, Engels and their immediate followers embraced a conception of the transition to socialism which left no room for political opposition, difference of opinion and dissent. They did not. As we have seen, Trotsky speaks plainly to the contrary and there is no reason to regard his idea as atypical. It has been said often, and rightly, that nothing in this tradition committed its authors to the notion of the single-party state. However, neither did anything spell out the requirement of a plurality of parties and there is, accordingly, a virtual silence on the issue. It may be reasonable, in that situation, for *us* to construe pluralist reflections like those I have quoted from Trotsky as allowing for organizational multiplicity. But it is impossible to overlook the circumstance that the Marxists of his epoch did not themselves habitually think in terms of such multiplicity and that the overwhelming weight of what they said lay, rather, upon unity of organizational focus, identifying representation of the interests of the working class with one political

23. 'The Russian Revolution', in Mary-Alice Waters (ed.), *Rosa Luxemburg Speaks*, New York 1970, p. 390.

party. Various considerations may be urged, historical, political and ideological, as to why this should have been so and the identification not, in context, objectionable or malign. But the locutions which it generated are associated, now, with another, repressive conceptual and political universe in which serious injury to the cause of socialism has been done. It is therefore proper that Marxists should look upon them critically, recognizing not only what produced them historically but also their theoretical limitations.

There is a familiar point in this. It has become a commonplace that amongst the several matters Marx did not speak much or in detail about must be counted the period of the dictatorship of the proletariat. In this he was more or less followed, until 1917, by his disciples and their motives were the same as his, that is, anti-speculative ones. There is, thus, nothing especially novel about pointing out a theoretical gap where the exact modes of proletarian representation are concerned. Today, however, no-one can continue to trade on the anti-speculative impulse as a reason for not attempting to make the lacuna good. Nor should anyone accept without close scrutiny whatever classical Marxism did bequeath on the problem of political representation and, in particular, a way of thinking and talking about it in unitary terms. For, a whole historical experience casts back sharp and questioning light on to the area of doctrinal deficiency by having offered a bureaucratic and authoritarian solution to that problem. One of our questions has to be whether some old intellectual and linguistic reflexes do not disclose a conception of workers' democracy which, understandable in its own historical time, must be viewed as too constricted nevertheless.

It may be objected that no univocal idea of party should be laid at Marx and Engels's door when the corpus of their writings displays, in fact, such fluidity of usage. Only during their lifetimes, it has been noted, did the modern concept of a political party take shape and they themselves used the term in a number of different senses.[24] But I do not suggest that there is just one usage in their work, only that a usage of interest in the context of

24. See Monty Johnstone, 'Marx and Engels and the Concept of the Party', in Ralph Miliband and John Saville (eds.), *The Socialist Register 1967*, London, p. 122; and David McLellan, *The Thought of Karl Marx: An Introduction*, London 1971, p. 167.

the present article can be argued to originate with them. Two amongst their meanings of party are relevant to the argument and they are neatly distinguished by Marx himself in a letter of 1860. Writing that after the dissolution of the Communist League in 1852 he 'did not belong any more . . . to any organization whether secret or public', he says that in that sense the party ceased to exist for him eight years previously. He goes on to add, however, that the League itself 'was only an episode in the history of the party which grows everywhere spontaneously from the soil of modern society' and he explains that, in this case, he means 'party in the great historical sense of the word.'[25] Let us then register these two meanings, a broad historical and a narrower organizational one. The broad can evidently encompass a plurality of particular organizations. It denotes a whole side, so to speak, in a large historical contest and the institutional embodiment of the party may here be multiplex, as well as changing over time. By contrast, in the other, narrower usage, it is rather a specific political organization that is referred to. Now, I think that there are to be found, in the thought of Marx and Engels, the premisses to encourage a slide between these two meanings, so that party in the narrow sense comes to stand for party in the broad and what is thus a part of the working-class movement to be taken for the whole of it.

Vanguard and Party

I shall seek to isolate them by inviting attention not, in this instance, to a personal letter but to that most public of documents, the *Communist Manifesto*. The relevant passage is a celebrated one in which the founders of historical materialism define the relationship of the Communists to the working class as a whole and, on the face of it, it goes directly against the case here being made. For, it does speak precisely of 'other working-class parties', insisting that the Communists do not form a 'separate' one, 'opposed' to them, or have interests 'separate and apart from those of the proletariat as a whole', or promote 'any sectarian principles of their own'; their conclusions only express 'actual relations springing from an existing class struggle'. These senti-

25. Marx to Freiligrath, in McLellan, pp. 173–74.

ments are part and parcel of an anti-sectarian, anti-'utopian socialist' outlook which Marx and Engels upheld their whole lives long. But the crux of this matter is what is said then to distinguish the Communists from the other working-class parties and that is: that, across the different national struggles, they stress 'the common interests of the entire proletariat' and, in various stages of the struggle against the bourgeoisie, 'represent the interests of the movement as a whole'; that, consequently, they are 'the most advanced and resolute section of the working-class parties' and possess the theoretical advantage 'of clearly understanding the line of march, the conditions, and the ultimate general results of the proletarian movement'.[26] The Communists are distinguished by being, in a word, the vanguard.

Once again, I must try to secure my argument against possible confusion with another that is common. In itself the idea of a proletarian vanguard does not necessarily carry with it any authoritarian or substitutionist logic. When coupled with the anti-sectarian emphasis which was one with the central theses of historical materialism at the moment of its birth, this idea is subject to a permanent democratic control. Socialism is the outcome of tendencies inherent in capitalism and, in particular, of the struggles of the working class, or else it is just a dream—the scheme of 'this or that would-be universal reformer'.[27] What is claimed for the putative vanguard, for a section of the working class already active politically, organized and aware; the objective interest it professes to look to and the political knowledge it purports to deploy; these are not, therefore, a truth to be imposed upon the workers willy-nilly, but something they will, it is held, discover in time for themselves through their own political experience. The claim has to be vindicated politically and representation of the workers democratically won.

However, in any historical circumstances, the association of a vanguard role with a single political tendency or organization is a much more dubious matter. For, it encourages two complementary assumptions each of which is highly questionable. The first is that one such current could represent, adequately and completely, the interests of the working class as a whole and not

26. 'Manifesto of the Communist Party', in Karl Marx and Frederick Engels, *Collected Works*, London 1975 ff., Vol. 6, pp. 497–98.
27. Ibid., p. 498.

need the critical opposition of other currents to help remedy omissions, emerging rigidities of political outlook or response, plain mistakes; or could command a type of knowledge always sufficient to its tasks. The second is that a vanguard need not be politically diverse, its functions shared, as it were, amongst a number of tendencies, all aiming to speak or even speaking for proletarian interests but divided along other lines; and relating to one another in a variety of ways, possibly as separate sections of one party, possibly as different parties in a united front, now as parts of a governing revolutionary coalition, now as competitors within the democratic structures of a proletarian state.

I have no wish to visit these assumptions on Marx and Engels, as in this form for sure they did not hold them. It must, nevertheless, be said that the claim made for the Communists in the *Manifesto*, for all its genuine modesty on one level, is a large one indeed and prone to be reproduced decked out with the two assumptions in question. From Marx and the Communist League to the present day, what single individual, political tendency or organization has understood, *clearly*, 'the line of march' *and* 'the conditions' *and* 'the ultimate general results' of the proletarian movement? Even the greatest respect for the historical contribution in this regard of Marx and Engels themselves, of Lenin and the Bolshevik Party in his lifetime, of Rosa Luxemburg and Leon Trotsky, cannot disguise that it is an implausible claim, and this for the sort of reasons we have seen stated here by the last-named pair, but which were stated also before them, in a different political idiom though no less eloquently or compellingly for being so, by John Stuart Mill.

Unfettering Socialist Democracy

Let us return now to Luxemburg and Trotsky and see how things stand with what both think of, and Trotsky repeatedly refers to, as 'the Party of the proletariat'.[28] As one would expect, there are statements which define the character of Social Democracy in terms that can be traced back to such passages from Marx and Engels as have been quoted above. According to Luxemburg, Social Democracy 'is called upon to represent...the totality of

28. OPT, pp. 7, 61, 123.

the interests of the proletariat as a class'; again, it 'is the representative of the class interests of the proletariat.' Its 'truth', says Trotsky echoing the *Manifesto*, is 'merely the theoretical expression of the broadening and deepening class struggle of the proletariat'.[29] But the equation of part with whole, Social Democracy with the workers' movement, is now a much clearer presence. Thus, in response to a notorious assertion from Lenin's *One Step Forward, Two Steps Back*, Luxemburg argues that 'Social Democracy is not bound up with the organization of the working classes; rather it is the very movement of the working class.'[30] Trotsky makes this same identification a matter of definition. Alluding to a formulation from the manifesto adopted by the First Congress of the Russian Party, he writes, 'It could not be better put. Social Democracy "*consciously wants* to be and to remain" the class movement of the proletariat...both yesterday and today, Social Democracy consciously wanted and still wants "to be and to remain" the class party of the proletariat, that is, to be itself: Social Democracy.'[31]

We must keep in mind here the broad, historical meaning of party since it is probable that something of it still attaches to these ways of talking about Social Democracy. It is clear in any event from their context that neither Luxemburg nor Trotsky mean by them to press for any rigid exclusivism, to confine the movement narrowly to one homogeneous political current. The very opposite is the case, and what they say construable in the generous sense: Social Democracy is large enough to embrace a political diversity. Still, even if it is true that they continue in some measure to think of the party of the proletariat in the 'great historical' meaning, the fact remains that it also has for them another connotation and this is the narrower, organizational one. For, they treat Social Democracy as a unitary political structure and defend the principle of centralism which makes it so. Whatever their other differences with Lenin, Luxemburg and Trotsky do not contest this issue. She sees the 'strong tendency toward

29. OQ, pp. 287, 303; OPT, p. 123.
30. OQ, p. 290. Lenin's assertion: 'A Jacobin who wholly identifies himself with the *organization* of the proletariat – a proletariat *conscious* of its class interests – is a *revolutionary Social-Democrat*.' See V. I. Lenin, *Collected Works*, Moscow 1960–1970, Vol. 7, p. 383.
31. OPT, p. 8.

centralism' in Social Democracy as following from the centralizing processes of capitalism and the bourgeois state, he argues
that 'organizational centralism is a powerful weapon of the *class*
struggle of the proletariat.' She speaks in this connection of 'a
unitary, compact labour party', he speaks likewise of 'a single
fighting Party organization'.[32] When all is said and done, therefore, representation of proletarian interests has come to be associated with one political organization and a party in the narrow
sense to 'usurp' the title of the broad, 'historical' party of the
working class.

A sense of historical proportion and political realism will be in
order finally. There are, first, straightforward empirical circumstances to explain in part the singularity of reference in these
usages of party. Where, as in Russia, there was not yet a socialist
organization commanding the allegiance of masses of the working
class, it was quite natural to talk of creating one, *a* proletarian
party; or where, as in Germany, there was such an organization
but only one, to talk of *the* proletarian party. Secondly, the
conception of a unitary party in itself expressed no aversion to
socialist pluralism or diversity, only an aspiration towards the
maximum unification and co-ordination of proletarian forces in
face of the centralism of the modern bourgeois state. However,
two things need to be said in this regard. One is that, while this
principle of co-ordination is perfectly valid for any effective
revolutionary strategy against the centralized political instruments of the bourgeoisie, it is not at all clear that its universal
form must be a single socialist party rather than an alliance of
such parties. The conception of one party should not be allowed
to become so ideologically regulative as to exclude this latter
possibility and, hence, the idea of a multiplex proletarian vanguard, a political representation channelled through more than
one working-class organization. The other thing is that socialists
need always to take care not to set up as a hard pattern of thought
what is prompted by some present reality, for as often as not this
will reflect a historical limit. So it was with 'the party of the
proletariat'. In most countries it described a historical experience.
But to generalize or make normative a conception in which
representation of proletarian interests is the business of one

32. OQ, p. 287, and see also pp. 285–86; OPT, p. 105; *Report of the Siberian
Delegation*, p. 38.

political organization is to put an artificial and potentially danger-ous limit on the scope of socialist democracy. Factions within one party are potential parties, tendencies potential factions, inchoate groupings potential tendencies—by a well-known logic the limits can begin to narrow. If its claims to go beyond bourgeois democ-racy are good, the norms of socialist democracy must allow, in unambiguous terms, for organizational pluralism. Under capital-ism, this means that no socialist tendency should pretend to any political monopoly. When the bourgeois state is overthrown, it means that there must be room for any organization that will respect a properly constituted democratic and socialist legality.

12.

Literature of Revolution
1978

Are we sensible enough of all the sources of our own literary heritage? The question is suggested to me by some of the writings of the young Trotsky. Upon reading them, it is quickly evident, even from the accessible fraction of a much larger output belonging to the years before the October Revolution, that here is one rich source. Where is its wealth appreciated? Naturally, anyone in the least familiar with Trotsky's life's work will know that within his wide range of concerns the literary-artistic occupied a prominent place, as they will know also the power and quality of his best writing. His biographer, in a work whose own towering literary achievement is undiminished by the passage of a decade and a half since its completion, gives due space and attention to these facets of Trotsky's personality. Others besides Isaac Deutscher have commented on the excellence of his prose.[1] And yet such is the imaginative force of some parts of Trotsky's early work, and so compelling their narrative drive, it is difficult to avoid the feeling that, as a contribution to revolutionary literature, they have not yet been properly valued. This appears to be a paradox, so let us explore it. I am not now speaking about the strictly scientific value of these writings, about their strengths and deficiencies as political theory or historical analysis (or, for that matter, literary criticism), although even in this respect many things still need to be spoken. Nor is it a matter of focusing, narrowly, on the nature of Trotsky's prose style, his manner of

1. See Perry Anderson, *Considerations on Western Marxism*, London 1976, p. 100.

construction or exposition. The question as to what is literature may be a particularly thorny one but I mean simply to draw attention to the way in which, in some basic sense at least, the techniques and inspirations of creative literature inform the productions of the young Trotsky in his activities as historian and journalist, revolutionary theoretician and polemicist. Theoretical analysis, historical narrative or political characterization may be illuminated by a sudden, compressed image. The language of Marxist objectivity (not, of course, the same thing as neutrality) is doubled by the vivid recreation of some lived experience, the subjectivity, so to speak, of that objectivity. Global historical forces in movement are set off against a small detail of individual humour or tragedy. A personal portrait is given depth by the invocation of impersonal structures. The results are usually effective and sometimes stunning: for each strained or misplaced metaphor, each occurrence of some exaggerated literary flourish —for these there sometimes are—there is many another passage of fine and whole conviction. One result, in particular, is that the book *1905*, as well as being a political text of capital importance, is a great book of the revolutionary experience of that year. Of lesser scope and maturity than Trotsky's subsequent *History of the Russian Revolution*, dwarfed by the massive stature of that work, it nevertheless displays many of the same qualities, and it does for 1905 some of the things that the *History* does for 1917, proffering, to be sure, a theory of the unfolding events, sketching the outlines of a history of them but, over and above this, communicating an acute *sense* of them.

Beyond a Boundary

Let me then pose another question, the answer to which I really do not know. When one speaks of revolutionary literature or art, when, as Marxists and socialists, we seek to define a tradition in this matter, to appraise its elements or provide a theory of its nature, is the view cast sufficiently wide that it will encompass also such elements as might lie beyond the boundary of works of literature and art in the strict sense? Can it take in not only Brecht but also Marx, Trotsky as well as Eisenstein? Even in the sober, matter-of-fact idiom of Lenin, a world away from the creative drama or fiction, one can be startled on occasion by the appearance of an unexpected image, telling in its own specific way beyond the possibilities of prosaic argument: as, for example, when towards the end of the relentlessly detailed polemic of *What Is To Be Done?*, Lenin abruptly unlocks a window from the Russian underground on to a more open revolutionary horizon by picturing himself at a party conference stoutly defending his right to dream; or when, in a swift phrase in *Two Tactics*, he encapsulates an essential truth about revolutions, calling them 'festivals of the oppressed'.[2] In any case, it is out of a conviction that Trotsky's early work, whose devices are far richer, contains as well as politics, theory, history, also some of the ingredients of a genuine *literature* of the socialist movement, above all and as certainly as any fictional construction, of a literature of revolution, that I am tempted into this essay of appraisal. Whatever may be the general answer to the questions just posed, the suspicion is a nagging one that, as they concern in particular the young Trotsky, the response is largely negative. Few would seek, or expect to find, here a valuable aesthetic source.

The reasons for this are not very difficult to identify. If we examine for a moment the other case, alluded to above, lying beyond that tightly-drawn boundary of creative literature, the case, namely, of Marx, things stand rather differently. So great today is the intellectual authority of the man that even those in the process of breaking from revolutionary politics seek for a shred of justification in his work, while others more distant still from Marxism will concede to him every sort of merit other than the essential ones. One of them is a powerful artistic vision and this has been widely acknowledged. It is impossible to read Marx's *magnum opus*, whatever difficulties it might otherwise present, and fail to be impressed by his rich satirical gift, by the cumulative impact of his documentary description and by his arresting use of metaphor and imagery.[3] The impersonal interplay of commodities with commodities, of capitals with each other, and the crushing weight of this world of automata are conveyed there with a force that puts to shame many a contemporary drama of human alienation. Marx's scrupulous depiction of the living and working

2. Lenin, *Collected Works*, vol. 5, p. 509; vol. 9, p. 113.

3. See Isaac Deutscher, 'Discovering *Das Kapital*', *Monthly Review*, December 1967, pp. 22–4; and Adèle Geras, 'The Language and Imagery of Capital', *Monthly Review*, November 1972, pp. 19–29.

conditions of labouring men and women, a vivid sketch of hell, belongs to a long line passing through such points as Engels' *Condition of the Working Class in England* and Jack London's *People of the Abyss*, Zola's *Germinal* and Upton Sinclair's *The Jungle*. Each type of discourse is clearly an important strand within a socialist literary tradition. But so, equally clearly, should be what one might call a discourse of the mass workers' movement, of its periods of calm and defeat as of those of stormy upsurge, of its vast organizations, of its leaders and of its masses. For this one has to look beyond Marx's time. Where Marx is revered or at least respected, Trotsky on nearly every side has been regarded with some mixture of hostility, contempt and ignorance. The phenomenon reaches far beyond the confines of a hard-nosed Stalinism of the 'old' sort into the consciousness even of some of the most independent thinking socialists. Amongst people who have been unwilling to approach Trotsky's political contribution to the workers' movement with the conscientious principle and seriousness which it merits, it is not surprising if a literary dimension of his earlier writings has been of no great interest.

However, a combination of reasons, good and not so good, may have been responsible also for its relative neglect by those nearer Trotsky's politics or more sympathetic to his person. Among the good, one can count the fact that, taken as a whole, the works of Trotsky's maturity do unquestionably overshadow those of the pre-October period and were bound, accordingly, to attract greater attention sooner. Their theoretical and political importance was of the most pressing immediacy. The effect, on supporters and sympathizers, of Trotsky's own ambivalent attitudes towards his anti-Leninist past ranks perhaps as a much less convincing argument for such a neglect of its products (as reflected, for example, in the large quantity of this material that has yet to be translated from Russian into the other major languages). Anyway, what follows is a small attempt to redress an imbalance. The scope of this essay is strictly circumscribed. It does not offer a detailed appraisal of the young Trotsky's political record, much less one of his subsequent career. It is not concerned with a general reconsideration either of his merits and achievements as a revolutionary or of his failures and political errors. In its broad outlines there is, evidently, a view of Trotsky involved here, one which I have made no effort to hide. But the substantive preoccupation of this essay is only a particular aspect of his politics as reflected in a part of his early work, namely, the quality of his writing. Trotsky being who he was, this is not, of course, a 'purely literary' enterprise, if such a thing is possible in any case. Important political themes and philosophical positions, concerning the modalities of political action, the nature of proletarian revolution, the human content of the struggle for socialism, and much else besides, are crucially at issue. However, they are treated in their relationship to the central question as I have presented it, the question of Trotsky's contribution to the literature of socialism. Such a focus is of interest and importance surely even for those, like myself, unfamiliar with any formal canon of literary criticism.

Tolstoy and Adler

Trotsky, then, is at work. He is discussing Tolstoy on the latter's eightieth birthday. Where Marx and Heine, he says, still appear contemporary with his own generation, this actual contemporary is already cut off from it by the flow of time. He pictures him, at first, as 'an enormous jagged cliff, moss-covered and from a different historical world'. Then, evoking that historical world, Trotsky quickly restores Tolstoy to his real physical, and social, setting. He grew up 'in an atmosphere of the old nobility, among inherited acres, in a spacious manorial home and in the shade of linden-tree alleys'. The 'short and narrow path' from the manor to the peasant's hut Tolstoy, the artist, trod lovingly before Tolstoy, the moralist, turned it into 'a road of salvation'. At the source of his creative being he is, according to Trotsky, an aristocrat. His is the world of landlord and muzhik; he hates the turmoil and disintegration brought by new social relations, the hum of city life. Although no apologist for serfdom, his heart belongs 'there where life is reproduced changelessly from one generation to the next', and this is reflected in the 'aesthetic pantheism' of his best work, *War and Peace*, as in his 'calm, unhurried, frugal' style. During the course of this appreciation, we are told of Tolstoy's abode: 'In the ancestral home of the Princes Volkonsky, inherited by the Tolstoy family, the author of *War and Peace* occupies a simple, plainly furnished room in which there hangs a handsaw, stands a scythe and lies an axe. But on the upper floor of this same dwelling, like stony guardians of its traditions, the illustrious ancestors of a whole number of generations keep watch from the walls.' It is, says Trotsky, an inverted symbol of Tolstoy himself. On 'the summits of consciousness' there lies a moral philosophy of the simple life and submergence within the people; below, at the origin of emotion and volition, the influence of the ancestors continues to make itself felt.[4]

Now Trotsky is describing Victor Adler, the leader of Austrian Social Democracy. He makes the scantest overt reference to Adler's 'opportunism'. He presents a shrewd politician of penetrating, analytic mind and a man of warmth and great charm. Disturbed early one Sunday morning during an election period, after a hectic speaking and editorial schedule the previous day, Adler is grumpily helpful to the young Russian arriving penniless in Vienna. Trotsky highlights his pragmatism, a flair for tactical improvisation and the diplomacy of compromise, a disrespectfully ironic regard towards all rigidity of principle and doctrinairism. Adler wants to drain dry all the possibilities of each political situation. He is deeply sceptical of attempts at objective prognosis. Trotsky recounts an incident. At the Stuttgart Congress of the Second International in 1907, an Australian trade unionist 'who turned out to be a mystic (this happens with the Anglo-Saxons)' reported having had a vision of the advent of social revolution in 1910. In translating, the French interpreter 'magnanimously' omitted the prophecy, while the 'honest German' said there had been a lot of rubbish at the end of the Australian's speech. Afterwards in the lobby, Victor Adler for his part joked that he preferred such forecasts to ones based on the materialist conception of history.[5]

Another occasion: we are on the threshold of the courtroom, about to be conducted by Trotsky into the trial of the Petersburg Soviet. Behind, there lie the sweep and the excitement of revolutionary days, ahead, the examination of charges of insurrectionary conspiracy. 'The indictment', says Trotsky, 'reflects the revolution in the same way as a dirty puddle in a police station

4. 'Tolstoy: Poet and Rebel' (1908), in Leon Trotsky, *On Literature and Art*, New York 1970, pp. 127–35.

5. 'Victor Adler' (1913) in Leon Trotsky, *Political Profiles*, London 1972, pp. 11–20.

yard reflects the sun.'[6] Or else he is discussing the professional intelligentsia, wanting to convey the spiritual as well as material dependence on bourgeois society of managers, doctors, professors and lawyers. An electrician, he tells us, can remain himself, installing wiring day after day in the offices or bedrooms of ministers and bankers. But it is different for the doctor 'who is obliged to find music in his soul and in his voice which will accord with the feelings and habits of these persons.'[7]

An idea is clothed in an image, some attributes are condensed into an event. From the generality or abstraction of an argument we are referred to a tangible, or visible, or audible, manifestation of its point, to a sense of time or an atmosphere of place. This concrete and specific mode does not replace the argument, standing in as it were for an absentee. It adds another dimension to it. The distance between the actualities of popular revolution and their police concept Trotsky expands at length as well as focusing it, nicely, in a pool of dirty water. His discussion of the intelligentsia has its complexities and qualifications, not to say its disputable propositions. But who has not heard the music? By the conjuring of physical, sensible images, sometimes metaphorical, sometimes realistic, Trotsky helps to fix in the mind of his readers an aspect of his subject matter, to enrich their understanding of political fact or literary artefact. He presents not only the evidence and the logic of an exposition but also a many-sided picture of its object, not a bare list of political characteristics but a human character in its own environment. The imposing, formidable stature of Tolstoy, and his survival from another historical time, are conveyed by Trotsky in one image of ungoverned nature. The space and the rhythms of *War and Peace* are related by him to the acres of an aristocratic estate and its rhythms through many generations of the Russian nobility. They are related but not reduced. He does not, once again, bypass the necessary effort of argument, an appreciation of the book's content and themes and pace, in trying to get at a sociological situation of its author. He analyses these. He does not abolish the independent existence, the 'autonomy' of the work of art. Very much to the contrary, he is acutely sensitive to its materiality as a

6. Leon Trotsky, *1905* (on the composition of this work, see the text to n. 37 below), London 1972, p. 353.
7. Leon Trotsky, *The Intelligentsia and Socialism* (1910), London 1966, pp. 9–11.

product. In his own words, 'It is a terrifying thing to say, but [Tolstoy] rewrote his colossal book *seven times*.'[8] Such facts of production no less than scenes of Tolstoy's life enter analysis of the manner in which *War and Peace*, slowly and massively, unfolds its 'limitless panorama'. However, no aversion from the supposed sin of historicism prevents Trotsky from attempting to portray the living being whose work this is. He scans the surroundings for us in a search for elements both of the artist's creative make-up and of his politico-philosophical allegiance, and he fastens the relationship between the two into a metaphor, taken from these surroundings, of the upper and lower floors of the ancestral home.

In this sort of way, what Trotsky succeeds in presenting acquires both depth and extension. It is a fully three-dimensional whole viewed from a shifting perspective where, little by little, more of the features under observation are disclosed. The diary he kept much later on records Trotsky's suggestion that 'only a participant can be a profound spectator',[9] and in his own best literary efforts it is as if he wanted to impart, together with his information, some sense of participation. It is so with Victor Adler. In the foreground of his portrait Trotsky places the political dimension—to which I too will shortly advert—Adler's political history, position and capacities. But he wants us also to 'know' Victor Adler: not in the philistine sense of knowing the 'real person' behind the political mask, a sense according to which one's politics are, for some extraordinary reason, extraneous to one's integral being; in the sense of being acquainted with the way in which the man bears himself, in his relationships political or otherwise. Thus we watch the 'Doctor' (this was Adler's familiar name, Trotsky tells us, drawing on other, kinder associations with the medical profession than those we just encountered). 'Round-shouldered', weary, grumbling mildly but sympathetic, he opens his door to the young Trotsky on a quiet Sunday morning in Vienna early in the century. Or he is at a congress of the International, amidst the several, national delegations, making an ironic remark which expresses something of his manner and something of his political outlook.

8. 'Tolstoy: Poet and Rebel', p. 132.
9. *Trotsky's Diary in Exile, 1935*, London 1959, p. 48.

Political Character and National Setting

I have begun from the somewhat primitive dialectic that contrasts the abstract with the concrete and the general with the specific. As I pursue my theme these pairs will recur but without always holding fast. They change their aspects and we meet new, but related couples: the great, historical movement and the small, local part; impersonal forces and human meanings; political tendency and psychological type; a fortitude, or fatalism, of the intelligence and an impatience of the will; the inert structures of order and the 'chaos' of change. On occasion the couples change partners. It is probably banal, from the point of view of any sophisticated aesthetic, to lay stress on a contrast between the great and the small. All the same, Trotsky employs this technique to good effect. It is not a matter here, evidently, of a purely formal device or mere literary artifice. It suits the whole cast of Trotsky's intellect, first as materialist, then as participant and activist. Equally at home whether trying to place a political fact or episode within its overall historical context, or bearing witness personally to the particular effect of a more profound, structural cause, he expands or shrinks, suddenly, the focus of attention. Sometimes he will hold larger and smaller aspects simultaneously in view.

Adler's political character, for example, he implants within the Austria of the Habsburgs. It is no accident, he proposes, that this formless country with so many national divisions, in which 'all the cards are so chaotically shuffled by the play of the historical process', should have produced a leader with such an 'ability to take into account empirical, temporary and particular combinations in political development'. The Austrian connection is not forced upon Adler but elicited. He himself, it is reported, has had frequent occasion to observe how thankless is the craft of the political prophet in Austria, and has even gone so far as to surmise that some insight into its disorder might have been vouchsafed to him by his psychiatric training. Nor is Trotsky proposing, in this, some sort of rigid geographical determinism of fixed, national types of political leader. He evokes a political setting and then indicates—no more—one kind of characteristic response to it. In fact, he also suggests another and opposite response, in the person and character of Kautsky. Formed within the same setting of disparate social realities, where 'the task of political generalization is extremely arduous', Kautsky learned to eliminate from his field of vision 'everything particular, secondary, accidental', to hold his 'capacity for abstraction in a state of perpetual tension', and consequently he has no rival in his ability to draw from the empirical turmoil of history its fundamental tendencies. Taking this path, he moved on, Trotsky reminds us, to Germany whilst Adler 'let all his roots become knitted into Austria.'[10] Trotsky's portrait of the very different personality of Jaurès is also set against the background of a national tradition. In two detailed sketches, one written before, the other during the First World War, he depicts 'a man of great dimensions' and a life of 'volcanic moral passion'. Trotsky builds by the cumulative association of many elements: identifying Jaurès's fundamental traits—'an impatient active idealism', 'a sort of infantile athletic sincerity'—offering a view of his powerful presence on the platform, emphasizing now his 'incomparable' oratory, now his zealous pursuit of backstage agreement in parliamentary corridors, alluding to his involvement, even here with the fervour typical of Jaurès, in the politics of opportunism and compromise, giving details of a conventional personal biography, describing his *un*compromising, intensely active commitment over the Dreyfus case. The energy, enthusiasm and temper of this figure, his tirelessness and the breadth of his ideals, the magnetic force and ample scope of his character, are brought together into a cogent, integrated whole. Trotsky begins his first sketch by seeking a source of Jaurès's political strength, beyond the politician's own inner resources or the influence of his party, in the revolutionary traditions of France. These traditions, he argues in an interesting passage, residing in material institutions and the consciousness of individuals but also, more deeply, at the level of the unconscious whence they return periodically to the streets from which they have been driven, are a real factor in French political life, bestowing on the workers' movement an influence incommensurate with its level of organization and parliamentary representation. This large, heroic heritage serves also to accentuate the degree and to define some of the specific quality of Jaurès's strength.[11]

Of examples of the opposite adjustment in perspective, where Trotsky will narrow down rather than enlarge the scale of things

10. 'Victor Adler'.
11. 'Jaurès' (1909) and 'Jean Jaurès' (1915), in *Political Profiles*, pp. 23–40.

so as to illustrate with a small, often personal detail, some greater historical point, there are plenty in the pages of *1905*. There is one chapter where he deals briefly with the 'moderate' opposition, discussing the short-lived sympathy of some of the organizations of capital for the workers' demands, the feebleness of Russian liberalism, the vacillating enthusiasm for the revolution of the radical petty bourgeois intelligentsia. At a certain point, he suspends the political narrative to recall a visit he made during these revolutionary days to the middle class family home of an acquaintance. The dialogue which he relates sums up all the man's political ambivalence, both his inclination towards the revolution's lofty ideals and the cautious, hesitant spirit of it. Regarding the Social-Democratic party with 'a mixture of worship and dread', the acquaintance wonders about committing himself to it—'Well . . . how does one really join?'—but draws back in the face of the situation's uncertainties.[12]

Russian Liberalism

Trotsky's attitude towards Russian liberalism, it is well known, was anything but warm. In open polemics he would employ against it as often as not the weapon of a harsh sarcasm or contempt; responding to Struve's mistimed declaration, just before 'Bloody Sunday' 1905, that Russia had no revolutionary people, with the suggestion that the words should be engraved upon his forehead did it not already resemble a tombstone covering other failed ideas;[13] or remarking later with regard to Menshevik expectations of the liberals: 'Without giving way to feelings of national pride, we can assert that the brief history of Russian liberalism was unparalleled in the history of the bourgeois countries for its intrinsic shoddiness and concentrated imbecility.'[14] In the context of historical narrative, and in keeping with its different aim, Trotsky is less brutal. Although not pretending by a long chalk to any impartiality, he adopts a milder, astringent rather than overtly mocking, tone. As with the

12. *1905*, pp. 157–65.
13. 'The Events in Petersburg' (1905), in Irving Howe (ed.), *The Basic Writings of Trotsky*, London 1964, p. 63.
14. 'The Proletariat and the Russian Revolution' (1908), appendix to *1905*, p. 293.

conversation just mentioned, he does not disguise his distance from those of another political hue but he tries to provide a view of them from where he stands, some psychological insight into their conduct as well as political analysis and criticism. There is another report, of an extraordinary episode this, in which Trotsky uses a personal experience to effective illustrative purpose. It is preceded by an account of a vigorous strike movement in November 1905, in protest against government repression of mutineers in the army and navy. The strike has spread to all major factories and plants in Petersburg, there have been tumultuous meetings, the Soviet has passed defiant resolutions, all as 'a cry of solidarity hurled by the proletariat over the heads of the government and the bourgeois opposition to the prisoners in the barracks'. The influence of the campaign within the army has been such that it has even touched its aristocratic officers. In dramatic contrast to what has gone before and with characteristic humour, Trotsky then recounts his attendance as a 'workers' speaker' at an unprecedented military gathering held during this period, where we encounter representatives of the moderate opposition. The venue is the home of a certain baroness, he is greeted there by a doorman who takes his coat and he is asked by a footman for his visiting card. Proferring his invitation to the meeting instead, he is conducted into the elegant company of officers and ladies who are being addressed by various journalists and radical lawyers. One liberal speech Trotsky reports as being 'dull and limp, the thoughts expressed . . . short and limp, and the applause at the end . . . limp too'; a professor hesitating between liberalism and Social Democracy talks 'about everything and nothing'. When Trotsky speaks, he says the workers and, with them, liberty are unarmed, and suggests to the officers that they should hand over the keys of the nation's arsenals at the decisive moment. 'It was the first, and probably the last time in my life that I had to address an audience of such a kind.'[15]

However, I shall leave the expansive images of freedom and movement and humour that belong to 1905, as well as some of horror, to later consideration. In the literary output of the young Trotsky they hold the same place of honour that the year itself occupies in his early political life. 'The Marxist politician', he

15. *1905*, pp. 166–77.

once remarked, 'feels that revolution is his natural element,'[16] and the force with which this remark was true about himself is evident not only from his own central, creative role in two revolutions but also in the dynamism and intensity which he imparted to the literary representation of revolution. When the workers began to move *en masse* Trotsky, indeed, was on his own favourite terrain. Nevertheless, let us first pursue him one step further in his portrayal of individual socialist leaders. Doing so will reveal both an image of inertia and an interesting, recurrent theme of restlessness, against which the better to appreciate the momentum of 1905.

Bureaucratic Immobility

Adler we saw rooted within Austria, but it is not a unique or one-dimensional historical location. As well as invoking the national milieu, Trotsky also carefully places him in his day-to-day political habitat, at the heart of a powerful organizational apparatus that at once 'links the leaders with the masses and . . . separates them from the masses.' Restraining and refracting the workers' passions, according to Trotsky, it accommodates within its structure not only 'living embodiments of the energy' of the proletariat but also elements 'too remote' from it, bureaucrats 'ready to counterpose their little ideas' to the development of the class struggle. Adler is represented as skilfully governing the play of different forces. He responds sensitively to the moods of the working class, deftly negotiates the pressures of differing tendencies and opinions. But with the growth of the party, his time is more and more consumed by the work of the leadership: tactical and parliamentary problems, complicated administrative tasks and political bargaining behind the scenes. His journalistic and agitational activity falls off and his main strength, a profound tie with the masses, is compromised as his direct contact with them is restricted.[17] What we encounter here, together with the political role of Victor Adler, is Trotsky's perception of a threat of immobility carried in the organizational routinism and bureaucracy of the socialist parties, a perception recorded in numerous

16. 'Our Differences' (1908), appendix to *1905*, p. 305.
17. 'Victor Adler', pp. 13–16.

passages of his early work, probably the best known of them being that in *Results and Prospects* where he explicitly projected the possibility that the 'inertia' and 'conservatism' within these parties might render them 'a direct obstacle' in the way of open revolutionary struggle.[18] This was not a freak insight on his part, merely one variant of a periodic line of thought, revealed as early as 1904 in *Our Political Tasks*. He had already affirmed there that the 'accumulated wisdom' of the older socialist parties often hindered the elaboration of novel political methods and, at a couple of points, he put forward the idea of 'the means turning against the end', each political period generating routines, tactics and an outlook which, becoming set, then tended to impose themselves upon the workers' movement beyond the limits of their own usefulness.[19] This represents, of course, a political rather than literary point. The manner in which it pervades Trotsky's early writings furnishes, perhaps, one clue to the fact that later it was precisely he who formulated a Marxist theory of the problem of bureaucracy within the workers' movement; he was, too, less disposed to any *religion* of the party when a whole generation of militants was going down on its knees before just that.

However, the theme also has its literary aspects. By its pervasiveness, it touches many of the images with which Trotsky tries to fix the reality of European Social Democracy, images of stasis or sluggishness, occasionally of embattlement, in any case of something other than an impetus to action. This is true, oddly enough, even when, against his own partial insights and in line with the illusions of the Marxism of that epoch, he puts an unqualified plus beside the organizations in question. Thus, in a short eulogy written on the occasion of the death of Paul Singer, co-chairman of the German Social Democracy, he refers to this party as 'a magnificent fortress of the proletariat' and recalls Singer's part in the work of erecting it, 'stone by stone'. Paying tribute to his diligence and thoroughness, his attention to detail and his unremitting, methodical effort on the party's behalf, Trotsky also points to his appreciation of the importance to the working class of 'every position where it can dig in, unfurl its

18. Leon Trotsky, *The Permanent Revolution and Results and Prospects* (1906), London 1962, p. 246.

19. Leon Trotsky, *Nos tâches politiques* (1904), Paris 1970, pp. 54, 73, 148.

banner and reinforce itself for further progress'.[20] Again, discussing the constraints of discipline imposed by Social Democracy upon the individualism of intellectuals coming into its ranks— 'sometimes in respect of their "opportunism" . . . sometimes . . . of their excessive "radicalism"'—Trotsky depicts the individual face to face with a 'colossal structure of working-class democracy . . . a solid apparatus at the head of which stand honoured veterans, of recognized authority'.[21] In the substance of passages like these there is no trace of critical distance on his part. Yet nor is there, in their imagery, any sense of revolutionary mobility. In each case, as fortification or gigantic construction, the organization, so to speak, 'stands', in place but inert. In fact, the direction of Trotsky's thinking here is presented most clearly of all through another metaphor deployed by him to deal with the relationship between political organization and mass movement; he was later, in some famous lines of the preface to his *History of the Russian Revolution*, to take up this metaphor again in modified form to express the same relationship. As he puts it in his treatment of Adler: 'The leader of a modern European workers' party is the nub of a powerful organizational apparatus. As with any mechanism this is in itself static and does not create energy: only its purposeful application can provide it. At the same time it can frequently present obstacles. In all great historical actions the movement of the masses has above all to overcome the dead inertia of the Social-Democratic organization. Thus, the living force of steam has to overcome the inertia of the machine before it can set the flywheel in motion.'[22]

Political Impatience

In the light of this it is quite surprising that Trotsky, in some degree sharing with Rosa Luxemburg, after the Russian revolutionary experience of 1905, her awareness of the limits to the

20. 'Paul Singer' (1911), in *Political Profiles*, pp. 3–5.
21. *The Intelligentsia and Socialism*, p. 7.
22. 'Victor Adler', p. 14. In the subsequent use of this metaphor Trotsky wrote, 'Without a guiding organization the energy of the masses would dissipate like steam not enclosed in a piston-box. But nevertheless what moves things is not the piston or the box, but the steam.' Leon Trotsky, *The History of the Russian Revolution*, Ann Arbor n.d., p. xix.

established routines of European socialism, should not have taken her part when she broke with Kautsky in 1910. The fact is that he did not. Nettl cites a letter written by him to Kautsky in August of that year, in which Trotsky attributes Luxemburg's positions to 'her noble impatience'. It is, he admits, 'a very fine quality' but not something to be adopted as a guiding principle by the German party.[23] How could he have have failed to recognize in Luxemburg's mass strike agitation an effort to overcome the very tendencies of inertia and conservatism that he too had identified? Was it for him, perhaps, just an example of that 'excessive radicalism' of the intellectual in need, quite properly, of organizational restraint and discipline? However it may be, we find Trotsky caught up here in a web of curious and revealing ambiguities. Their abiding theme is precisely impatience. But he detects this behind political errors, or supposed errors, of an entirely opposite character and, moreover, he displays a different attitude, negative or positive, depending upon whether it is the error itself or its psychological dimension that is to the fore.

The characteristic of impatience we have just seen qualified as noble and very fine in the case of Rosa Luxemburg's mass strike tactic. Trotsky was also wont to represent it as a feature of Social-Democratic opportunism. However, it is impossible to overlook the indulgence with which he generally viewed it even then, when seeing it not in a tactical difference over the potentialities for revolutionary mobilization but in tendencies of reformism and integration alien to his whole political being. This was so with regard to the urge he ascribed to Adler 'to seize each historical moment by the throat' and exhaust its possibilities,[24] and it is very prominently so in his portrait of Jaurès. For, seeking there the 'psychological knot' which can tie Jaurès, the heir of a heroic tradition that is expressed through an immense personal vigour and idealism, to Jaurès the parliamentary operator, engineer of the backstage deal and the 'ambiguous compromise', Trotsky finds it in the fact that he is essentially a 'figure of *action*'. At the expense very often of the longer historical perspective and his own 'higher aim', he is too thoroughly engrossed in the task of the

23. 'Letter to Kautsky' (1910), quoted in J. P. Nettl, *Rosa Luxemburg*, London 1966, vol. 1, p. 433. Nettl surmises that Kautsky probably borrowed his own characterization of Luxemburg's positions ('rebel's impatience') from this letter.
24. 'Victor Adler', p. 16.

moment, 'wholly and completely here amid the evil of the hour' expending 'his passion, energy and talent with such a spontaneous extravagance, as if the outcome of the great struggle of the two worlds depended on each political question' taken on its own. Born for great times, Jaurès's misfortune according to Trotsky was to have been in political life during a long period of reaction. He lacked 'the ability to *wait*', so added his enthusiasm and capacity 'to go through to the end' to the politics of compromise.[25] Now, plainly in these instances, Trotsky's tone is informed by the keen admiration he felt for both Adler and Jaurès, his political differences with them notwithstanding, and this needs to be borne in mind when taking note as I have of his favourable regard for the trait of impatience even when present in some political error. There is in fact a text in which the two things, trait and error, are brought together by him into a wholly negative picture, the polemical object of this being the more mediocre Menshevik figures of Cherevanin and Martynov. In their case too Trotsky speaks of opportunism's 'inability to wait', only, with a somewhat different inflection: it is, he says, 'devoured by impatience . . . It hurls itself avidly upon the dung-heap of liberalism . . . implores it . . . appeals to it . . . It rushes from place to place, grabbing possible allies by their coat tails . . . it rushes to the government, pleading, arguing . . .' All of which seems clear enough. Yet something interesting then occurs. Not five pages later, Trotsky casts his mind for contrast back to the 'great founders of Marxism', in particular to a correspondence thick with their 'anticipation of revolution'. This anticipation he qualifies as 'tireless'. But as though prompted by an unconscious desire to remind himself that the attribute generally keeps such, more dignified political company, he cannot refrain from qualifying it also as 'impatient'.[26]

It is only a word, but the word is a sign. In its recurrent and ambiguous role, announcing an impulse, usually but not always benign, behind widely different political choices, many but not all of them mistaken, it is the visible representative of another, larger 'ambiguity' if such this can be called. Rosa Luxemburg next to Adler and Jaurès; radicalism beside opportunism; a quick will to action at the heart of political error; the restraints of

25. 'Jaurès', pp. 23–7.
26. 'Our Differences', *1905*, pp. 300–1, 304.

organization embodying history's slower necessities, amongst them the goal of revolution; but then: bureaucratic inertia against the sources of revolutionary mobility; Marx's impatient expectation of revolution and the 'obstacles' presented by Social Democracy; the nobility of Luxemburg's radical impatience as against the undignified frenzy of Menshevism's opportunist impatience . . . subjacent to these several oppositions are two sides of the political soul of Leon Trotsky, Marxist and revolutionary. The two sides are related intimately—not externally but internally. The Marxism, like every authentic one, is not only objective and theoretical but also committed and revolutionary, the revolutionism not only activist but also theorized. Still, they are not identical, and in an unceasing dialogue they interrogate one another, the voice of history, its accent on objective conditions and laws, and the voice of revolutionary engagement stressing a will and the need for action. Now one and now the other is heard more clearly and, refracted on the instrument of Trotsky's political judgement, they resonate in different ways depending on the object of the discourse. In the generosity towards a certain type of political impatience there speak the exigencies of struggle, a will to contention, the urgency of liberation, a protest against the unyielding facticities of a history with its own time. There speaks, surely, some of the specificity of the young Trotsky's own political persona, part of himself recognized and then represented in other of the political figures of his age: an active, restless instinct full of energy, even exuberance, and of a readiness to do battle; a keen alertness to all signs of movement, sharpened by the knowledge that structures of inertia may not rest upon any longer rhythm or necessity of history but only on bureaucratic prejudice, privilege and routine. In the chastisement, on the other hand, of the assorted mistakes of impatience, are heard the legitimate, materialist claims of an objective historical process, a resistance to those who would cheat it one way and another, a care for the historic goals and interests of the working class in their integrity, as lodged putatively within its own class organizations. Against the advancement of aims not yet within reach or an unseemly haste to compromise and abandon them because of their distance, are affirmed the necessity and ability to wait.

'Fatalism'

Fatalist endurance and impatience face to face: the dialogue drops out of politics into the cosmos where it merges with a larger human theme. Two voices are again audible as they echo back and forth, the one of an animate, suffering, striving humanity, the other an advocate of vaster forces, themselves impersonal and mute. In one of his first published pieces, written at the age of twenty-one, Trotsky proclaims why for him, as a man, world history should be all-important, 'everything'. It is the arena in which a human future 'of beauty, joy and happiness' will be won. It is a terrain of battle and of hope. On the scale of eternity, by contrast, he knows it to be a 'negligible' quantity and the earth just a 'miserable ball of dust and dirt'.[27] Or, as he also says in counterposing the conviction of the materialist to Tolstoy's faith in a God of love, in human society and the human individual there is 'only a particle of the universe, subject to general laws'.[28] In this perspective, history represents the sphere of human need, human effort and human meaning within a boundless, unrelenting cosmos whose only deity—if I can take the liberty of speaking in this way about an outlook free of any trace of theism—is a being that is utterly indifferent.

By a shift of significance, however, it is history at other times that becomes the relentless, inexorable force. At best people act as its 'executive organ',[29] at worst it is a foe to their purposes. In that case, by devices of personification and reification, Trotsky will conjure up another being, actively cruel and pitiless now, still not a God of love. For political mistakes it exacts its due of living flesh, like Shylock;[30] those who look back, as does the bourgeoisie in retreat from progress, it strikes 'like Lot's wife . . . with a fearful punishment'.[31] Inherently ambiguous then, a vehicle of both hope and death, history evokes from its subjects a

27. 'On Optimism and Pessimism; on the Twentieth Century and on Many Other Issues' (1901), in Isaac Deutscher (ed.), *The Age of Permanent Revolution: A Trotsky Anthology*, New York 1964, p. 40.
28. 'On Tolstoy's Death' (1910), in *On Literature and Art*, p. 145.
29. 'La douma et la révolution' (1907), appendix to Alain Brossat, *Aux origines de la révolution permanente*, Paris 1974, p. 269.
30. Leon Trotsky, *Rapport de la délégation sibérienne* (1903), Paris 1970, p. 60.
31. 'A "Declaration of Rights" and a "Velvet Book"' (1901), in *Trotsky's Writings on Britain*, London 1974, vol. I, p. 40.

double, contradictory language, of impatient protest, or of fortitude biding its time. In this wider, universal space, also, Trotsky
makes use of the two idioms. Sometimes, it is the vocal impatience
and revolutionary humanity that ring out: 'The whole of history is
an enormous machine in the service of our ideals. It works with
barbarous slowness, with insensitive cruelty, but it works. We are
sure of it. But when its omnivorous mechanism swallows up our
life's blood for fuel, we feel like calling out to it with all the strength
we still possess: "Faster! Do it faster!"'[32] On other occasions he
will sound a quieter note, one of resignation without defeat, of a
readiness and the stamina to endure while larger, impersonal
forces work themselves out. Not surprisingly—and what speaks
here is some of the specificity of Trotsky's political *fate*—this
note is often associated with the circumstances of deportation and
exile.

Thus, on his way for the second time into the remoteness of
Siberia, condemned to it for his part in the Soviet of Workers'
Deputies, Trotsky writes to Sedova, his wife and companion. The
letters are posted by sympathetic soldiers in the escort. Being
conveyed daily further north together with the other prisoners,
also members of the Soviet, he is destined for Obdorsk inside the
Arctic circle. They travel by sleigh, too slowly. 'Luckily the frost
is not very severe—20, 25 or 30 degrees below zero', but there are
'no newspapers, no letters, no news of any kind'. After travelling
for a month they still have no clearer idea of what their place of
exile will be like. Trotsky wonders if escape will be possible or if
he must wait for the revolution to turn his release 'from a
technical question into a political one'. If necessary he will sit and
wait, and work; from Sedova, he requests 'books and newspapers,
newspapers and books'. Who knows how long he will have to
wait? He asks her whether she regards such thoughts as too
fatalistic. 'Dear friend,' he observes, 'when one is travelling to
Obdorsk under escort there's no harm in a little fatalism.'[33] (As
it happens, not long afterwards he executed a daring, lonely
escape.) Twenty-two years later, in the opening pages of his
autobiography, Trotsky will echo this thought liberating it from
the wry understatement and the geography. In Turkey, 'camping
—but not for the first time—and patiently waiting for what is to

32. *1905*, p. 351.
33. Ibid., pp. 401–13.

follow', he will make its application general, maintaining: 'The life of a revolutionary would be quite impossible without a certain amount of "fatalism"'; and 'I know well enough, from my own experience, the historical ebb and flow. They are governed by their own laws. Mere impatience will not expedite their change . . . To understand the causal sequence of events and to find somewhere in the sequence one's own place—that is the first duty of a revolutionary.'[34]

1905

When we turn to Trotsky's account of the year 1905, the whole scene changes. The same dialectic of the human and the impersonal may still preside. Indeed it is here, on the broadest, as it were most open, social stage that the conception and its artistic execution are the most compelling. The rumble of great, objective causes and effects is punctuated by live notes of subjective

34. Leon Trotsky, *My Life*, New York 1960, pp. xiii, xix. Is it necessary to say that the themes being pursued here have nothing whatever to do with certain well-known 'criticisms' of Trotsky concerning impatient ultra-leftism and 'fatalistic Marxism'? The credibility of criticism in this mode must be gauged against the fact that its purveyors in the socialist movement have been unable to date to put together *one* appraisal of Trotsky with the accuracy, scruple and thoroughness to withstand close scrutiny. This is not a question of pretending that Trotsky was immune from political mistakes. But they can be stated with exactitude and care. Generic charges, *de rigueur* since straight slander fell into disuse, and purporting to compromise all of Trotsky's political activity as a revolutionary, charges like ultra-leftism, fatalism, economism (this last, from certain quarters, supposedly connecting him with the Stalinism he fought so long; for these superficial oppositions can so often conceal, don't you see, the signs of a deeper complicity), these are worse than useless—they are intellectually derisory. For the rest, I will just add that the literary side of Trotsky's work indicates not, yet again, deviation and sin, but together with more important evidence, the subtlety and richness of his Marxist understanding. The density of *literary* texture, with its manifold levels of reference, reflects an underlying *conceptual* wealth. Resistant to all the reductionisms alleged against him, Trotsky ranged over many areas of knowledge and aspects of human existence in an effort thereby to fathom the complexities of history: taking in class structure, political movement, national tradition and personal character, setting the politics of today beside the literature of yesterday and the aspirations of tomorrow, seeing in the present struggle not only its immediacy and urgency or its obstacles and delays, but also its historical development and material basis, also the human qualities brought into play there, and then the cultural specificities defining its peculiar character as well as the universal preoccupations beneath its surface. That is more than all the Pharisees can contend with.

experience. Individual action and incident throw their light on to the social forces in motion. The story of revolution gains depth, solidity and colour, as well as a powerful narrative thrust, from the ceaseless, fluctuating encounters between historical law and human volition. But all the signs over people and things are now clearly different. Restlessness is no more of the will. It is in the facts. The voice of 'fatalism' is still heard from time to time but it speaks other lines. History, elsewhere blocked against revolutionary engagement, presents to it a more hospitable aspect here, not the empty stillness of the Siberian landscape, not the silence of a Sunday in Vienna or the slow, mechanical routine of a bureaucratic organization, but a noisy, thronging movement, vast yet of abundant detail, replete with moments of heroism and drama, of humour, incongruity and life. I said earlier of *1905* that it merits a position of honour in the young Trotsky's literary output. Others have commented in passing on its excellence. The first volume of Isaac Deutscher's trilogy, although drawing on some of its episodes for the chapter covering Trotsky's part in the revolutionary events, contains no discussion of it, but in an extensive critical appreciation of *My Life* and *The History of the Russian Revolution* in the third volume, Deutscher remarks that Trotsky's descriptions of 1905, showing early the promise of his subsequent achievement as the historian of October, 'provide till this day the most vivid panorama of that "general rehearsal" for 1917.'[35] Edmund Wilson expressed a similar view, writing of *1905* as 'a brilliant forerunner' of the *History* and of its 'dramatic sense of life'.[36]

Despite the stylistic features common to both works, in overall design *1905* does not have either the continuity or comprehensiveness of the *History*. It is not a systematic narrative of the revolutionary events throughout the Russian Empire. The first and longer part of the book covers the development, and ultimately defeat, of the revolution as such; the second deals with the trial of the Soviet, then exile and escape. Geographically, the first part is concentrated mainly, but not wholly, in Petersburg. Chronologically, it picks out key episodes, institutions, persons, held by Trotsky to express some essential stage or facet of the

35. Isaac Deutscher, *The Prophet Outcast*, London 1963, p. 218. And see *The Prophet Armed*, London 1954, pp. 117–74 *passim*.
36. See Edmund Wilson, *To the Finland Station*, London 1962, p. 429.

revolution. This general design matches the manner of the book's composition. Trotsky prepared it for a German edition during 1908–9, writing much of it especially for that purpose but also incorporating material, some of it intact, some with modifications, which had already been written at various dates from 1905 to 1907.[37] However, the chronicle is far from being fragmentary or untidy in effect. Its multiple sketches do not leave an impression of being so many scattered or disconnected essays. They have a cumulative, coherent impact. This is due partly to the coherence and sharpness of Trotsky's explanatory historical framework, the effective setting for all the separate sections. In so far as one can make the distinction for analytical purposes (the power of the whole residing precisely in his remarkable capacity for synthesis of the explanatory and the artistic), it is due also to a unity of aesthetic conception, which from the beginning of the book to its end takes the reader from historical argument to vivid reportage and then back, to and fro between political analysis and an imaginative reconstruction of events, each of these enriching the content of the other. The historical setting, which will account for the specific characteristics of the unfolding revolution, is laid out at once in the opening chapters, in an analysis of the Tsarist state, Russian capitalism and the configuration of classes, that had earlier been formulated as the basis of the theory of permanent revolution. Thereafter, Trotsky welds together that analysis with the deeds of the participants, offering general reflections on the dynamics of the revolutionary process amidst a wealth of observation and incident.

Organization and Chaos

As to dynamics, to the revolution's point of departure and arrival across an apparent chaos, the following passage from another essay of the same period sums up Trotsky's perception of its essence beneath its unruly, turbulent surface: 'The popular masses revolt, set in motion by elemental vital impulses and interests, often without any conception of the paths and goals of the movement: one party writes "law and justice" on its banners,

37. See *1905*, pp. x, xiv.

another "order"; the "heroes" of the revolution are guided by a consciousness of "duty", or are carried away by ambition; the behaviour of the army is determined by discipline, which does not reason, by fear, which consumes discipline, or, at last, by revolutionary insight, which conquers both discipline and fear; enthusiasm, self-interest, routine, soaring flights of thought, superstition, self-sacrifice—thousands of feelings, ideas, moods, capabilities, passions, throw themselves into the mighty whirlpool, are seized by it, perish or rise to the surface; but the objective sense of a revolution is this—it is a struggle for state power in the name of the reconstruction of antiquated social relationships.'[38] There are many similar passages. To evoke what he calls the revolution's 'elemental pressure',[39] Trotsky avails himself, naturally, of an imagery of the elements that likens it to some natural phenomenon with its own motive power—to carry people along or sweep them away. The revolution is a mighty whirlpool. The strike movement 'leaps from place to place, then takes off again and rushes forward like a whirlwind.'[40] The masses themselves rush forward 'like the ocean tide whipped by a storm'. Sometimes, Trotsky will couple such with other images of social upheaval, less naturalistic, less familiar, but which also convey that sense of a power greater than the participants, and something of its disordered aspect. As the masses rush forward, each day brings 'new strata of the population to their feet' and unfolds 'new possibilities'. It is 'as though someone were stirring the social cauldron, right to its very bottom, with a gigantic spoon'. During 1905, the country, Trotsky says, 'did not know a moment of quiet. Workers' strikes, incessant meetings, street processions, wreckings of country estates, strikes of policemen and janitors, and finally unrest and mutiny among the soldiers and sailors. Everything disintegrated, everything turned to chaos.'[41]

This chaos is *just* chaos, of course, only in certain eyes, not those of Trotsky. The deeper meaning of events being a class struggle for power, he does not fail to stress the need that an order, but another, 'democratic order', with its own embryonic

38. 'Thirty-five Years After: 1871–1906' (1905), in Leon Trotsky, *On the Paris Commune*, New York 1970, p. 11.

39. *1905*, p. 106.

40. Ibid., p. 82.

41. Ibid., p. 198.

'organs of power', should begin to define itself from within the turmoil. Throughout his account of 1905, there are descriptions of the realities of an emerging dual power and they are accompanied by one of the clearest formulations of that concept to be found in the literature of the time. The greater the anarchy caused by the movement of strikes and mass actions, the more 'they disorganize state power', the nearer, so Trotsky argues at one point, is the working class to victory. 'But on one condition only: the anarchy must not be created by anarchic means. The class which, by simultaneous cessation of work, paralyses the production apparatus and with it the centralized apparatus of power . . . must itself be sufficiently organized not to become the first victim of the anarchy it has created. The more completely a strike renders the state organization obsolete, the more the organization of the strike itself is obliged to assume state functions.'[42]

Once this necessary point about organization has been made, however, there remains the 'chaotic' side, an inevitable product and integral feature of the upheaval in social routines. In the fabric of Trotsky's argument there are literary, theoretical and polemical threads to it. The literary is our main concern here and will be taken up again presently. The theoretical thread traces out a reminder for those wedded to the Marxist tradition that revolution, as the disintegration of an exploitative social order—not only that, but all the same, that—will carry some look of disintegration in its countenance. The polemical thread Trotsky weaves in for all who, refusing to acknowledge this, want both socialism and unbroken peace and quiet. Them he chides with metaphors of fussy calculation or nice, neat choice. They imagine it possible to replace the class struggle by 'bookkeeping'.[43] Unable to grasp the revolution as a whole, they think it can be treated 'like a stick of asparagus, the edible part being separated at will from the useless part'. Within the disorder of 1905, he himself points out, 'there arose a need for a new order, and elements of that order began to crystallize. Regularly recurring meetings in themselves introduced the principle of organization. The meetings elected deputations, the deputations grew into representative assemblies.' But at the same time, 'the desire for action left the feverish

42. Ibid., pp. 252–3; and see also pp. 101–2, 156, 236, 251, 256–7, 384–400.
43. Ibid., p. 263.

attempts at organization far behind. Therein lies the weakness of the revolution—*any* revolution—but therein also lies its strength.'[44] And thence derives some of its elemental, disorderly quality. This perception, given life in his vivid recreation of the climate and atmosphere of upheaval, Trotsky shared with the other outstanding thinkers of classical Marxism, with Marx, with Engels, with Lenin and Rosa Luxemburg. The literature which embodies it displays a more profound understanding of the nature of socialist revolution than is contained in a dozen of the careful disquisitions on state apparatuses and the mechanisms of hegemony—important subjects for Marxist research though these obviously are; very eminent Marxist theoreticians though the authors of such disquisitions may be—which are today being written to obscure the idea of a 'disruptive' revolutionary *break* behind an edifying picture of political continuity. But that is another story.

Scenes of Revolution

Our themes, for the time being, are the whirlpool and the storm. It is a common enough device, this summoning of the elements to assist at the revolutionary drama, a suggestion by nature's own forces of great and spontaneous energy. Other examples of its use come readily to mind, from the 'ceaselessly moving, changing sea' perceived by Rosa Luxemburg in the phenomena of the mass strike,[45] to the 'revolutionary wave' which, rising or ebbing, has found its way on to innumerable pages of political argument. However, in Trotsky's *1905* the elemental metaphor is not trite. At the centre of the whirlpool are the moods and the passion, and the ideas; in the area of the storm there are active people. As the revolutionary chaos secretes its own emerging order, so the onward rush and the loud clash of great forces are composed of a thousand smaller actions, episodes of life, and death, recalled by Trotsky with that feeling for the concrete to which I earlier referred. It is these, with their graphic impression of immediacy, individuality, interiority and multiform variety, as much as the allusions to natural turbulence, that communicate the sense of uncommon, dramatic movement.

44. Ibid., p. 198.
45. Mary-Alice Waters (ed.), *Rosa Luxemburg Speaks*, New York 1970, p. 182.

There are the scenes of tense emotion. During the struggle for an eight-hour day, the workers of Petersburg, faced with lockout and dismissal on a massive scale, had come to severe straits. Reckoning with probable defeat, the Soviet met to consider sounding a retreat and the meeting, as Trotsky reports it, was sharply divided. The Putilov works were against going on with the campaign, others were in favour. Trotsky remembers one participant: 'A middle-aged woman weaver from Maxwell's factory rose to speak. She had a fine, open face; she wore a faded cotton dress although it was late autumn. Her hand trembled with excitement as she nervously fingered her collar. "You've let your wives get accustomed to sleeping in soft beds and eating sweet food," she hurled at the Putilov delegates. "That's why you are afraid of losing your jobs. But we aren't afraid. We're prepared to die, but we'll get the eight-hour day. We'll fight to the end. Victory or death! Long live the eight-hour day!" . . . The ringing voice came to a halt. There was a moment of painful silence. Then a storm of passionate applause.' The delegates, Trotsky remarks, though they later adopted the resolution to retreat, 'were applauding their future victory over cruelty and inhumanity.'[46]

There are the scenes of unrest in the army and navy: big street meetings with soldiers and sailors participating, a sailors' orchestra playing the *Marseillaise* at the head of a revolutionary demonstration, 'in short', as Trotsky comments, 'total "demoralization"'. He tells of the sailor Petrov who, when his company is forbidden to attend political meetings, steps out of the ranks and shoots two of the officers responsible for imposing the order. When he is placed under arrest, other sailors press forward and demand his release. 'An officer, trying to find a solution, question(s) Petrov: "Petrov, did you fire accidentally?" "How accidentally? I stepped forward, I charged my rifle, I took aim. What's accidental about that?" "But they're asking for your release . . ."' And Petrov is released.[47]

There are the fine pages on 'the revolutionary word . . . out in the open, astonished and intoxicated by its own power'—pages that, for well-known historical reasons, are even more valuable today than they were when originally written. Trotsky recalls the long difficulties of the underground socialist press, symbol and representative of the movement's sole initial weapon, 'the word'. He

46. *1905*, pp. 182–4.
47. Ibid., pp. 199–201.

recalls the 'traps and pitfalls . . . between the illegal writer and the illegal reader', the presses confiscated, the literature burned, the work wasted, the 'many existences ruined'. 'We, the Russian journalists of socialism, who for many years had led, like moles, the life of the revolution's underground, knew the value of open skies, fresh air and the free word.' In the fresh air of 1905, he recounts, the revolutionary press enjoyed a 'colossal success', selling tens of thousands of papers and generally evading the controls of a temporarily half-hearted censorship, and he recaptures the climate of novelty and excitement, of avid interest in the latest news, that prevailed during those days. It is nicely summed up in the following picture: 'The provinces devoured the capital's press like manna from heaven. Long queues of newspaper buyers waited at railway stations for the arrival of postal trains. Vendors were practically torn to pieces. People would open a fresh issue of *Russkaya Gazeta* and start reading the main articles out loud. The railway station would become filled to capacity and transformed into a tumultuous auditorium. This happened for two days, three days, and then became part of the system.'[48]

The October Strike

There are many other such memorable images of an animated, just awakened political life: images of working people beginning to have their say, of boisterous meetings and swiftly spreading strikes; images of peasant gatherings or of the 'red cockerel' illuminating the rural sky; images, finally, of confrontation, uncertain, hesitant and peaceful, or open and bloody, between the people and the troops. Of all of Trotsky's sketches, three, perhaps, stand out above the others in narrative brilliance and they deserve especial mention here, although I can do scant justice to them. The first is devoted to the October strike which quickly wrung from the Tsar his Manifesto promising a constitution. The sketch was written just after the event itself,[49] and is a masterpiece of revolutionary journalism.

It begins with the facts of the strike's early days: an action by typesetters in Moscow extending quickly to fifty printing works,

48. Ibid., pp. 146–7.
49. See ibid., pp. xv–xvi.

a strike of the Moscow bakers, growing ferment on the railways, all this against the background of large political gatherings in the universities, attended by masses of workers. The idea of a general strike of the railways begins to gain ground, but then the ferment appears to subside as many return to work. 'The strike', Trotsky interjects, 'had not yet made up its mind. It was still pondering and hesitating.' But the hesitation is deceptive. 'In reality the strike was preparing to go into action at full tilt.' Throughout the factual account, Trotsky employs this device, gradually building up within his narrative a personification of the strike that imparts a strong impression of its autonomous momentum. A general strike is declared on the railways and it spreads from one line to another. One town after another begins to report that the lines are failing. Slogans are formulated which transcend local and trade concerns. As the strike begins to 'take over the country', it acquires 'unprecedented daring', begins 'to feel that it (is) a revolution'. Finally, it sweeps ahead: 'The strike rushed forward along the rails and stopped all movement in its wake . . . It followed a grandiose plan—that of halting industrial and commercial life in the country at large . . . it did not overlook a single detail. Where the telegraph refused to serve it, it cut the wires or overturned the telegraph poles. It halted railway engines and let off their steam. It brought the electric power stations to a standstill . . . Where it met stubborn resistance, it did not hesitate to disrupt lines, break signals, overturn engines, put obstacles across lines or place railway carriages across bridges. It penetrated into lift systems and stopped the hoisting winches. It halted goods trains wherever it found them, while passenger trains were usually run to the nearest junction or to the place of destination. Only for its own purposes did the strike allow itself to break the vow of immobility. When it needed news bulletins of the revolution it opened a printing works; it used the telegraph to send out strike instructions . . . Nothing else was exempt: the strike closed down industrial plants, chemists' and grocers' shops, courts of law, everything . . . It used every possible means. It appealed, convinced, implored; it begged on its knees—that is what a woman orator did at the Kursky station in Moscow— it threatened, terrorized, threw stones, finally fired off its Brownings.'

Trotsky's approach here works to fuse the global movement and its constituent details into a closely packed tableau. By itself, the device of personification would be merely commonplace, and its results, inevitably, flat. If it carries conviction, it is only because the strike's independent dynamic is shown *in* and *through* a multitude of specific details, so that we grasp not only the sense of this powerful, rapidly moving force—a sense sharpened by the cumulative effect of Trotsky's quickness and brevity of phrase— but also a graphic, almost *photo*graphic, impression of the activities of the strike's participants. There is a constant interplay between the two. The strike racing ahead; railway carriages placed across a bridge. The movement carrying all before it; an orator literally beseeching her listeners in the Kursky station. This reference back and forth is in the end clinched in one splendid scene when the strike, having brought the railways to a complete standstill, and aiming still beyond them, is itself seen making its way into the working-class throng, thereby reuniting with its own active 'bearers': 'Having let the steam out of the engines and put out the station lights, it joins the crowds of railway workers on their way to town. It halts trams, stops the horses of hackney carriages and obliges the passengers to dismount, closes down shops, restaurants, cafés and taverns, and confidently approaches the factory gates. Inside they are already waiting. The alarm whistle starts, work stops, the crowd in the street swells. The strike marches forward, now carrying a red banner.' Withal, Trotsky does not neglect his journalistic responsibility in the interests of aesthetic effect. From the typesetters' action to the Tsar's Manifesto, through the general political strike proclaimed across the urban centres of Russia in the course of one hectic week, his narrative carefully lays out its factual report of the strike's development in the lines of evocative prose.[50]

The Trial of the Soviet

Of the second of the chosen episodes, the trial of the Soviet of Workers' Deputies, I will only touch on its opening sequence. This is described in a passage of sharp contrasts where the fact of the revolution's defeat stands alongside symbols of enthusiasm and goodwill, and where the initial atmosphere of humour and

50. Ibid., pp. 83–96.

defiance is suddenly brought up short before another, more gruesome reality. Trotsky strikingly depicts the scene in court, the whole building surrounded by soldiers and cossacks, and, inside, gendarmes with drawn sabres everywhere—'at the backs of the defendants, at every corner, probably even inside the chimney stack'. They were supposed to separate the defendants from the public but, as Trotsky relates, this wall was constantly being pierced by the defence lawyers who conveyed from the public 'newspapers, letters, sweets and flowers—infinite quantities of flowers!' The flowers lay all about the accused. When the court officer opened the door to the courtroom, revolutionary songs could be heard from the workers gathered in the witness room. Trotsky then goes on to tell how, at the beginning of the trial, the court's president called only fifty-one of the fifty-two defendants. Challenged by one of the defence lawyers as to the whereabouts of the missing defendant, he was obliged to inform the court that the man in question had already been executed.[51]

The counterpoint in this scene, light at first and then brutal, is, evidently, part of the occasion itself described. The concentrated drama of this occasion comes out in many of the passages Trotsky devotes to it as well as in the transcript of his own impassioned speech before the court. All the same, his account of that opening scene well illustrates his capacity for representing, in a few compressed images of some given political episode, all the contradictory forces in play there, his eye for just that detail of an event which will express something of the wider, social background. If this is true in relation to the single incident, it is equally so on the great historic canvas as a whole. There too, as I have tried to show, he seizes the variety in the ever moving conflict, there too picks out the item symbolic of a larger social meaning. We have so far seen upon this canvas the revolution's own colours. But there too others, the colours of counter-revolution glimpsed only fleetingly in court, are seen right out in the open. The third of the sketches mentioned earlier is an account by Trotsky of a pogrom, such as swept many of Russia's towns in the days following the October strike. The picture is one of irredeemable degradation, unrelieved brutality and pain, and the experience is communicated with an unequalled intensity and emotional power. Given the horrific nature of this experience, it may seem morally

51. Ibid., pp. 356–7.

insensitive to invoke an account of it as an exemplification of narrative skills. However, the reality in question has tormented socialism since its inception and torments it still today. *Its* images, disgorged by so many counter-revolutionary movements granted only the opportunity, are also in their tragic way a part of the literature of socialism, one which we forget at our peril. Marx's indignant, accusing pages on the butchery that followed the crushing of the Paris Commune; in a slightly different vein, Luxemburg's moving conclusion to the *Junius Pamphlet*, marking outrage, sadness, a deep sense of loss, at the barbarities and the waste of the mutual slaughter of peoples on the battlefields of the First World War[52]—these writings, and others, have bequeathed to the workers' movement the record and memory of its terrible defeats. To them Trotsky adds his own angry indictment. As a witness to the events of 1905, he does not neglect this hideous dimension of them, the face of counter-revolutionary mobilization.

A Pogrom

In his account of the November strike that effectively stopped the punishment otherwise threatening mutineers in the navy, there is a point where Trotsky poses the question of the overall significance of this successful action. It lay, he says, not in the fact that it 'removed the noose from the necks of a few dozen sailors— what do a few lives matter in a revolution that devours tens of thousands?'—but in the circumstance of being a warning by the workers that they were ready 'to give blow for blow' against any more generalized reactionary attempt.[53] In that one harsh interpellation, it is the discourse of eternity that is heard once again. A few lives weighed against many, in the vast scale of things what does it matter? The fatalist discourse must reckon with fatalities. But then elsewhere, the other, human voice tells only too lucidly why it does matter. I quote Trotsky here at length, no 'critical appreciation' being either possible or necessary.

'Here (is) the petty shopkeeper and the beggar, the publican

---

52. See Karl Marx and Frederick Engels, *Selected Works*, Moscow 1969, vol. 2, pp. 235 ff.; and *Rosa Luxemburg Speaks*, pp. 326–8.

53. *1905*, p. 174.

and his perennial clients, the janitor and the police spy, the professional thief and the amateur housebreaker, the small artisan and the brothel doorkeeper, the hungry, dumb muzhik and yesterday's villager deafened by the roar of the machine . . . Everyone knows about a coming pogrom in advance. Pogrom proclamations are distributed, bloodthirsty articles come out in the official Provincial Gazettes, sometimes a special newspaper begins to appear. The town governor of Odessa issues a provocational proclamation in his own name. When the ground has been prepared, a visiting company of "specialists" appears. They spread sinister rumours among the ignorant masses: the Jews are planning an attack on the Russians, some socialists have defiled a holy icon, some students have torn up the Tsar's portrait . . . A patriotic procession starts out, with the clergy in the front, with a portrait of the Tsar taken from police headquarters, with many national flags. A military band plays without cease . . . To start with a few windows are smashed, a few passers-by beaten up; the wreckers enter every tavern on their way and drink, drink, drink. The band never stops playing "God Save the Tsar", that hymn of the pogroms . . . Protected in the front and rear by army patrols, with a cossack detachment for reconnaissance, with policemen and professional provocateurs as leaders, with mercenaries filling the secondary roles, with volunteers out for easy profit, the gang rushes through the town, drunk on vodka and the smell of blood. The doss-house tramp is king. A trembling slave an hour ago, hounded by police and starvation, he now feels himself an unlimited despot. Everything is allowed to him, he is capable of anything, he is the master of property and honour, of life and death. If he wants to, he can throw an old woman out of a third-floor window together with a grand piano, he can smash a chair against a baby's head, rape a little girl while the entire crowd looks on, hammer a nail into a living human body . . . He exterminates whole families, he pours petrol over a house, transforms it into a mass of flames, and if anyone attempts to escape, he finishes him off with a cudgel. A savage horde comes tearing into an Armenian almshouse, knifing old people, sick people, women, children . . . There exist no tortures, figments of a feverish brain maddened by alcohol and fury, at which he need ever stop. He is capable of anything, he dares everything. God save the Tsar! Here is a young man who has seen the face of death: his hair has turned white within an instant. Here is a ten-year-old boy who has gone mad over the mutilated corpses of his parents. Here is an army doctor who went through all the horrors of the siege of Port Arthur, but who, unable to stand a few hours of pogrom in Odessa, has sunk into the eternal night of madness. God save the Tsar! The victims, bloodstained, charred, driven frantic, still search for salvation within the nightmare. Some put on the bloodstained clothes of people already dead, lie down in a pile of corpses and stay there for a whole day, for two or three days . . . Others fall on their knees before the officers, the policemen, the raider, they stretch out their arms, crawl in the dust, kiss the soldiers' boots, beg for mercy. In reply they hear only drunken laughter. "You wanted freedom? Here, look, this is it." . . . During this black October bacchanalia, compared with which St Bartholomew's night looks like the most innocent piece of theatre, 3,500 to 4,000 people were killed and as many as 10,000 maimed in 100 towns.'[54]

Human Experience and Emancipation

There I will leave Trotsky's *1905*. It has been in the nature of the present exercise to focus on its representation of a lived experience, and to allude only in passing to its political analyses and historical argument. The book is rich in both, but my intention was to get at the creative imagination which, fused together with them, contributes so much to its power as a document of socialist literature, to its effort to grasp a part of the human experience of our times. Since Althusser's essays on Marx, it has, of course, become something of a fashion in Marxist research to cleave to the principles of an '*anti*-humanism', and in face of these such an effort may be thought not to count for very much. However, the anti-humanist tendency is doubly misguided. It is misguided theoretically because the principle which sustains it, that

---

54. Ibid., pp. 131–6. The two discourses are found also in Rosa Luxemburg. With the closing pages of the *Junius Pamphlet* compare these lines from one of her wartime letters: 'the longer it lasts, and the more the infamy and the monstrosity of the daily happenings surpasses all bounds, the more tranquil and more confident becomes my personal outlook. I say to myself that it is absurd to apply moral standards to the great elemental forces that manifest themselves in a hurricane, a flood, or an eclipse of the sun. We have to accept them simply as data for investigation, as subjects of study.' *Rosa Luxemburg Speaks*, p. 337.

individuals are merely constituted by the ensemble of social relations, is incompatible with a materialist science. It is an idealist fiction, collapsing the material constitution of human beings into history, immersing the real processes of human evolution and transformation within an over-historicized conception of the social 'structure' that presents every appearance, despite protestations to the contrary, of being just one more version of the transcendent *subject*. When all due distance has been taken from the compromised and reactionary usages of the idea of 'human nature', when every necessary point has been made regarding the historical production of new human needs and social values, there remains, as Timpanaro has eloquently argued,[55] an infrastructure of biological and psycho-physical continuities. Marxism does not neglect them. In the construction of its most basic explanatory concept, the concept of mode of production very dear to the intellectual children of Althusser, they are a vital constitutive element.

Moreover, it is only because of them, because, that is to say, human beings are not infinitely malleable, that the project conditional upon, but also broader and more far-reaching than, the abolition of capitalist exploitation, the commitment to *human emancipation*, can be embodied meaningfully within the perspectives of Marxism. If the 'myth of man' had truly disappeared from its horizon, 'reduced to ashes' in Althusser's phrase, that idea would be deprived of all sense. But Marxism does embody it: not as an alien incursion or as a merely useful instrument of 'ideological practice'; as a central, normative, (dare it be said?) *moral* commitment. With it Marxism lives or dies. It is in the name of it that Marx condemned capitalism, in its name that the socialist enterprise sets itself against a situation of oppression, of countless lives lived in need and toil, of so many deaths experienced in loneliness, terror or agony, when the means to end or to alleviate these sufferings are available. This is a commitment to a society where human beings can lead lives of freedom, dignity and happiness, where pain, grief, loss, want, boredom, fear, can be subdued as far as possible, be reduced and integrated within a decent existence, where people can eat and find shelter, achieve health and sexual gratification, develop their intellectual powers, enjoy their physical powers, enjoy work, play, laughter, music

55. Sebastiano Timpanaro, *On Materialism*, London 1975.

and the sun; and the rest is but an interesting diversion for the leisure of philosophers. It in no way compromises Marx's achievement that he inherited from others a very old aspiration, that of human liberation. On the contrary, it is an essential and enduring feature of his greatness, that he sought to release it from religious obfuscation, philosophical discussion, liberal political rhetoric, to support it with a materialist, scientific knowledge, and to put this at the service of the only forces capable of giving reality to the hope.

Trotsky, for his part, had no doubts on this score. The human principle affirmed by him at the very beginning of his political life was reaffirmed as strongly in the testament written just before its premature end: 'Natasha has just come up to the window from the courtyard and opened it wider so that the air may enter more freely into my room. I can see the bright green strip of grass beneath the wall, and the clear blue sky above the wall, and sunlight everywhere. Life is beautiful. Let the future generations cleanse it of all evil, oppression and violence, and enjoy it to the full . . . I shall die with unshaken faith in the communist future. This faith in man and in his future gives me even now such power of resistance as cannot be given by any religion.'[56] It would be easy to respond to this by saying that such moral affirmations come relatively cheaply. The response itself would be cheap. For it is not a question of the bare affirmation of principle, but of its realization in word and deed. As to deed, it is not my purpose to offer here an assessment of Trotsky's political record, though I believe it to have been on many issues as honourable as, and on decisive issues more honourable than, any other contemporary with it. As to word, however, which is my concern here, the life which Trotsky's writings gave to that affirmation is not something that comes relatively cheaply. It is, indeed, extremely rare in the pages of socialist argument. Its rarity is a measure of his literary achievement.

Individuals and Masses

There is a passage in Isaac Deutscher's treatment of the *History*,

56. *Trotsky's Diary in Exile*, pp. 140–1.

but which applies with equal force to *1905*, where the point is expressed with characteristic lucidity. Comparing Trotsky's depiction of the revolutionary crowd in action with Eisenstein's method in *The Battleship Potemkin*, Deutscher draws attention to the way in which he will let an individual phrase or gesture foreshadow some wider action of the mass, to his perpetual movement, in both conception and image, between the particular and the general. Trotsky's revolutionary masses, Deutscher goes on, 'think and reflect. They are elemental; yet they are human . . . He lets us feel that here and now men make their own history; and that they do it in accordance with the "laws of history", but also by acts of their consciousness and will.'[57] What is true of the revolutionary crowd is true also of Trotsky's individuals. They have a political formation, are constrained by an objective historical situation, represent in themselves various, often contradictory, aspects of the struggle of classes: Jaurès, heir to a great revolutionary tradition, and caught in the 'shallows' of the Third Republic; Adler, adapted in his whole being to the politics of Austria, and attuned by experience to the life of a large organization. But then we 'see' Jaurès and Adler on the platform, the demeanour and presence of the person before his audience, the quality of an individual thought seeking to express itself. Trotsky attempts to capture the distinctive tones of the orator's voice.

In the case of Jaurès, it is 'a voice with the ring of wonder': 'On the platform, he seems huge and yet he is below average height. Thick-set, with a head sitting squarely on his neck, with expressive "dancing" cheekbones, nostrils which swell up as he speaks wholly releasing the stream of his passion, he in appearance too belongs to the same human type as Mirabeau and Danton. As an orator he is incomparable and has met no comparison. There is not that finished and at times irritating refinement in his speech with which Vandervelde shines. He cannot be compared with Bebel for a logical force of attraction. The cruel and venomous irony of Victor Adler is foreign to him. But in spirit, in passion and in his verve he is the equal of them all . . . It is not his rich technique nor his enormous, miraculous sounding voice nor the generous profusity of his gestures but the *genius's naiveté of his enthusiasm* which brings Jaurès close to the masses and makes him

57. *The Prophet Outcast*, pp. 232–3.

what he is . . .'[58] Adler's voice is more halting but in its own way effective. 'He has an innately good voice but it is not strong and Adler moreover cannot take control of it: he squanders it wastefully and by the end of his speech he gets hoarse and coughs. His gestures are not rich though very expressive. One must add that Adler has quite a strong stammer particularly at the beginning of his speech. And yet he is one of the most remarkable orators in Europe . . . Each speech of his is one apart. He never develops already prepared positions *with regard to* the given occasion but unfolds the *inner logic* of each occasion. He loves the personal characterization and the characterization of the peculiarity of the moment and as he speaks he ponders the question. He does not simply place a figure or a phenomenon within a known political category but he stands in front of his object like a scientific analyst (frequently like a psychiatrist) and slowly turns the object around on its axis and relates what he finds there. If this object is a living figure, a political opponent, then the latter must during this operation have the feeling that he is on a spit being roasted on all sides . . . even the organic defect in his speech seems to be essential: the short pauses are so arranged as to coincide with his stammers as if they might bring the listener closer to the creative work of the orator—as though the material is resisting and does not yield at once to the chisel.'[59]

There is something else in these political sketches, beyond their sensitive portrayal of individual personality, that deserves to be articulated although it is by now very evident. That is the warmth and the generosity which Trotsky could feel and display towards figures quite distant, politically, from himself. The point is not to suggest that he was incapable or even shy of a much sharper and more hostile tone. In polemic and invective Trotsky could more than hold his own. One need only glance at his writings from the period of the First World War, devoted to the renegacy of Plekhanov or to the depth of Kautsky's fall, more generally, to the wave of patriotic apologetics sweeping over the socialist press, to witness examples of his bitter irony and of his angry, scathing condemnation.[60] Nor is the point even to argue that this other, polemical tone should have no place in socialist writing. The

58. 'Jean Jaurès' and 'Jaurès', pp. 33, 25–6.
59. 'Victor Adler', pp. 17–8.
60. See 'Stop Worrying Us' (1915), in *Political Profiles*, pp. 90–93; Leon

stakes being what they are, episodes of socialist betrayal and socialist crime (and no apology is necessary for these phrases), not to speak of those of ruling-class persecution and counter-revolutionary brutality, have evoked their own appropriate linguistic response. However, a whole history has already conspired to focus attention on *this* side of socialist discussion, to exaggerate it, to evoke it when it was not appropriate, to dignify it with the status almost of a principle of discussion as such, and to give it the vilest of forms. In that situation, to recall a style of socialist journalism that could identify the merits of a political opponent is very much to the point. In Victor Adler, Trotsky was capable of perceiving not only an 'opportunist degeneration' but also 'one of the most attractive figures of the Second International', a man 'too good for mitigating circumstances not to be found'; in Jaurès, not just a reformist politician but a true fighter who, in another period, would 'move off the shallows out to the open sea'.[61] This lack of sectarian narrowness was displayed also, indeed above all, on issues of culture and morals. It is summed up in the generous tribute 'On Tolstoy's Death'. Trotsky did not there disguise or attempt to fudge the question of differences, saying plainly that Tolstoy was no revolutionary socialist and taking clear distance from his beliefs in pacifist non-resistance and in God. But in Tolstoy's honesty and courage in the renunciation of all social slavery, Trotsky sought out the 'deep moral affinity'; in that sense, he wrote, 'everything in Tolstoy's teaching that is lasting and permanent flows into socialism as naturally as a river into the ocean.'[62] With that repeated image of revolutionary socialism before us, as open and receptive as the sea to the finest qualities of the human character and intellect, I now proceed to a few tentative conclusions and some outstanding questions.

Trotsky, *The War and the International* (1914), Colombo 1971, pp. 30, 48–49. Trotsky's contempt for these apologetics is expressed in one fierce image of putrefaction: 'This is simply a case of an ulcer of slavish sentiments bursting open and foul pus crawling over the pages of the working men's press.'

61. 'Victor Adler' and 'Jaurès', pp. 16, 20, 19, 27.

62. 'On Tolstoy's Death', pp. 143–7. With a singular lack of generosity, one recent commentator sees this as a 'transparently facile . . . attempt by Trotsky to "adopt" or "mobilize" Tolstoy for revolutionary socialism', and wonders if 'he did not write it with tongue in cheek'. The judgement would carry some weight had Trotsky pretended to a greater community of belief with Tolstoy than there was—and he did not. See Baruch Knei-Paz, *The Social and Political Thought of Leon Trotsky*, Oxford 1978, p. 461.

Image and Theory

It is an image, quite obviously, at odds with that other familiar one of a total *rupture* between Marxism and all its antecedents, humanist, empiricist, idealist, rationalist, liberal, utopian social-ist, political-economist, and virtually any other that one cares to name. Equally, the texture of image and of value that has been the main concern of this essay appears very remote from the rigours and the structures of 'high theory' which that idea of rupture did so much to legitimate. But as there is, in socialist thought, a place of theory, so also is there a place of image and imagination, portrait, description and evaluation. We too have our images and portraits. What is more, though their relationship to knowledge is certainly a complex one, they are not so far removed from the site where theoretical issues are contested. They have definite cog-nitive functions, both positive and negative. To take the negative first, it is enough only to think of some of those images, charged with reverence or with animus, that the socialist movement still carries as a part of its inheritance. An image of Marx, for example, in which the very features of his physical countenance seem to reflect a mature, superior, unquestionable wisdom; or another in which those same features are the sign of a dogmatic, almost religious intolerance. Familiar images of Lenin: strong and calm, utterly selfless, meticulous and free of excess or ex-travagance, the standard of dedicated militancy; or else ruthless and unprincipled in the pursuit both of personal vindication and of political power. Images of Trotsky himself: brilliant, right, the lonely, unfaltering defender of all the works of Lenin; or— arrogant, authoritarian and impatient, a little too *clever*, and flamboyant, ostentatious, individualistic, in the style of his cleverness, his voice generally just a shade too loud. How many other caricatures, possessing, like all such, some actual basis in fact, do we continue to secrete and to articulate? The extremes of hostility and veneration which they display can be set against a long history of acute divisions and of beleaguered self-defence. Yet, they are so many barriers to the real knowledge of its leading figures that the socialist movement indispensably requires: a knowledge beyond mere images, free of myth, founded on close historical, biographical and textual study, and combining the respect and loyalty due from it to its own best products with a critical, exacting regard for all the shortcomings in their political and intellectual records.

On the other hand, just as theory can avail itself of metaphor for good reasons as well as bad, so portrait and imagery can sometimes assist knowledge instead of crippling it. As opposed to the flat, caricatural picture which, behind a parade of heroes and villains, blocks off every effort to grasp the complex reality of individual lives, there is a mode of perceiving and depicting these that, by its detail, nuance and contradiction, precisely *releases* some of the most pertinent questions about them, opening up lines of thought that might lead into the very heart of their complexity. Trotsky, at his best, employed this mode. He could make the description of a physical bearing, episodes of a personal history, say something about the harmonies, or the conflicts, between a style of thought and its physical expression, between the political positions and the personal temperament of an individual; images of the social and physical milieu he could use to expand upon the relationship between a political record and the historical period or national tradition within which it unfolded. At his best, he thus provoked serious thought about his subject, clearing a space upon which a real biographical and intellectual interrogation might take place. This is not to say that the validity of all his judgements is guaranteed by that alone. It would be possible, obviously, to take issue with aspects of his treatment of Jaurès or Adler or Tolstoy. Had Jaurès lived, would he have moved off the shallows? A mode of writing and an intellectual style cannot, by themselves, validate the theoretical substance whose vehicle they are. It is to be doubted, all the same, that what is at stake is a matter of mere literary 'style' in the narrowest, most formal sense of the word.

Form and Substance

What confronts us here is, in fact, the central and most difficult question that has been posed by the foregoing discussion of Trotsky: a question of the relationship between literary form and theoretical substance, or truth, in the work of a political writer. From what has just been said, this clearly cannot be a straightforward or expressive one, but nor is it wholly external and accidental. If sound arguments can sometimes be presented in a stumbling or clumsy prose, and deficiencies often be concealed by a powerful and compelling one, it is also the case that in the style of an author we already read *something* of the content of his or her ideas. The language of *Capital*—by turns systematic, technical and explicative; dignified and dramatic; mordant and impassioned —matches its purposes, at once scientific, prophetic and engaged. The single-mindedly political character of Lenin's revolutionary intellect is conveyed not only by the number of his theoretical contributions to the politics of Marxism but also in the qualities of his tireless prose: qualities of appositeness, simplicity and clarity, of patient repetition, of persistent argument, delivered in an implacable, sometimes hectoring, tone. Active in every particular case of the relation between style and substance is a more general question, and this only an aspect, though a neglected one, of the Althusserian question 'What is it to read?'[63] For, in the texts of the revolutionary tradition, in their overt forms and in their omissions, what we read as well as the theoretical and political content is invariably also a specific way of talking. Within a literary tradition whose vocation it has been to explain and to educate, to persuade, to engage, the specificities are bound to be of consequence. There is not one idiom of revolutionary communication. There have been, and are, many. To overlook this, or to pass it by as a matter of *mere* style not relevant to the serious business of theory, is to devalue both the difficulty and the originality of the contributions of those who spoke and wrote in them. At the other extreme, to attempt simply to mimic one or another of these idioms is to kill it stone dead, depriving it of what efficacy it may once have possessed. Only by an analysis of the pecularities of each idiom, by asking *how* an author tried to speak in relation to *what* he or she had to say, can we take a real measure of the value and effectiveness of the individual discourse in the context of a collective socialist debate. The analysis I have undertaken in this essay provides some elements of a provisional answer to this question as it applies to the character of Trotsky's writing.

A caution needs to be entered here. I spoke just now of Trotsky at his best, and I have tended throughout to concentrate on the strengths of his prose. No author, however, writes in a uniform, much less in a uniformly cogent and illuminating, way; and Trotsky was no exception to this. To be mindful of the quality

63. See *Reading Capital*, London 1970, p. 15 and *passim*.

and force of much of his writing is in no way to suggest that it did not also contain weaknesses and lapses or, simply, pages of an ordinary, not exceptionally forceful kind. There is no point in trying to exemplify this by lengthy quotation. But it is relevant to one of the preoccupations of this essay to register, for example, that while the sketches of some of his leading contemporaries, occasional pieces of revolutionary journalism, could be both revealing in their personal detail and politically educative in their form, Trotsky's treatment of certain lesser figures in the same period was often less convincing. His sketches of Paul Singer, Franz Schuhmeier, Gustav Eckstein,[64] though not without political interest, appear now somewhat inflated and 'over-written'. No doubt, their character as obituaries is partly responsible for this, but they show nevertheless that Trotsky's touch was occasionally less sure, his language too large for his subject. On the same terrain and during the same period, one cannot escape the contrast between his rounded and discerning picture of, say, Adler, and the glaring misappraisal of Lenin that is embodied in a number of his remarks scattered through these early writings. At the time of the Bolshevik-Menshevik split, Trotsky wrote of Lenin as a 'disorganizer', of his 'will to power', 'poverty of thought' and 'malevolent distrust'; he characterized him as 'an agile statistician and adroit barrister'.[65] As late as 1916 he could see in Leninism only a 'lack of ideas', 'the most primitive vulgarization of social radicalism', 'paucity of theoretical content', 'the product of an amorphous, uncultivated social background, where the first historical movement of the proletariat necessarily requires simplification and vulgarization of theory and politics'.[66] The blind spot manifest in such characterizations of Lenin and his ideas, homogeneous with a larger political error on the part of the young Trotsky, shows how distance and difference could also cloud his personal judgements.

There is a related point. I referred above to some of the more negative features in the tradition of socialist polemic. Trotsky

64. 'Paul Singer', 'At the Coffin of Franz Schuhmeier' (1913) and 'Gustav Eckstein' (1916), in *Political Profiles*, pp. 3–5, 7–9, 53–4.

65. *Rapport de la délégation sibérienne*, pp. 60, 72; *Nos tâches politiques*, pp. 43, 192, 195. This is not to say that everything in Trotsky's polemic against Lenin at this time was misdirected: see 'Lenin, Trotsky and the Party' above.

66. 'Letter to Roland Holst' (1916), Leon Trotsky, *A Rediscovered Document*, Spokesman Offprint No. 2, Nottingham 1973, p. 24.

himself bears, along with many others, some share of the responsibility for them. Although separated by a chasm from the lying and the slander of Stalinism, he was capable at times of abusing his literary capacities in the interests of excessive polemic. His disparagement of Lenin in *Our Political Tasks* is one example of this: in some of the *ad hominem* epithets, Trotsky clearly overreached the necessary or proper limits of socialist debate, a fact that is not excused by Lenin's own frequent, reciprocal excesses of personal abuse and denigration. One could also identify, without too much trouble, cases where the flow of Trotsky's argument is interrupted by some dubious or ugly flourish. One of these we have already encountered: an image in which the forehead of a political opponent is said by him to merit disfigurement;[67] an image, in other words, of physical brutality against the person introduced, however obliquely or humorously, into a discussion of political differences. Another example, of old Marxist pedigree but no less unfortunate for all that, occurs in *1905* where Trotsky at one point does not hesitate to align side by side the interests of Mendelssohn and Rothschild, 'the laws of the stock exchange', and the laws 'of Moses'.[68]

Language and Truth

However, the real problem we are concerned with goes much deeper than is registered by such qualifications regarding local misjudgements or literary blemishes in Trotsky's work. The problem of literary form and theoretical substance is posed more acutely in fact by considering the very strengths of his writings to which I have given attention here. There are at least two sides to it. Firstly, in any work of theory properly speaking, equally in serious historiography, there will be a core of analysis and argument whose level of abstraction—from the phenomenological 'surface' of life; from the immediate experience, the moral concerns and the psychological motivations of the social actors; from the underlying commitments and the peculiarities of outlook of the author—must make it relatively indifferent to the form of literary expression. Beyond the elementary requirements of

67. See text to n. 13 above.
68. *1905*, p. 128.

clarity, precision and logical rigour, the validity or otherwise of this basic conceptual content will not depend on how well an author wrote. We can revert to the case of Marx's *Capital* to elucidate the point. The cognitive status of the theory of value, which is being fought over so vigorously today, depends finally on whether it can be shown that the theory provides coherent foundation for an account of profits and prices in the capitalist economy—for otherwise it is merely fanciful to suppose that it could adequately explain the 'laws of motion' of capitalism; it does not depend upon Marx's powerful portrayal of the vampiric tendencies of capital, on his vivid documentation of the oppressive situation of the proletariat, or on his sharp exposure of the ideological hypocrisies of bourgeois society. It is possible to argue, of course, that Marx's literary representation of these features of capitalism is only effective because he did understand something of the realities of capitalist development. But the theory of value cannot be sustained by this alone. In the absence of an independent validation at the level of abstraction and rigour appropriate to it, Marxists would have to begin to reformulate the substantive truths of Marx's major work in terms and concepts other than those of the theory of value.

A similar point can be made about Trotsky's *1905* even though this is a work of a rather different kind. I have emphasized repeatedly, however, that it is more than just a work of reportage. Keenly and dramatically evocative of a proximate historical experience, it embodies also an early formulation of the theory of permanent revolution, theoretical considerations on the nature of proletarian revolution, and the elements of a history of one such upheaval that ended in defeat. Clearly, the quality of Trotsky's prose in this book, its drama and its colour, do not establish the theory of permanent revolution. The validity of that theory, the truth of its central insights, and some of the shortcomings in its original presentation, these are matters of a separate analysis. Trotsky's arguments, *ante litteram*, on the significance of dual power can be extricated too from the particular context of the experience of 1905, integrated into subsequent and current debates about the contours of an effective strategy for socialism, and judged on that terrain. Finally, as a work of history, *1905* has to be tested against the criteria of historical knowledge: the analysis of the disposition of class forces that unleashed the revolution, the construction of particular events during its course, and the explanation as to why it failed, can only be measured by historical argument over evidence and interpretation.

The second aspect of the problem consists in the fact that a particular political language can be both a rich and powerful medium for the most acute insights of its author, and simultaneously, just because of its wealth and power, the site of errors that are hidden or partly hidden when they would be more readily evident in a more prosaic statement of the same arguments. As regards the young Trotsky, there is an important and relevant case of this. We have seen how images of organizational stasis crystallized his perception of the bureaucratic tendencies within European socialism, and how his own exceptional grasp of the dynamics of the revolutionary process could be conveyed in writing sharply suggestive of their eruptive, uneven, 'chaotic' and contradictory character. At the same time, his political understanding here, a proper and salutary emphasis on the centrality of the self-activity of the masses in the struggle for, and in the goals of, socialism, sat beside a serious underestimation of the place in this process of the workers' political organizations. This underestimation is consistently present, but the flow and movement of the argument on revolutionary dynamics, some of the images of spontaneity, serve to glide over it, so to speak, and it must be caught here and there when it surfaces briefly in a revealing formula. This happens in *1905*, for example, in a vivid passage on 'the climate of the revolution' where Trotsky observes how the masses will 'sweep the party forward' as well as being led by it. In such a climate, he also says, 'the subjective will of a party, even a "dominant" party, is only one of the factors involved, and not by any means the most important one.' Again, in connection with the revolution's 'elemental pressure', he suggests in passing that the Soviet's tactics during 1905 were 'determined in advance' and 'obvious' because of it, as if the problem of tactical choices could really be dissolved by the momentum of revolutionary events.[69] Similar examples could be given from other works of this epoch, from *Our Political Tasks* and *Results and Prospects*. The error involved is one which Trotsky was later to recognize, admit and correct.[70] The point here is not so much that his literary gifts did

69. Ibid., pp. 263–4, 106.
70. On this, see Ernest Mandel's replies to Nicolas Krassó in *New Left Review*, Nos. 47 and 56, and 'Political Participation in the Revolutionary Thought of Leon Trotsky' above.

not rescue Trotsky from this mistake or from others: his failure to grasp the significance of Rosa Luxemburg's break with Kautsky, some unilateral assertions on the national question, the inability he shared with all his contemporaries to reckon with the prospect of a proletarian regime isolated *for decades* in a hostile capitalist world. That should go without saying. Exceptional literary talents provide no special guarantee against error. The point is rather to illustrate how these could sometimes help to conceal a weakness in the theoretical discussion, buried away as it might be in a cogently written presentation of other valuable observations.

A Second Discourse

There is then no simple, linear relation between literature and politics in this context. An individual idiom may be more or less neutral vis-à-vis the argument it is called upon to express; it may serve as an effective medium for an author's most fertile ideas; or it may partially disguise intellectual problems and failures. Must we conclude that literary form has no special bearing on theoretical content in the area of social and political inquiry? It seems to me that such a conclusion would be unwarranted. Though the relation in question is a complex, even 'loose' one, so soon as we attend to the specificities of an authorial style, we can generally detect how they do bear on the writer's substantive concerns in a sense beyond mere ornament or eccentricity.

In Trotsky's case at least I think it possible, from the appraisal attempted above, to identify the cognitive function that was served by the literary modes he employed. These were, as I have tried to show, an important if secondary and supportive part of his theoretical equipment, now reinforcing a particular political argument, now condensing the elements of a historical analysis into some lively image or bringing out the play of social contradictions in the detail of a local incident. In a broader perspective, however, their function was much more fundamental. Trotsky was above all a political writer and a political actor, and accordingly his discourse was in the first place a political one, dealing in all those concepts familiar to the tradition he embraced: concepts of class, party and state, of capitalism and socialism, of tactics, strategy, revolution and history. But into the rhythms of this first, political discourse he habitually inserted a second one, by which he tried to extend the horizon of his readers, outwards from the immediate problems at stake to the very limits of the political narrowly conceived. He sought thereby, simultaneously and in counterpoint with his analysis of the problems of politics, to raise the whole range of questions residing at the margins where politics and morality, politics and the personal, politics and the 'universal', politics and experience, politics and philosophy, meet or intersect. One could say that, in a sense, the literary forms of Trotsky's writing sought to extend the boundaries of political understanding itself, by considering the relationship between political and such other preoccupations, the place of politics in the wider human environment. The function of his imagery, to return to that, was more than merely decorative, more even than just supportive of the political point he was pursuing. It was a *generalizing* function, serving to open up the political discussion to questions or observations not immediately evident there, and to lift it on to another level of reflection. As I have already indicated, the fruits of this other reflection would not necessarily substantiate the political case Trotsky might be trying to make; but they had their effects on it, usually inflected it, and frequently enriched it. In so far as they did the latter, they constituted and constitute a definite gain, not only in style but also in knowledge, to the political thought of socialism.

I shall develop this contention in a moment. It is worth pointing out first that, if the cognitive function of Trotsky's 'literature of revolution' has been correctly identified above, then that function can be defined as in part a philosophical one. Trotsky, significantly, produced no major work of overt philosophical reflection. Marx and Engels, Lenin, Gramsci, these other central figures in the Marxist tradition all did so. Their ears close to the ground, attentive as they had to be to the most current political and economic developments of their day, they nevertheless also gave independent and intensive treatment, at some time or another, to philosophical problems of one kind and another. Trotsky's *Their Morals and Ours*, or his discussion of the dialectic in *In Defence of Marxism*, represent a much more limited excursion into that area than was undertaken by any of them. But this absence of concentrated philosophical discussion from his work coexisted with the presence of something else, a way of writing about politics that consistently evoked some of those questions, both very general and very personal, that have traditionally been the object of philosophical inquiry. His own philosophical positions are present throughout his work, as it were 'horizontally', contained there in the literary dimension. The same point can perhaps be made by considering another, this time more localized, presence in Trotsky's output, one that is as atypical as the absence. Imagine the consternation it would provoke amongst those interested in the life of Lenin to discover that he had written a work of autobiography. Everything known about the man renders the suggestion bizarre. Trotsky precisely did write such a work, and it is far from being bizarre. Like everything else he wrote, *My Life* is manifestly the product of a revolutionary politician. But it is the product of this revolutionary politician and no other: powerfully synthesizing the great political issues of the time, the personal experiences of a life, ethical questions, cultural questions, and a perception of contemporaries and events. From a certain angle it can even be said that it is the most concrete embodiment, between the covers of one volume, of the specificities of Trotsky's writing that have been the concern of this essay (though, on a smaller scale, his *Diary in Exile* is also relevant here). *My Life* is not a work of philosophy. However, in the scope of its concerns, in the range of questions it inscribes into its record of political development and conflict, it is a work of theoretical, as well as biographical and historical interest. Its unusual character within the canon of classical Marxism does not deprive it of its status as an outstanding work of socialist literature, in its own way as valuable as the *Economic and Philosophical Manuscripts*, *Anti-Dühring* or Lenin's *Philosophical Notebooks*.

The Individual Moment

We have seen examples of how the young Trotsky's political discourse could be inflected by more general, philosophical themes. The dialectic of revolutionary will and historical causation—a dialectic as old as Marxism itself, and expressing a philosophical problem that is very much older—to which he returned so often in his discussion of political strategy and political personality, is one of these. Naturally the mere allusion to this problem, the dialogue of determinism and freedom however pungently recalled, is sufficient to solve no specific question of socialist strategy. By its very nature, such a general philosophical reference could not furnish the political *knowledge* of both structure and conjuncture necessary to adjudicate the issues in contention at any time. In evoking it, Trotsky simply tried to indicate how strategic differences might mediate, and the varieties of the 'socialist personality' refract, a wider set of existential concerns. The generalizing tendencies of his prose are clearly evident in this case. Similarly, his capacity to convey the subjective, experiential aspect of revolutionary movement and event pointed, as I have tried to argue, towards positions concerning the human dimension of the struggle for socialism that were not theorized by him separately or at any great length. In particular here, his effort to fuse, within the literary representation of socialist experience, its individual with its class dimensions, reflected a constant preoccupation with the individual moment of the collective socialist project as an indispensable complement of its attempt to grasp the tendency of social and economic forces. This moment of individuality, integral to the original Marxist vision, was kept alive, so to speak, in his manner of treating the political present (as also in his interest in literary and cultural criticism), rather than being situated simply, as ultimate value or maximal goal, at the end of a long historical process. Now, does this preoccuaption, which can legitimately be termed a philosophical one, enrich Trotsky's political discourse in a substantive as well as a stylistic sense? It seems to me that it does, and that the discussion of *1905* serves partly to illustrate in what way. In the response of Trotsky's peers to the same events, in Rosa Luxemburg's *Mass Strike, Party and Trade Unions*, in Lenin's *Two Tactics* or in his other articles on 1905, there is much that unites him and them. Like Trotsky, Luxemburg and Lenin in their own way both seized and tried to communicate, out of the atmosphere of this revolutionary upheaval, those class dynamics which defined for the proletariat a central and dominant role in it, the experience of a direct eruption of the masses on to the political arena, the crucial educative importance of their autonomous initiatives, and the significance of this Russian example in the wider European context. Rosa Luxemburg's pamphlet is written with a powerful sense of the ebb and flow of the overall movement and conjures up the intricate pattern of relations between economic and political struggles over the breadth of the Russian Empire, in an effort to stress the historical scope and implications of 1905. Lenin's work in this period, acutely sensitive to the enormous potentialities contained in the same wave of events, insistently drawing attention to them, focuses more sharply on immediate political tasks and problems; it reads, simultaneously, the aspirations of the masses, the agenda of the party, and the inter-relationship between the two. Despite their deep understanding, each from their own perspective, of the tendency of class forces, Lenin and Luxemburg do not usually focus, however, on the way in which individual experience and action refract or concentrate the historical process. Their viewpoint is, in *that* sense, more unilateral, and also more typical of the generality of Marxist political discourse. Trotsky's special achievement within the literature of classical Marxism was his exceptional capacity to summon up the interplay of individuals and masses within the maelstrom of events and to do so, moreover, in ways which preclude some of the false antitheses that occupy this terrain: eschewing, alike, the perspective in which the reality of social forces is reduced to a multiplicity of individual wills, a collectivist denial of the individual dimension, and a 'Jacobin' identification of the interests of the masses with the personality of the heroic leader. This special quality was part and parcel of his political writing. To that extent, and within the limits of a particular theme, the suggestion is borne out that his political ideas as such could be enhanced by the literary forms he employed.

This discussion can be brought to its conclusion on that note. Trotsky was no stranger to the necessities and the demands of theory, but he brought also to his writing a power of historical synthesis and a keen faculty of perception which added another dimension to it. Thereby he tried to capture for the workers' movement the many-sided reality of its history, to hold before it the experiences of victory and defeat, the emotions and the deeds of individuals and of masses. He gave these a literary as well as theoretical expression. When so many have been prepared to play fast and loose with this same history, the importance of his effort, for a picture of the truth in the round, should not be undervalued.

Index